RELIGION AND COMMON SENSE

Religion and Common Sense

by

SIDNEY SWAIM ROBINS

PHILOSOPHICAL LIBRARY, INC.

New York

Library of Congress Catalog Card No. 65-28764

FOREWORD

by Harold E. B. Speight

THIS BOOK is offered to lay men and women who are disturbed by the wide gap between modern knowledge of man and nature and the teachings of the churches. For those who are finding that organized religion does not give them the guidance, the inspiration, or the challenge to think for themselves which they need as they face far-reaching changes in the economic and political climate there are, throughout the book, insights which open up the neglected field of personal religion.

The conventional words from the pulpit, too often timid in approaching everyday problems, fail to answer the layman's questions. If he drifts away from the church he is regarded as a member of the "careless, pleasure-loving and materialistic masses." If he continues to support the church, harboring unspoken and unanswered questions, he suffers an uneasy feeling that he is helping to maintain an institution that has no relevance to his life.

Some laymen resent being asked to accept and recite publicly statements of faith which offend their intelligence; they do not find in creeds adopted hundreds of years ago any connection with what they are learning about the universe. Others are unhappy about the form of church organizations which have come down to us from civilizations very different from our own. The lack of a democratic atmosphere disturbs many more.

We live in a period in which once-revered dogmas are being undermined by freedom of thought and trivial activities of the churches are ceasing to interest people who are every day facing really significant issues. Such an era as ours challenges clergy and laity alike. Here and there we can see evidences of a new willingness on the part of members of the clergy to recognize lay dissatisfaction with credal statements. For example, two bishops have recently criticized theological positions which lay people find to be stumbling blocks. Bishop James Pike, of California, is reported as having said, significantly in Trinity Church, New York, that the doctrine of the Trinity was not one of the beliefs of the earliest Christians, that Jesus never heard of it, that the apostles never knew it, and that Christian missionaries have often found it a piece of heavy baggage. Bishop Robinson, of Woolwich, England, recently wrote a book, *Honest to God,* in which he deplored the perpetuation of ideas derived from primitive times, which placed God "up there" somewhere in space above the earth. Leaders in various denominations, and even in the Second Vatican Council, have given much thought to the place of laymen in the church.

For lay men and women who have begun to lose confidence in the traditions of their churches, the loss of authoritative guide-lines for their thinking can be very disturbing. Many find themselves handicapped in their effort to cope with moral issues that arise in the home, in the course of their daily lives, in their communities, and in the larger world. The confusions of life become burdensome. Tensions between capital and labor, partisan proposals for national policy, changes of educational methods, wars and rumors of war in what cannot any longer be thought of as distant countries, and countless other challenges to their judgment and integrity—these all tax their serenity and their endurance. Facing such complex and persistent problems, the layman meets obstacles as he tries to maintain a positive direction for his life. He senses that whatever may be his technical skills, or his intelligence or his economic security, these are not enough to satisfy him. But he is not sure that religion has guidance or encouragement for him.

Readers who are encountering such difficulties will find help in this book. It is not much concerned with inherited doctrines, organizations, or ceremonies of traditional Christianity. The approach to religion is positive. It is based upon the needs of men and women of today. After essaying a suggestive definition of religion and taking note of the forms that evolved for early men, the author sketches the development of Judaism and Christianity. This review throws a great deal of light on our inheritance. The later chapters help the reader to appraise these legacies and stimulate him to move forward into a free and fruitful pursuit of "goodness, truth, and beauty."

The author, long a student, for some years a teacher of

philosophy, for more years a minister in college and university towns, brings to the service of the questioning layman both an informed appreciation of the issues at stake and a positive attitude. He has no interest in undermining the sincere loyalty of any reader to points of view which he himself no longer finds acceptable. He has always welcomed opportunities for fellowship with adherents of churches in which he would not be quite at home. He has never sought to be different for the sake of being different. Affirmations are more important to him than negations, although a negation is sometimes necessary in order to clear the way for an affirmation. His many years of thoughtful study of both philosophy and religion have borne the fruits of personal devotion and commitment which all who know him admire, to whatever church, if any, they may belong.

Dr. Robins offers not only information that throws light on the history of religion, but also insights that awaken a new interest in the improvement of the prospect for human beings. He challenges the too easy and superficial approval of what we know to be untrue. He brings seekers after truth, whatever their label, into a fellowship which asks for sincerity in all professions of faith and in all action for the common good.

TABLE OF CONTENTS

ACKNOWLEDGMENTS

PEMISSION TO USE at the head of certain chapters quotations from copyrighted material is gratefully acknowledged: Chapter III, from *Alfred the Great,* by P. J. Helm, published by Robert Hale, Ltd., London; Chapter IV, from *An Historical Approach to Religion,* by Arnold Toynbee, published by Oxford University Press, New York; Chapter VII, from *The Birth of the Christian Religion,* by Alfred Loisy, translated by L. P. Jacks, published by George Allen and Unwin, London; Chapter X, from *A Sense of Humus,* by Bertha Damon, published by Simon and Schuster, Inc., New York; Chapter XXI, from *God's Frozen People,* by Mark Gibbs and T. Ralph Morton, copyright 1964 by Mark Gibbs and T. Ralph Morton, copyright 1965 by W. L. Jenkins, published in the U.S.A. by Westminster Press, Philadelphia.

RELIGION AND COMMON SENSE

I. Religion a Positive Concern

This is the master-key to the whole moral nature: what does
a man secretly admire and worship? What haunts him with the
deepest wonder? What fills him with most earnest aspiration?
What should we overhear in the soliloquies of his unguarded
mind? This it is which, in the truth of things, constitutes his
religion.

—JAMES MARTINEAU

In some lyceums they tell me that they have voted to exclude
the subject of religion. But how do I know what their religion
is, and when I am near to it or far from it? I have walked
into such an arena and done my best to make a clean breast of
what religion I have experienced, and the audience never sus-
pected what I was about. The lecture was as harmless as moonshine to them.

—THOREAU

RELIGION HAS ROLLED AWAY burdens from the shoulders of men
like St. Augustine and John Bunyan. It has been on the one
hand man's search for the Lost Chord, and on the other his
discovery of himself in what he referred to as a New Birth, a
change of heart, or a vocation. It has given men the sense of
being at home in this always most problematic life and this
most mysterious universe. It has produced men who "spoke as
having authority," whether or not they were all entitled to
recognition as great human leaders. It has called the Spirit to
witness before Diets and in the presence of tyrants, and has
made champions able to stand against any kind of external
authority, danger, or fate. It is probably the most personal concern there is, and involves the strongest convictions and engage-
ments. It has a broad path of workings in every region of our
old earth, among all people of historic memory or note.

But at the same time many people are today estranged or
turned into purely passive onlookers at public worship and are
left without much company in their deepest thoughts and feel-

1

ings. They find the creeds wholly inacceptable. They feel the need of frank recognition that public worship is based on myth and drama. They find more of prerogative, sectarianism and peculiarity operating in the public religion than is inviting or endurable to the democratic spirit.

The clergy still tend to operate as official custodians of mysteries and sacred books. Priests were originally masters in the art of public sacrifice and pastors were originally, in the meaning of the word, sheeptenders. But the prophets long ago tried to draw our attention to the inward sacrifices which are of the heart or the spirit and the sheep-mind is somewhat less prevalent than it was when the name of pastor was given.

Critics of religion in our day are inclined to echo the dictum of Cicero, who declared that fear made the gods; and to accept the view of his Greek contemporary, the poet Lucretius, who said that religion is man's worst enemy because instead of allowing men to live out their days with only the natural human fears and anxieties, it insists upon adding others of a purely superstitious nature, such as those based upon supposed punishments in another life. This charge is repeated often by the Marxists of today, who declare religion to be a system of mystifications and terrors on the one hand and of promises of "pie in the sky" on the other. As we well know, they claim it is all motivated and triggered by the exploiting classes and the priests working together to keep the masses in subjection and passive endurance while they are being robbed of their birthright of equal privileges and equal opportunities.

At the same time we have every reason for believing there really is something positive in religion for which no other name has as yet been suggested or found a lively hearing.

The word "fear," which Cicero and Lucretius used so much in their condemnation of religion, itself really covers too much. But we can think of the shivers and shudders which attend the millions of taboos that cluttered up the ways of primitive life; that dread of punishment visited upon men in this life, of which Job's friends spoke so eloquently; that anxiety about Nemesis and Hell, or things to befall us after death; and that "fear of God," or fear of doing wrong, which the Old Testament declares to be the beginning of knowledge, or in some of the older renderings the beginning of wisdom. This last kind of fear can be and is associated sometimes with a positive sense of duty or a desire to be right. It can even be associated with a false pride in being righteous, just as it can be connected with some of those older notions of divine punishment behind it. In spite of being surrounded by such fears men have emerged who have had a sense of mission or high purpose, with a corresponding fear of doing wrong or of making a bad mistake. Horace Mann said: "Be ashamed to die until you have won some victory for humanity"; and that was his religion. To be sure, when we get to the higher branches of the topic there is something to be said for Thomas Carlyle's positive and forthright terminology: "Love is ever the beginning of knowledge, as fire is of light." But fear is the reverse side of love, and inevitably attends it all the way from the lowest levels to the heights.

We should not be subject to fears of any kind at all if we did not in the first place have positive concern and devotion. Life is an affirmation. The seeking of some kind of goal runs through the whole range of it from bottom to top, from savages to saints and seers. And on the whole the goal becomes constantly wider, takes in more, as intelligence rises in level. There is love of food along with the fear of missing it. There is love of creature comforts and pleasures, of horse and dog, of woman and child, of tribe and clan, of nation and even of humankind. There is curiosity and the love of seeking what is over the hills or inside the atom. There is pride of skill which develops in and through the crafts and arts. There is truth-seeking. There is social endeavor which requires tact and management along with the ability to stand up under abuse or denunciation. It takes real ambition and love of achievement to enable men to enjoy responsible public office. There is admiration for persons, taking the forms of reverence, emulation, discipleship. Fear, a mere negative, dogs our footsteps with nose to the ground wherever we go. It follows us from the bottom to the top of humanity's pursuits and attainments.

Who is there that is not constantly pushing aside some of the ordinary fears to become engaged in new and more pervasive ones, which may be incidental to greater or wider concerns? And the higher we go up in our contemplation of human affairs the less central are those superstitious fears which Cicero and Lucretius had in mind when they were assessing the role of fear in religion. It is not even necessary to ignore the fact that some childish and superstitious fears do hold their ground to some

3

extent in people who have got beyond them in their active lives and perhaps in their minds. William Ellery Channing once said that while his mind had grown liberal his nerves were still Calvinist. There is both a psychological and a social lag in human progress. But we are compelled to recognize Jesus and Mahatma Gandhi as religious leaders in a high and positive sense of the word. Neither of them was a leader in running away, or in retiring to the rear.

It has been said that religion is an activity of the whole man. We may have been in some doubt as to whether the person who says this is not just trying to make room for his self-centered emotions. But we seem bound by respect for humanity to make more than that of it in many cases. If religion is to concern as many different kinds of men as it does and always has, there must be something of the life abundant attached to it in many places. Without our being totally idealistic in the matter, we judge there must be room for all of a human being's major drives, his gifts, his possibilities, his gradual education, his sense of beauty and his admiration, his developing sense of justice, his awakening sense of the brotherhood of all men, his cosmic feeling of one kind or another in the face of all the widening horizons. In short, religion must be concerned with, in real contact with, all the ground of vital activity and search that men cover. It cannot be held down by either conventions or critics to some common denominator of lower emotions and desires, such as primitive men knew perfectly well.

Of course it is possible to call mankind's higher aspirations by some other name than religion. In many fields today we are engaged in struggles over vocabulary or for new words to express our sensitivity. All words tend to spoil or lose some of their impact as they lose their freshness. We even rename restaurants by the roadside every two or three years in order to make fresh appeal to the imagination. Eminent writers are always complaining of the inadequacy of all the old words, and many of them make for themselves a new vocabulary. They naturally want their new and creative ideas to hit us without the burden of the dust, confusion, manifold meanings and confusing applications, that have accumulated upon certain familiar words. There is far from being any law of common sense to forbid our distinguishing between the interests of religion and those of human life itself. We need renewal of glamor and romance in

4

religion, or in life, whichever we are talking about, as well as in multifarious momentary interests. Some of that need applies to the names we give things. No doubt at all, religion and atheism have many times already worn one another's names, for that is the way realities defeat conventionalities and bring forward progressive views. Much of our rebellion against things as they are, and against religion as it looms and glooms upon the public street corners, is itself religious. A good deal of it is plainly traceable to religious prophets and poets who were rebels in other days. We need rebels; but along with our rebellion against the past, rebellion against names, rebellion in favor of unspoiled slogans and new beginnings, we need some sympathy with the past and a recognition that our own struggle and rebellion is not entirely a new thing. "Brave men lived before Agamemnon."

*   *   *   *

The idea behind the present study and presentation of religion is that there is religion too near, too simple, too universal, also too youthful and of the dawn, to be everywhere and by all people dignified by any one name. Inspiration is always a fresh subject. Who does not know that much of the best religion of earth exists apart from any and all conventionalities, whether of name, place, or canonization? The prophets told people to concern themselves with other matters than bringing bloody sacrifices to Jehovah. And in Leigh Hunt's well-known poem, *Abou Ben Adhem*, when the humble hero asks to be set down as one who loves his fellow men if not the deity, the recording angel puts his name at the very top of those who love the Lord. And many individuals, neither circumcised nor baptized, have brought needed, perhaps new, truth to their contemporaries. If the most important affairs of human life, our universal concerns, our responsible criticism, our free choices, have no vital religious significance, we must feel that all of the prophets and most of our seers have missed their vocation.

We pass from this introduction to the topic of worship and the social forms of religious expression.

II. The Meaning of Worship

Worship's deeper meaning lies
In mercy, and not sacrifice,
Not proud humilities of sense
And posturing of penitence,
But love's unforced obedience.
—JOHN GREENLEAF WHITTIER

FROM THE HANDBOOKS of the history of religions we certainly
learn that, like humanity itself, religious worship began in barbarism and savagery and has evolved, the world over, into
more civilized forms. But there is one other fact which stands
out with equal clarity upon the pages of the history of religion
as well as elsewhere. That is the tendency to assume that religion, or the worship part of it, consists chiefly or altogether of
public and official pieties. It seems to be taken for granted that
whatever business is transacted with a medicine man or a priest
taking the lead, whatever public proceeding bears a religious
name or acquires one from us onlookers through underground
association with things we do today in church, is "worship."
Of course that is the easy part of our worship for travellers to
find and report on, although we are reminded in this connection
of the fact that icebergs travel with the vast portion of their
bulk under water. Perhaps there is more religion in our daily
activities, in our business, in our homes, and in all our practical
dealings with our neighbors, than there is in our Sabbath observances, creeds, and a few other things that we may call our
religion.

If an inquiring gentleman from Mars or some asteroid came
along and asked about Earth's religion, he might very likely be
directed to a steeple and told to go and listen underneath. That
would be religion, we might tell him; at least in the theory of
it. And he might be further told to observe particularly and
closely the gentlemen who pass the plates, and to follow them
around outside and through the week to learn how the theory

6

of religion is applied. The conventions confuse and overpower us. We are all too ready to assume that whatever echoes out of a pulpit or is exemplified in a prominent churchman's daily walk is the most important revelation of religion. One recalls an old army surgeon who claimed to have lost all his religion in youthful days, when a barrel of apples bought from a deacon of the church turned out to be good only in the top layer.

But this approach to religion or worship is surely no more justifiable than identifying education with the imperfections of our public schools or measuring it by the possession of college diplomas; or than identifying democracy with the misrepresentation or travesty we sometimes make of it in some areas of our American life. The conventions of a subject are important to know about but they are not thoroughly reliable advisers, especially if any ideals are involved.

Even the dictionary can occasionally force us out of this formal approach to a subject. It may do this by the very variety of the definitions it assembles. We need go no further than Webster's Unabridged to observe this in the present case. Here is Webster's list of definitions of religion as nearly as one can abstract them in brief from two-thirds of a column:

(1) The outward act or form by which men indicate their recognition of the existence of a god or gods having power over their destiny, to whom obedience, honor, and service are due.
(2) The feeling or expression of human love, fear, or awe, of some superhuman or overruling power, whether by profession of belief, by observance of rites and ceremonies, or by the conduct of life.
(3) A system of faith and worship.
(4) A manifestation of piety.
(5) Conformity to the faith and precepts of the Bible.
(6) Devotion or fidelity, as to a principle or practice.

The first of these definitions applies at all well only to those forms of worship which have developed as far along as the early Greek and Roman polytheism, let us say of the time of Homer; or as that of the Old Testament at the time when the Israelites were wandering around with the Ark of the Covenant, making incursions or seeking a homeland. It does not go back to the more primitive forms described in any textbook of the history of religions, in some of which there is nothing to be found that you would ordinarily call a God. Also this definition is restricted to outward acts and forms.

The second definition takes in more of the primitive background. Like the first, it emphasizes obeisance to overruling power. It is broader in outlook than Cicero and Lucretius, both of whom thought that the belief in gods arose out of fear, in that it brings in love and awe as well. It makes a considerable extension of the subject by bringing in the conduct of life at large, although it cannot be said to offer any anticipation of the Old Testament's and Jesus' teaching to the effect that real love of God is to be accompanied by, or as Jesus had it, to be proved by, a love for one's brother and neighbor.

Webster's third alternative makes religion squarely a public affair and practically identifies it with formal creeds and established forms of worship. The fourth brings in "piety," which may be almost a synonym for worship although it also breathes a suggestion of conventional "good works." This definition seems to be moving largely in a circle. The fifth, since Jews do not accept the New Testament as authoritative, applies only to Christianity.

The sixth of Webster's definitions brings in what we know some will regard as merely a metaphorical extension of religion, not to be taken with too much seriousness. It defines in terms of an attitude which can be taken or observed in others, either personally or socially, either informally or ritually: namely "devotion." However, devotion is sufficiently akin to love, aspiration, and the like to come alive and evince the same expansiveness as those terms which are by universal consent so important in religion. It fits in well enough with the tendency of Barthians and others to emphasize "anxiety" in religion, or of Quakers to feel a religious "concern." Strong devotion covers all that ground in a positive way. It is, at the other extreme, in line with our way of saying that a certain man makes a religion of his golf, his money bags, his art, or his morning exercises. This definition has no difficulty of course in continuing to be in touch with the primitive beginnings of religion.

Some may think a definition of religion as simply "devotion" too broad, threatening us either with a return to the primitive or abandoning all separation between religion and secular life. However these critics are doubtless ready to admit that any

8

man's religion can be good or bad, for him and others. So the fact of religion being always open to debasement or caricature can hardly be a serious objection to the definition.

Included in such a perspective as we are now taking is the devotion of the most radical and God-denying type of "Humanists," of the Marxists, and indeed of many professed "atheists." Anybody at all can be an example of mistaken or misplaced devotion. At the same time, included in such a perspective, and reached by a plainly obvious stairway within human life, one of many steps, is the highest kind of devotion and loyalty evoked by a great prophet like Amos, Mahatma Gandhi, Gautama Buddha, or Christ. For after all, what these leaders show is not where our devotion now lies, but where we ought above all to be concerned.

What is the real objection to religion's being defined as devotion? It can still be plentifully full of the call to grow up, to mature, to "come up higher." In the case of children we readily recognize, indeed we dwell upon, their potential for development in the future. Some of the modern prophets are telling us that we are all children too.

Not only the Hebrew prophets, but all of them, have always had to be critical of men's conventional and actual devotions. They have all been hard on mere Sabbath observances or what corresponds, on altar gifts, on praying in public and on the kind of religion which is for public show, on circumcision, on saying "Lord, Lord," on being in and out of the synagogue or the church, on forgetting "the greater matters of the law" while leaning hard on ritual performance. If we are going to take the religious evolution of mankind seriously; that is to say, look upon it in the same way as we look upon evolution in all sorts of important affairs, then it is not useful for students of religion merely to go around collecting oddities of public devotion or practice, or even of beliefs. These things will not take us to the gravity and importance of the subject. They will be far from showing us the breadth of it. Without recognition that there are lower and higher forms of religious devotion running all through life and into its every precinct and office, not just through the sanctuary in the public square, no historical examples such as those Sir James Frazer, for instance, gathered to display in the *Golden Bough*, will be very enlightening. Frazer's studies in anthropology led him to concentrate too fully

9

on primitive propitiation or conciliation ceremonies. There is danger that such limited views of religion will clutter up the subject, make us unable to see the woods for the trees, cast a reflection on the higher forms of religion and dampen enthusiasm. It is only a progressive view of devotion and a view of its evolution as involving a kind of growing up that can save us from the erosive effects upon great words like "love," and upon great personalities, that have been wrought by some Freudian psychoanalysts.

This leads up to a very interesting fact which students of primitive tribes come upon and which helps to confirm us here. These students find that men begin acting in certain ways which we ourselves probably feel like classifying as religious before they have any theology at all, or any clear beliefs beyond that of its being a good thing to do. Undoubtedly some religious ritual began in what in other connections is referred to as imitative magic. In the midst of a long drought some medicine-man-priest would climb a tree and shake the branches in the hope of bringing on a storm of wind with rain. You might say men have notions of *mana* attaching to some of the tools they handle instead of any theology, and something of that general animistic outlook which nearly all primitives have. Their clearest ideas are about their tribal needs (it might be for rain, it might be for a victory in battle), and about their ritual procedures being old tribal custom. Their fathers engaged in the kind of dramatics they are now carrying on, and got results. We might say that early people's religion is likely to begin in mass activities and rites instead of in any clear beliefs in gods or spirits. And this is an important lump of factuality that we can easily understand, because it continues undissolved all the way up into the worship of modern man and our own day. People can and do go to church on Sunday morning, and can even form the habit, without being able to tell what if any religious beliefs they hold. Some confess to inquirers that their conscious motive is social. They go to meet other people. They have no belief in the creed that is read out in church, or in any particular part thereof which stands out in prominence.

This fact of religion beginning as a practice rather than as a developed theory has even a very high range of exemplification. One is not at all led to suppose that Jesus' disciples understood what was the attraction about him when they first turned to follow. He, himself, was content to say, "Come and see." They were not asked to accept any dogmas. He simply deepened those fishermen's concern as they listened to him and followed him around. We are talking from the Gospel pages. In so far as the disciples were led at all by beliefs, a good part of it must have been belief that it was good or worthwhile to be with Jesus.

To finish with the point: we all know that the way to get an education in any great subject or in the comprehension of any art like music or painting, is to follow a leader or to associate with people of taste. Even so religion in its higher manifestations just has to begin in gravitation or attraction to persons. Attraction is a word which gets its start in physics, and then moves on from that field to biology and psychology, and even sociology. The early Greek philosophers used "love" as a synonym for "attraction." So we have at least three words for what moves in life from the bottom to the top: "attraction," "love," "devotion."

We have to thank Plato for explaining the growth of men as a maturing in love. He pointed out how naturally love grows from bodily attraction and the love of some one person to love of the many and of ideal beauty. Both the Neo-Platonic and the Christian-mystical supreme goals, contemplation and blessedness, spring historically from what he said about the development of love. It is true that Plato is accused of having thrown away the ladder by means of which men rise.

In fact Plato is accused of the fault opposite to that which reduces high phenomena to lower ones. That is, he contrasts directly with the Freudians who go around debunking all sublimities. Plato is accused of other-worldliness, which may be the general fault of a certain type of idealism. They say Plato forgot the base materials out of which men are put together and hoped to turn some of them at least into philosophers, just as later Christian teachers tried to turn men into saints—the ones that were not predestined for hell.

Christian teachers used Plato's thought to great effect in more ways than one when it came to building a structure of ideas that might stand out to match the cathedrals of stone. But on the secular side, "Platonic love" came to be popularly regarded as having little or no heat and passion in it. It was supposed to be disembodied, cool, impersonal; which may not be so far from saying other-worldly or saintly. Anyhow this love is "agape," not love as ordinary humans can know it.

Plato can also be taken to mean that every upward step in love is an abandonment of humbler devotions, and that no genuine root-growth is involved. Some of his words may partly justify this interpretation. But it is an unnecessary inference from his story of how love can grow and mature. The close-at-home loves do not necessarily exclude the wider ones. The home affections sometimes promote the high idealism and normally are themselves improved by the association. Theodore Roosevelt once said that the man who does not love his native land will make a poor internationalist. We might buttress that by saying that a man who does not love his family or have some kind of high regard for himself is poor material for citizenship. In fact that ladder which Plato, in the *Phaedrus,* described a-building is properly and naturally pictured as of twisted living vines, growing filaments, from bottom rootage to the top.

We have seen the difficulty of any attempt to define or describe religion in too restrictive a fashion. Our survey of the meaning of religion has, with Webster's help, covered some of the many available definitions and focussed on one of them as most nearly doing justice to the whole subject-matter as it has developed from the world of primitive man to the modern scene. And we have seen the danger of isolating religion in a compartment of life instead of finding it parallel to life itself. That danger appears all too often in books designed to interpret religion, especially when the authors introduce two other subjects, magic and morals. Frequently, usually indeed, they have contrasted religion with magic in the way of making it a personalized form of "supernaturalism." And frequently they have contrasted it with morals to make it appear to be mystical, and to open the way for talking about a distinctive "Christian ethics."

We shall in the next chapter see how common sense views these distinctions and separations.

III. Religion, Magic and Morals

An Anglo-Saxon remedy for a "fiend-sick" man:

Collect cockle, lupin, wood betony, cockspur, wild iris, fennel, lovage, lichen, from a church and from a crucifix. Place the mixture in clean ale and sing seven Masses over it; put it in garlic and holy water and put some drops of the mixture into every drink that the patient drinks.

Let the patient sing the Psalms *Blessed are those who are undefiled, Let God arise and let his enemies be scattered,* and *Help me, O Lord,* and then let him drink of this drink from a church bell. After he has drunk, let the priest sing over him, *Domine, Sancte Pater Omnipotens.*

—ALFRED THE GREAT,
P. J. Helm, 1963
(Robert Hale Limited, London)

A DISTINCTION between religion and magic has been proposed. It is based on the idea that magic is mechanical procedure, a pulling of tricks and triggers to get results; whereas religion is always a transaction between personal agents. In magic you use spells; in religion you offer sacrifices to gods or spirits, and hopefully these respond. Of course this distinction is not well-founded if, as has been suggested, the place to find men's religion, from the very beginning of religious history, is in their realistic devotions. For then we have to say that wherever men resort to magic, white or black, in pursuit of their liveliest and deepest concerns, it involves their religion, such as that is at a particular stage of growth.

Moreover, and even more directly to the point, it is quite unrealistic to suppose that savages, Neanderthalers, or any kind of primitive men, ever had in their minds any clear-cut distinction between mechanical and spiritual agencies or operations. Exorcisms have always been used, and still are, to drive unwholesome spirits out of a man's body or mischievous ones out of his house. In the Arabian Nights a genie is imprisoned in a bottle in the form of smoke, and others are called up for service by

13

the rubbing of a lamp. Explorer Stefansson tells of certain Eskimos asking him for some new prayers to bring back the caribou herds, and complaining that the old prayers which they had formerly got from the missionaries were now worn out. Prayer-wheels of Tibet may be set to catch the breezes like other wind-mills; but surely there is some expectation of wandering spirits passing by and having their attention caught by such artfulness of petition. Mechanical and personal are confused. Jesus had to rebuke some of his contemporaries who hoped to be heard for their "much speaking."

Let us lay aside particular illustrations and put the matter in a form which would seem to settle the question: the animistic notions of nature, which we now learn to have once been world-wide, the feeling that the waving grass, the waters, the winds, and all interesting objects and artifacts are alive and on their way towards being self-conscious, show on the widest scale how unlikely it is that early man could have seen any real partition dividing mechanical forces from personal, or religion from magic. The very concept of "mechanical," however you take it, is a recent development.

In the same way the separation of religion from ethics and morality, involving the notion of a "mere morality" somewhere existent, can be disposed of if we think of religion as devotion. Earliest religion undoubtedly supported the family customs and the mores of the tribe. In all probability every tribesman always felt his own welfare to be wrapped up to a very large extent in that of the tribe to which he belonged. To a great extent he shared the same superstitions as everybody else; and he believed a good deal of what he was told about where lay the tribal interest. If he heard everywhere that breaking certain taboos brought bad luck to the whole clan, he believed it. He picked up prejudices and like his betters swallowed medicine men's advice. Slavery, segregation, wars of aggression, even genocide, have been defended at times by religions representing wide-spread prejudices and popular concerns and devotions. Established religions everywhere, and always, have helped things to stay established in the familiar forms and ruts. Their leaders have not been backward or unhelpful in finding catch-words and slogans for the purpose of popular appeal.

Of course, as civilization or evolution progresses none of these conservative forces keeps the individual from becoming more responsible and independent, a center of rebellion against the Establishment. Moral growth works through minorities of all sizes, beginning with the single queer duck of a fellow. Especially where rulers are unpopular a minority begins to doubt what it is told about where lies the good of the tribe. A minority usually sees further on any question that comes up at any period of history. A small minority helped to work out something approaching the Golden Rule in one country after another. The idea that all men are brothers is broached here and there before it can be made in the least degree popular. Of course the greatest service of any minority lies in its efforts towards turning itself into a majority. And sometimes it achieves even that. It does this, gradually winning the majority's admiration, respect and emulation. But it would at any time be fatal not to continue having minorities, even of one person.

It has been made a criticism of religions at large that men make gods in their own image. No doubt they do just that. An old Greek philosopher said that the animals would do the same if they ever came to the point of thinking about it, or of having gods. But the critics carry a stinger in their tail and go on from there to maintain that it is the mores and the ideals of yesteryear that are represented in the images of the gods. Euripides cited the Homeric gods which were widely recognized in his own day and accused a lot of his fellow Greeks of worshipping gods not even as good as the average men of their times. Which properly leads us to exclaim: "How natural it is to cling to an idol of our youth! How possible it is for progress engineered by minorities to leave our mass attachments stranded." But there is no rule to the effect that pictures of gods must be backward looking. There is merely a question of progress, with majority and minority involved. Euripides was speaking for a minority of intelligent people of the time who had left Homer behind and were brave enough to say so. Aristophanes helped him out by criticizing current religion, and some popular figures besides, in his comedies. Whether Euripides and some of the other poets, and also Socrates and Plato, were practically giving up the term "gods" as spoiled by usage, at least in the plural form, is not much to the point. Euripides commented on certain ancient and famous stories of the gods that, if the gods really did these things, then they were not gods. The concept of Zeus as supreme above all the other gods, or as the one God (Aeschylus), and

15

as not quite such a quarrelsome deity as Ares, already had in it something that helped Greek civilization to join in the monotheistic current that was soon to flow in from Judea. We know that the Stoics, for example, had just one God and his name was sometimes Reason. The Greek poets, like the Hebrew prophets, were after all dreaming ideals of justice and a unity of mankind. And they were probably incarnating in their own persons higher ideals than just the common. It may be very much to the point to see that a whole lot of this lay-prophecy in Greece was a genuine part of religion, and that these poets are a part of the process by which religion evermore grows, casting off old forms and preparing new ones. If we are unwilling to grant that men's realistic religion is their real devotion, we are in danger of ignoring and disrespecting evolution and humanity itself. If we are going to allow religion to stick fast in the ruts and the conventionalities, we shall need otherwise unnecessary miracles to haul us out.

The Egyptians tried making use of some of the animals in their pantheon of gods as well as in their ethical teaching; and the Egyptians were a civilized people, bent for a long time and on a grand scale upon bettering themselves. As a matter of fact we all use the animals in inculcating certain virtues: the spider to teach patience, the ant industry, the dog obedience, and more than one animal to teach fidelity or loyalty. But that road is no wide thoroughfare. Only of a man can we idealize the whole figure. The incarnation has to be anthropomorphic. It has to be some atavar, some Gautama sitting cross-legged under his Bo tree and letting the world go by, some little child (at Christmas it is the Christchild), some saint who visits the poor and sick, some sinless and perfect Christ or some legendary figure tailored to meet our present ideal.

* * * *

When we encounter organized or conventional forms of religion we find a serious confusion between worship or religion on one hand and ethics or good works on the other. The two parties to that argument have represented religion and ethics as entirely separate; as hangers-on, the one to the other; or as if the one or the other was to be superseded. This difficulty, however, is disposed of if we start with the idea of our religion consisting of our devotions.

One finds a separation of religion and ethics in the talk, if not in the life and walk, of as admirable a man as the late Albert Einstein. In the magazine section of the *New York Times* for November 9, 1930, he is quoted as speaking of religion as a vision of cosmic law and order, transcendently beautiful and inspiring. Then he says: "The ethical behavior of men is better based on sympathy, education, and social relationships, and requires no support from religion." But further on he adds: "The cosmic religious experience is the strongest and noblest driving support behind scientific research." Of course Mr. Einstein is distinguishing between social ethics on the one hand and a kind of noble personal morale among intellectuals on the other. Thus his view of what constitutes religion is a far cry from that of the Hebrew prophets, who made religion largely a social question; or from that of ordinary people; or from our view that religion should be defined as our highest and deepest devotion in all fields.

Apparently there was an ancient confusion about the relation of ethics and religion, found even in the Ten Commandments, which Mr. Einstein was trying to clear up and have done with because he felt it to be unwholesome. The first four planks of our decalogue concern duties owed directly to Jehovah, or Jahweh. They prohibit the worship of other gods; the making of graven images or idols which might either encourage idolatry or bring the idea of God too close to our faulty human nature; the utterance of his sacred name. The fourth commandment imposes observance of the Sabbath Day. The remaining planks are in the field of social ethics. They concern duties to parents and to fellow-men, and anticipate the teaching later developed in Judea to the effect that the way to serve and honor God is to love your brother. But the God of the first four commandments is of course not Mr. Einstein's God, although it stands in the foreground of his inherited religious outlook in such a way as to make it very difficult for the ethical spirit which is in the later planks to seem to him to have anything to do with "God" at all. Of course there is a god he is plentifully devoted to in the spirit of friendship and humanity as well as in musical appreciation, contemplation of the cosmic, and in a lesser degree in all approaches to beauty and order. Personally Mr. Einstein is substituting an aesthetic religion for the social one of the Jewish prophets. He may be within his legal rights in wishing to be free of the word "God" on account of certain conventional associations. The question of the importance of words is one which must come up even in theology, in its own place. But finding a man's religion in his deepest devotion destroys the particular separation Mr. Einstein makes between religion and ethics.

St. Paul's separation of religion and ethics is more important historically, although it comes out only when he is riding a theological high horse. He teaches that we are saved by faith alone and not by works, and brings those two terms into a kind of opposition that has lasted unto this day. On the other hand, on many heads and at many points Paul appears as a grand ethical teacher. In First Corinthians 13 he teaches that love, or charity, is the greatest of virtues and makes it seem as native to man as faith or hope. For a time he almost lets it sound like the whole duty of man. Moreover, Paul was an active center within a religious movement which came to teach in other prominent writings, such as John's Gospel and the Epistles of John, that God is love. Yet in St. Paul, as in ancient Judaism itself, and in some modern Christian teaching, God is so far separated from man, so far from being a penetrative spirit, and (for those who are content with the Pauline theology) his kind of love so distinct and different from any ordinary human kind, that God or Christ must impart a new kind of love, not native to us, before we can do anything good at all. Our righteousness, as has been well enough said, is in such a view naught but filthy rags. The supposed Pauline teaching on this head would certainly kill the root of ethics if it were at all possible to kill it by words or talk. Fortunately, good clergymen have a way of getting around Pauline theology by saying that good behavior, or the best pretense of it we can muster, is a divine requirement even while its positive worth is precisely nil, even while the rags of righteousness are all holes.

It *is* difficult to express religious truth because we come upon paradox wherever the water is deep. As Whitehead says somewhere: "A man knows that he must fight with himself, for himself; and he knows that he himself must do the fighting." That is paradox. If he had said that the divine which is in the higher part of a man must fight the demonic or supernatural which is in the lower parts, that could be only more paradox, or a plain figure of speech. Possibly we might imagine St. Paul meaning, at least when he is in the vein of that speech he made

18

at Athens, that all the good, all the expansive love, and all the aspiration which is in man, is God already and originally there; and that all the individual does or can do—not as if alone or fragmented off—is to help develop his own divine potentialities. Even the Psalmist had long since said something about God working within us to do his own good will. If the moral process, like many other processes in nature, is bi-polar; if it works from above and below, then perhaps good men will always give the credit and the glory to God when they do not ascribe it to good parents or some other external influence. Some stout men say they owe everything they have achieved in life to Mother. It is a fine modesty and better than the boast of the "self-made" man. So Paulinists may ascribe all moral achievement as well as their very salvation to God alone.

But clearly Paul misled the world in making man as helpless and really unresponsible as he did; and on that issue he should be plainly reckoned with.

As to the general idea of religion superseding ethics or the other way around, we have first the highly respectable forms of those notions. For ethics being ready to take over from religion we have the Ethical Culture movement. And for religion taking over from ethics we have what is prominently called and written about as "Christian Ethics," of which the motive and the capacity is supposed to be divinely imparted at conversion, so that Christian love, or agape, is something quite different from native human devotion of the best kind. This is in the Pauline tradition.

So is the extreme form of it, or "antinomianism," within the Pauline tradition, although less respectable. By that long word we understand the notion that religion, as a love imparted to the converted or sanctified ones, can carry men into a freedom beyond responsibility to the law, social or moral. St. Paul can be quoted as saying that love is the end of the Law. In fact he said it was the Gospel; and that right there was the *differentia* of Christianity from Judaism. He plainly felt that Judaism was all tied up in its Law, just as Gulliver was all entwined and tied down to the dirt when he woke up among the Lilliputians. And so Paul raked the Pharisees fore and aft. There is no question about that. And he said that those who were "in Christ" were no longer under the Law. With that start, Antinomians of the Reformation times concluded that if we loved God enough

19

and showed it by keeping the commandments which glorified and honored him directly, then God would let us off from some of the lower laws which embody our human duties.

Once assume that right and wrong are divine commands instead of partial names for God himself and then of course he can issue permits to break some of the laws he made. In fact, you can reason that God would not grudge a great preacher, an Elmer Gantry let us say, engaged hours on end in the sacred business of saving human souls, some let-down and easement in between religious services. It would be merely releasing the spring for an hour, so that it might not lose its tension. But if religion is inner devotion of the spirit to high human ends, and no mere obedience to fiats of men or of God, and if ethics is the same thing within the field of human relationships; then we must learn to take our pleasures and relaxations from a high table, being made over if necessary to give us that kind of taste. Then we must be one and the same person all the time. Our greatest need will include wholeness of spirit and our whole life must invite the open sunlight.

Again it is fortunate that not many good-willed clergymen, not many plain people, and indeed not many rogues, have ever been deceived by the idea that saints are privileged characters, or that God issues permits to flaunt what of course we describe as his laws. *Whatever else is the mark of a religious man, we readily recognize that the deep devotion of his whole life, the constant sense of a calling and of a single aim, the evidence of constant practical application and of unvaryingly pressing on towards the same high mark, is a part of it.*

At the beginning of this chapter we introduced the topic of "supernaturalism," and we are reminded of the fact that many people, in spite of anything we have said, adhere to the notion that religion implies worship of what they think of as a "personal God." And modernists of a sort, especially those who like to make something very clear-cut out of such words as "atheist" and "atheism," like to make a cleavage between those who believe in a "personal God" and those who don't, or between supernaturalists and naturalists in religion. The next chapter will endeavor to show how such a distinction appears in the history of religion as a whole, up to modern times. And it will sum up the history of theology itself in terms that are, in the widest view of the subject, all naturalistic. Nothing more so! The proof is in the historic facts.

IV. Main Highways in Theology

In the earliest civilizations . . . at the earliest dates to which
we can trace their histories back, we find Primitive Man's leg-
acy of Nature-worship not only co-existing with, but associated
with, an undisguised worship of the parochial communities into
which the nascent civilization has articulated itself.

In Egypt, for example, we find the worship of the Sun, the
Corn, and the Nile surviving side by side with the self-worship
of the cantons. In Sumer and Akkad we find the worship of
Tammuz and Ishtar surviving side by side with the self-worship
of the city-states. In China we find an agricultural ritual in
which the prince communes with Heaven and ploughs the first
furrow of the new agricultural year, surviving side by side with
the self-worship of the contending states and of the oecumenical
empire by which the gods are superseded. In Canaan we find
the worship of the fertility-gods, the ba'als and the ashteroths,
and the agricultural rites embodied in the Pentateuch, surviving side by side with the self-worship of the city-states and
cantons.

—Arnold Toynbee,
*An Historian's
Approach to Religion*
(Oxford University Press,
New York)

All problems of religion ultimately go back to this one—
the experience I have of God within myself differs from the
knowledge concerning him which I derive from the world. In
the world He appears to me as the mysterious, marvellous creative force; within He reveals Himself as ethical will. In the
world He is impersonal force, within me He reveals Himself
as Personality. The God who is known through philosophy and
the God whom I experience as ethical Will do not coincide.
They are one; but how they are one I do not understand.
—Albert Schweitzer

THE WORD "theology" is sometimes used to mean the science of
gods; at other times to mean an explanation or systematizing of
the tenets about the One God. In the former or scientific sense
of it, an important observation would appear to be eminently

21

apropos: namely that the gods who have been formally worshipped by sizeable groups of men seem to fall under one of three general classifications. There are natural gods, tribal gods, and gods that one thinks should be distinguished from both of these and called spiritual gods.

The classification is not rigid or, for that matter, exactly final. Rather it is historical and in line with convenient approach and study. The distinction of natural gods, for instance, was somewhat clearer before men stopped thinking of themselves as merely confronted by an outdoor, or purely objective, nature of which they themselves were in no sense a part—clearer indeed than it has ever been since. But the distinctions are marked on the map of theology and they still identify main approaches to religious experience.

(1) In the first place, gods have been personifications of features of the outdoors like the Sun and the River Nile; likewise of pools and waterfalls; of winds and storms; of planets including Earth; of the Underworld and the Sky; sometimes of some literal Creator of the whole of Nature or of some outstanding feature thereof. These gods have for people's thoughts and feelings ruled over some portion of the outer world and have possessed a corresponding control over man's destiny.

(2) In the second place, gods have been and are our own group or tribe, as Toynbee makes clear; or personifications of the same in some supernatural leader or hero of the past, or in some present king, emperor, or Fuehrer.

(3) In the third place, gods are life-forces within or through nature and, within man in particular, a possessing energy or spirit that raises us above everyday consciousness into an exalted state of being, energy, and power.

Of course when the Nile was thought of as a source of fertility at large, and when the corn was thought of, as so often it has been in religion, as a champion exhibit of the life-force working throughout nature including man, the Egyptians reached a junction of the natural and the spiritual highways of theology. There have been junctions of the social and spiritual highways too, because many of the moving and possessing forces of life are social, contagious, and even epidemic. But our present objective is a walk on the main streets of theology.

It seems as if that group of peoples known as Aryans followed the natural or outdoors highway of theology and philosophy in a distinctive way and for a very long time. Not only did the Aryans have their share of the less important nature gods that everybody else had—gods of rivers, mountains, and groves. All their major deities were personifications of the great features and forces of nature. It seems as if no other grouping of peoples were ever quite so possessed along this line. Through sacrifices and offerings they sought favors or protection from these powers of the external world.

The Hindus worshipped Fire and Storm under divine names. The Greeks martyred Iphigenia at the outset of the Trojan expedition to get a favorable breeze from the god of the winds. Old Poseidon was honored with endless worship from all sailors and had many temples built in his honor, where shields of innumerable warriors who had escaped from shipwreck were hung up in honor of him as god of the seas. Oddly enough, Zeus, he of the heavens and king of the gods, received less than his share of worship. He was ever too far off, above the battle, and rather impartial. His wife, Hera, more splenetic, had much of his share. Hades (in the Roman world Pluto) got a full share as god of the under world and the kingdom of the dead. Athena, goddess of wisdom, was given a grand share of worship; but her worship, while associated with the owl as symbol, was confused with the self-worship of the city-state of Athens. The Romans long copied the Greeks in religion as in so many other things.

The religion of Homer and Vergil is no total picture of the religion of those two great Aryan nations, but it is one of the main tracks. The great reformers of Greek religion, like Euripides and Lucretius, knew that Homer was the point from which to start their higher criticism.

The prominence of this kind of religion in India, Greece, Rome, Germany, probably has something to do with the fact of these Aryan nations producing more than their share of cosmology, ontology, and metaphysics of the highest order.

After lawfulness in nature was more and more observed, as it was everywhere bound to be, the main-track of religion in India and Greece moved on through polytheism into monotheism, and on the philosophic side into dualism and monism. The whole religion of these lands gradually acquired something of an over-intellectual cast, because pointed at the outer and the vast. The Stoics of Greece and Rome identified God with nature as a whole except when they were teaching ethics and morals.

Then they shifted to thinking of him as Law or Reason overall and in all. The Stoics certainly helped prepare the way for a philosopher of later days, Spinoza, to write a book about the One Substance, with its attributes, modes, and accidents; and to call this book *Ethics*. This title he used in spite of the fact that there was no room in Spinoza's grand intellectual system for his noble ethics. How could there be when there was no valid individual or private person to be found in the system, but all was wheels within wheels and really called for nothing so much as silent midnight contemplation? But Spinoza's is a magnificent form of cosmic- or nature-religion, as is also Mr. Einstein's.

Taking the world as a whole, the second kind of religion, the kind in which mankind worships itself in a body or in some kind of hero, seems both more prevalent and more obsessive than the ancient worship of the powers or system of the surrounding natural world. Covering a great deal of the ground there is ancestor-worship, with its piety centered in the family. The Greeks and Latins had their Lares and Penates as well as their goddesses of the hearth, Hestia or Vesta. They concerned themselves more with these gods than old Homer makes us see. The ancient Hebrews had their household gods such as Rachel stole when she and Jacob, her husband, ran away from Laban, her father.

But the Chinese were long most conspicuous of all in this field. Until recently at least, we were advised that birth control was not practical politics in China because every household needed all the sons it could possibly get, in order to render fullest honor to its ancestors. The Chinese even created a literary and highbrow form of this ancestral piety, a form called Confucianism. Confucius, the founder, has been called an Atheist by people travelling along some other theological road; but it was he who taught the educated Chinese to worship their ancestors in the way of celebrating the good old days as until very lately they continued to do.

The totem-pole of Northwest America is supposed to be a symbol of tribal worship not so very different in effect or style from patriarchal or family worship. And among our other Amerinds, various clans of a tribe often traced their ancestry to some animal: fox or wolf, bear or serpent. The longest mound south of Chilicothe is in the form of a snake with a round moon or a world within his open jaws. Our Indians went apart sometimes to commune with their ancestors as well as the Manitou in connection with their initiation ceremonies. And the same kind of piety is found in Australia and at many other points of the compass, with the same accompaniment of ritual or worship involving forefathers and heroes.

Romulus and Remus were very sacred founders and at times treated as gods. And in Greece, Hercules was probably a tribal hero who got idealized, or else a Paul Bunyan who came to be taken more or less in earnest.

The highly civilized Egyptians worshipped their Pharaohs and the later Romans their Emperors, and demanded top allegiance for their state-religion while sometimes, at least in the case of the Romans, tolerating other kinds of worship alongside. Emperor Julian, the Apostate, usually referred to Christianity as either a superstition or an "atheism," keeping the name of true religion for what was to him the more realistic kind of piety which worshipped the Emperor, while retaining or trying to rebuild shrines for all sorts of local deities. The obvious fact that the Emperor supplied daily bread and held the destiny of his subjects in his hand made him a kind of God, and reverence before him a kind of religion in comparison with which Jewish and Christian worship was viewed as nothing but moonshine.

So, when Hitler and Rosenberg set up their religion of race, blood, and the state, they were engaged in no new-fangled business, but in a kind of worship as old as any on earth; and they were travelling one of the main highways of theology.

As to the Marxists, they probably accept the name of "atheists" for themselves mainly because they make a butt of the accepted Western religion, connecting it with an unconfessed worship of the Capitalistic System. It is natural indeed for the established and all the other churches of Europe and America to support our economic system, insofar as we have one; because that system is a part of our whole way of life. We do not actually worship it in monolithic aspect though, as our critics claim. It has been subject always to both qualifications and modifications. From Jefferson's time on we have believed to some extent in both individual and social enterprise. As Alexander Hamilton said in the Federalist papers, the militia and the navy were social and public undertakings. So are the schools and the Department of Agriculture. Recently we have had our Square

Deal, New Deal, Fair Deal, Regulated Deal, and Better Deal. Devotion to details and features of the "system" follows no fixed pattern and is subject to majorities and minorities of the day. Sometimes we make use of a little mythology to pretend that we have a system more fixed and sacred than has actually ever been the case. That is typical to a degree of the work of any religion, and it is easy for Marxists to exploit their kind of theology and, in opposition to our system as they interpret it, to call themselves "atheists." Conversely some of us make a devil of Socialism, hardly distinguish it from Communism—which is supposed to be worse—or from Stalinism. And all of these things are practically "atheism" to us.

The question is why Marx and Lenin, and their followers, have not given their way of life more of the outer trappings of a religion. They may have done so to a much larger extent than we realize. They have their sacred text or Bible in *Das Kapital*. The pictures of heroes and the banners used in their political halls begin to make them into temples. Solemn memorial rites and ceremonies are on the worship road. The Marxists say their devotion to the Communistic cause is more realistic and more of this world than Christian piety. They say their devotion is to the welfare of the workers, whereas that of Christianity and Judaism is a spurious and superstitious one, whipped up and exploited by robbers of the people. The same accusation awaits Buddhism and Islam undoubtedly, whenever these systems appear more notably on the stage of international affairs. Denying the religion of others, have the Marxists left a religious vacuum for themselves? Hardly. In the language of historian Toynbee, they are worshipping themselves and their avatars, or incarnations.

We come to the third highway, which we called spiritual religion, signifying thereby a religion of sheer inwardness. On this highway, the main thing is religious experience and that is the medium whereby and wherein God is manifested. This highway also goes back to the dim origins of all things profoundly human. When we first begin to note the trail it is running through dance-intoxications, vineyard festivals, war manoeuvers, drama, exciting oratory, and "speaking with tongues."

King Saul travelled with the whirling dervishes for a time in his youth. These were the first seers of Israel, along with the witch of Endor and her kin. King David danced before Jehovah with all his might, when they brought the Ark of the Covenant to Jerusalem and into the Temple. The Delphic priestess danced in her cave-mouth before she delivered her prophecies; and other priests and hierophants danced themselves dizzy or intoxicated in line of official business. No doubt they still do this in back-places of Africa and elsewhere.

When men discovered wine, they founded a religion of Dionysus, or Bacchus, or whoever was locally the god of the grape. Mystery religions like the Dionysian had their initiation ceremonies, their ritualistic bandaging and unbandaging of eyes, their visions, conversions, illuminations, along with sacrifice of victims. They had their resurrections from the dead, both as a celebration of historic fact or faith and as an experience of the initiate at a point of ritual. As we know, they contributed symbols and mythological elements to Christian worship. They made religion into something which, in revivalistic vocabulary, you "get," or the other way round, something which takes possession of you.

One of the deservedly most popular of Christian hymns, Whittier's "Dear Lord and Father of Mankind," is the conclusion or final coda of a long poem on the brewing of *soma,* which, distilled from a plant of the same name, was the ancient Hindu substitute for whiskey. The poet pictures the priests singing incantations or invocations while they pile on the faggots around the pot and wield the big spoon. Needless to say, Whittier had in mind a relevance to the politics of his day, in which men became intoxicated by slogans, oratory, and panegyric made to fit their passions and prejudices.

Somewhere along the line of this highway of development of the inner spirit, or we might say of the development of the arts themselves, came musical rhapsodies of the martial kind such as Tyrtaeus wrote and Plato approved; and of another kind which caused Plato to disapprove of all music except the martial. Again, and especially in the religion of Isis and Osiris, came in the celebration of the Corn, and of the god of fertility, this worship connected too with springtime and the yearly rebirth of vegetation. In time arrived poetical inspiration of the kind invoked by Homer: "Sing, goddess, the wrath of Achilles." Somewhere worship of Phoebus-Apollo, God of light and of beauty, with all the Graces in his train, patrons and inspirers of beauty and of all the arts.

The word "intoxication" embodies a Greek root meaning "poison"; hence it is replaced when we come to the civilized ranges of this religious highway by such a word as "enthusiasm," which embodies a root meaning "god." Men glow with enthusiasm forever, but we must remember that all our words require replacing ever and anon. We are always needing substitutes for debased or overworked words, as we seek to utter something that is felt to be finer and rarer 'than anything previously recognized. At times men have vitalizing experiences, breathe inspiration, undergo new birth, discover themselves, are smitten with light or visited by revelations. In turn we cheapen all these phrases and labor for new ones; but at times many of them still come from the heart with utter seriousness. As always, though, bystanders are given their chance to say: "These men are drunk with new wine." And at times the critics are correct.

From physical intoxication through creative momentum of the enthusiasm that is in all the crafts and all the arts, up to the highest intellectual and moral kindling, to a sense of support when we feel ourselves in a minority of one with God or truth, or to enthusiasm in the cause of justice and active good will to all men, is a long road. But it is so straight and so clearly marked with graduated steps all the way from barbarism to humanity, that it would seem as if there must be some pull or drawing-power, some lodestone central to nature and not only man's part of nature, and greater than any of its works up to this date. Through it all, man remains an unfinished creature, and the best men are those most conscious of that fact. Man seems to be the kind of thing that hardly can be finished. Forward prospect and the beyond are of his very life until he weakens and drops like a falling stone.

All these theological main streets have been followed throughout history under the impulsion of the deepest devotion that men of the age, or at a given stage of evolution, were capable of. As men have worshipped one kind of god or another, have followed their devotional instinct upon one highway or another, their well-being and future have always been felt to be at stake. Nature gods, were, of course, applied to for assistance in all sorts of felt needs. Tribal gods were appealed to and worshipped for aid in war and, perhaps, for augmenting the superiority complex of the tribe in every way. The life-forces themselves were followed after as gods in the search for health and vigor, for release and power, for élan, for new and transcendent self-consciousness. Even when we come to that search for "salvation" which is the goal of many of the great religions,

> *'Tis of life our nerves are scant,*
> *More and fuller life we want.*

Back in the Eighteenth Century, conservative Christian theologians insisted that Christianity was a "positive" or "revealed" religion over against the deistic or rationalistic religion which had come out of the Enlightenment and had deeply influenced such men as our own Franklin and Jefferson. That was their way of emphasizing the importance of history for religion, history with Moses and Jesus in it, supernaturally sent and appointed. They were right about the importance of history. History gives us founders, saints, hallowed customs or rituals, as well as a proportion of myth. History is itself revelation. It stirs the imagination. It focusses the eye upon high moments of the past. It kindles high devotion, launches or continues discipleship, offers samples of "the blessed community." Through history religion becomes to an extent *our* religion. And it seems to be clear that in time, and in the course of evolution, religion is displayed in closest contact with the whole of human nature and all its problems. I do not suppose there is any way of studying religion at large very well, or of criticizing what goes by the name very well, without going to history. And probably we should always begin with the familiar current of history and of religion which is ours by inheritance. For there we see more clearly than anywhere else. A great philosopher (Hegel) said that philosophy is its own history. I think it is just as true, or nearly true, to say the same thing of religion. At least religion so far is its history so far. So we now turn to our own historic line of descent, which surely had to be fraught with both successes and failures in quantities that have to be honestly measured by each new generation. And we begin of course with the Hebrews.

V. The Old Testament and Judaism

THERE IS no other nation than the Hebrews, not even the Hindus, whose religious literature is or could be collected to make anything like as good a handbook as the Old Testament, not only of their own religious development but of mankind's everywhere. The collection of books in the Old Testament is representative enough to produce something like a graduated story of progress from the beginnings to the highest kind of prophetic religion.

So far as Jahweh, or Jehovah, came into it, as he did more and more until he won out over all rivals, Judaism was always a tribal and social religion rather than a religion of nature or one of the spirit. We do not know too much about the Elohim, who were perhaps the chief older gods of Israel and whose worship may have gradually been carried over into Jahweh's. Some of them appear to have been gods of localities, as is witnessed by such names as Beth-el and Penu-el. Their name is also grafted on Isra-el, and in many given names that either begin or end with "el."

Omitting the mythological tales of the patriarchs Abraham, Isaac and Jacob, the religion of Jahweh begins when the Hebrews were nomads raiding settled folk. They carried around with them the symbol of their war-making religion in the Ark of the Covenant, as in later times at least it was called. I remember George Foote Moore expressing the opinion that the ark, or sacred box, contained just sacred stones. Why he was confident of that does not matter. The later claim was that it had contained a pot of manna and the "tables" of the law. Of course, that made a good story to be told to later generations. In any event, the Ark of the Covenant was very sacred. When they were on the march one day, and came to a rough stretch which caused "the oxen to stumble" as they pulled it along, a leading citizen, Uzzah by name, put forth his hand to steady the Ark and was struck dead for his presumption. Holiness in those ages was as physical as that, and as deadly as lightning to all save anointed or priestly

30

hands. On the other hand, it was believed that the presence of the Ark guaranteed success in battle or foray, acting either as a talisman or as seat of the divinity.

When the Ark of the Covenant was captured by the Philistines, the religion of the Hebrews may have come close to dying. One phase of it actually came to an end. There was an interval before the Hebrews recovered, as they always did, with another interpretation of tribal faith. Under King David they presently consecrated the City of Jerusalem, the King dancing before the returned Ark as it was brought into the city to be given a place in the Holy of Holies of the Temple. That made the Temple and the city sacred in the public eye, defended as they were now supposed to be by the Ark and a divinely established kingship. Of course, the adventures and misadventures of Hebrew faith were just beginning.

Years ago a curious little girl asked me what finally became of the Ark of the Covenant. I told her I supposed it just rotted to pieces in the course of ages, was swept up as dust by the acolyte or whoever had such menial tasks in sacred precincts, and was cast to the winds. We hear no more of it except that when Roman Pompey pried open the Holy of Holies out of curiosity to see what was in it, he had the surprise of his life. For there was absolutely nothing there. Perhaps tradition served just as well as fact.

There were many ideas of sacredness and taboo during those times, and often attached to the same objects. There was a sacred mountain, Horeb-Sinai, which was supposed to be deadly to all who approached save only Moses and Aaron. Then there was the taboo on speaking Jahweh's name. And the familiar one on pig-meat. The sacred Sabbath, with attendant taboos, may have been extremely ancient. Vjalmar Stefansson tells of one Esquimo facing down all his neighbors on the question of who had the most brains, the white man or themselves. He demanded to be told who would ever have thought of a whole day being taboo until the white man brought that piece of knowledge.

Of course, the sacred or holy thing was not always destructive to the touch, even in earliest days. It could act as a cure, or as an alibi. In one place we read of the people being cured of a plague by gazing upon a bronze serpent set up by their leaders under orders from Jahweh. On another occasion, the high priest solemnly puts the sins of the whole nation upon the head of a scape-goat—a real goat this—and then sends the goat out into the wilderness to die for the whole tribe as an expiation. As time went on, no doubt rites of this kind became in part symbolic and perhaps also as cathartic as some good modern drama.

In the time of the prophets we first clearly trace the process of "holiness" turning ethical. The prophets were the instrument of that change. The reason we do not see the great prophets standing out in even fuller relief than they do is probably that ancient notions do not die when new ones are born to supplant them. They remain attached to the religion of the backward portion of the community, which may be the majority. Isaiah told the people that their bloody sacrifices, their burnt offerings, their assemblies and rites, their new moons and their holy days, were not pleasing to Jahweh, who preferred they should act justly and love mercy instead. But a long time after Isaiah, public sacrificial rites were still going on. In the reign of Josiah leaders tried to put a stop to sacrifices on the hilltops for the purpose of concentrating them in the temple of Jerusalem, where they could be controlled and kept free from taint of idolatry. Temple offerings were still being made in the time of Christ. In fact, the ideas of sacrificial lamb and of scapegoat were lively enough after the time of Jesus to win a place in familiar Christian ideas of the Atonement. Even the great prophets could not kill it. You do not kill an idea as great as sacrifice. At best they could only discredit it with some men or possibly start turning it into a symbol of something spiritual.

The earliest plainly labeled version of the Decalogue or Ten Commandments, that in Exodus 34, deals with nothing but bloody sacrifices, meal offerings, taboos, and duties honorific to God above. It is the same with the larger grouping of commandments in Exodus 23, not yet restricted to the number of ten to give the people a rosary of principal duties to tell over and remember. In our familiar versions of the Decalogue, Exodus 20 and Deuteronomy 5, we find obligations of the people to one another coming into the picture: honoring parents, not killing, stealing, or committing adultery. There are also in surrounding chapters references to duties owed to strangers or aliens. This represents a later age, and is plain evidence of growth and of some influence from the prophetic voices which had been heard.

As for human sacrifice, the logic of that is inescapable and the Hebrews did not escape it. Logic requires that we give God our very best gifts, the most valuable things we have. In the story of the call which Abraham received to sacrifice his first-born son, Isaac, we see this logic at work. What could there be so precious, so revealing of devotion, except for moderns a first-born daughter?

Editors of the Old Testament in later times did what they could to obscure the fact that human sacrifice had been prevalent at a stage of Israel's growth. It peeps out at us though in a phrase in those passages which refer to the people making their children "pass through the fire." Of course, the Hebrew editors like to associate this with Moloch, which might excuse Jahweh but not his people. A plain case, with Jahweh involved, is in the story of Jephthah's daughter (Judges 11), which must have been too circumstantial and traditional to be omitted. And probably the story of Abraham preparing to sacrifice Isaac, at Jahweh's summons, represents the moment when some prophetic leader reinterpreted the covenant, and reinterpreted deity itself and its demands, by saying that what God wants is devoted lives and careers rather than bloody deaths. It would be natural that such a great insight should be referred back in literature to the first of the patriarchs.

After the founding of the sacred city of Jerusalem, the covenant with Jahweh was supposed to cover protection of a settled nation rather than a wandering tribe. The political form of this faith lasted for only a relatively short time. All the tribes became lost or carried into captivity, and Jerusalem was destroyed in 586 B.C. After the Babylonian captivity ended, Jerusalem was rebuilt, and about this time the synagogue, or place of meeting, replaced the temple as the lively center of national worship. This change was accompanied by a new interpretation of Judaism as a law rather than a political experiment. The Law and the Prophets were something you could carry around with you, even in captivity. But the conservatives revived the nationalist form of the religion, or preserved it, by dreaming their Messianic dream about the coming of a second David and a millennium. This new dream was embroidered with variant imaginative features until the time of Christ. But some of the prophets, like Jeremiah, had long ago given up the faith that Judea, a little country between the upper and nether millstones of Egypt and Persia, could ever be a great nation. These prophets dis-

33

covered that Jahweh was god of the whole earth and perhaps that he had other names, or could have. He had one righteous law which he had revealed to Israel, and this law, in a sense their own, was nevertheless destined to cover the whole earth "like as the waters cover the sea." A great and universal faith!

These universalizers went as far as to teach that the whole Law of God could be summed up in two commandments, loving God and loving one's neighbor. Along this line there was just one further step to take, to discover and teach that the way to really love God is to love your neighbor, who is any human being who needs your help. It does not appear that the Judaism of ancient days ever took this humanistic step, though it became a universal religion and learned to think of Jahweh as the one and only God, the same in his love to all men.

Somehow the Jewish religion always deepened and widened in time of trouble. Of course, this was brought about through a minority or what Isaiah called "a remnant" of the people. But that only reminds us of the usual role of minorities in all great things. They are the small seed of the future. A religious minority kept Judaism alive wherever one of its conservative forms was dying, and gave it a new birth with a promise of something better in the future.

As in the case of Isaiah's condemnation of bloody sacrifices and the mere conventionalities of religion in his time, this new penetrating insight which made Judaism into a law of loving God and neighbor could be either forgotten, cheapened, or misapprehended. People could move forward to acceptance of the idea of law, and then turn to the law's external side, the mere legalities. That is what some of the people called Pharisees were proving in the time of Jesus of Nazareth. The law to them was a matter not of the spirit but of dotting the i's and crossing the t's. Even in the time of St. Peter, Jewish Christians were all for circumcision and for avoiding certain meats. And it was still possible to believe that if you kept the forms of the law, God would be with you in battle. Just as today it is possible for Jehovah's Witnesses to believe that failure to maintain old-fashioned and literal New Testament religion was the cause of our two World Wars.

Christian teaching that religion is a matter of love and the spirit, with the added point that the proof of loving God is loving your fellow-man, is built on top of Judaism in somewhat the same way that you splice a new section on to a mast or a flag pole. The new piece runs back a way on the lower one, and is clamped on sideways to the other before it begins to run free into the upper air. Christianity began as a Jewish sect. But Jesus quoted that saying about love to God and man, and went on then to say that the way to prove love of God is to manifest love to your neighbor.

As we said, so far as we can see from where we now stand, that humanistic teaching of Jesus appears to be like a masthead added to the structure of Judaism as it existed in his day. However, we cannot claim that no Hebrew prophet or rabbi had reached such a height. Admittedly, commentaries on the law which were the work of rabbis of the time of Jesus closely approached his insight. In any case, where and by whom new ideas were first broached is a secondary question.

In the meantime, Christians are unaware how much they have taken over from Judaism that was purely Jewish, not universal at all. It is part of a real Jewish conquest of the world. In Christian churches all the ancient books of Judaism are sometimes read as if they had as much religious light in them as the grand passages of the prophets. The Psalms, without very much discrimination or selection, are used full-length as responsive readings. In such readings Jehovah is besought to take a hand against our enemies, or he even offers to do so: "Ask of me and I will give you the nations for thine inheritance, and the uttermost parts of the earth for thy possession; thou shalt break them with a rod of iron." Jehovah is presented as wrathful to sinners, and loving to the righteous—as if there were in reality any such classes of people. Promises are made to the upright—which cannot apply to any of us. Elsewhere Christianity's teaching is that we are all sinners; but this it forgets, with the help of the Old Testament. A tendency to moralism which is in that book at least confirms the tendency to moralize and preach to other people which is a fault of most of us. All of this is illustrated by that image of the flag pole, the new top piece running back down the side. To refer to such long-continued influence of the Old Testament as a "Jewish conquest of the world," however, may unduly obscure the positive contributions made by Judaism.

In comparing the Hebrews with the Greeks—for we have a religious inheritance from both—we are confronting Mt. Sinai with Mount Olympus. The Hebrews were moralists par excellence, sometimes, like many of us, too much so; while the Greeks leaned to intellectualism and aesthetics, where they also could lean too far. The Jews regarded all human error of conduct as Sin. That came from tracing wrong behavior back to disloyalty or breach of covenant. They separated saints and sinners, righteous and unrighteous, although that could be done only by basing judgments on smaller, instead of greater, matters. We sometimes wonder how they could have done so. But they did. And we took that over in the very notions of sin and conversion. The Greeks took a more naturalistic view, regarding evil as negative rather than positive, or as a matter of failure, so far, to grow up and attain. Nearly all our physicians are on their side. The Greeks set up such ideals as order and harmony of life, self-realization, maturation. To them at least these goals were lofty and divine.

Judaism taught that "out of the heart are the issues of life." Those words faithfully reflect the fact that the Jews knew a man's heart can be molten in his breast, and sometimes needs to be. We can sometimes get a new heart and can faithfully interpret the experience as being born again. The Greeks and their spiritual descendants put their emphasis upon education, admiration, ambition, aspiration, as the tools for improving mankind. They did not deny the importance of the depths of feeling, but they did not view life as a purely moral or ethical conflict.

The Hebrew religion taught obedience and humility under the Covenant; and early Christianity and much of the later teaching of it makes these the central virtues if not the only ones. We are bidden to give up our self, and as some of us feel it, our very manliness. Susannah Wesley's idea of the first thing to do with a boy was "to break his will"; and that is the grand idea her son John carried far and wide. Many other Christians joined him in spreading it. The Greeks however, applied the teaching of Jesus himself even in this field: the saying, "I am come not to destroy but to fulfill." They believed in fulfilling the individual according to the divine pattern in him, as Plato explained. They strongly felt the need of civilizing the barbarian within the breast, or you might say of subduing "the old Adam." But they felt no need of grovelling or self-abasement, no place for asceticism or despising the body.

The Hebrew religion, being a tribal one, needed to be widened into something for all men. And it was. The Greek religion, being a religion of nature, needed to be humanized and spiritualized. This extension was made, too, at the top of their flagpole. They did not finish their task, or carry it out with all their people. We are not finished either, at this day. For one thing, the Greeks had slaves among them. But so do great modern nations have segregated lower classes.

The part of our Christianity which came to us from the Greeks has been demoted by critics under the name of "naturalism." Here we come to the conflict between naturalism and supernaturalism as it stands today. As a matter of fact, we need to see what meaning we are giving to "nature" before we touch that controversy. Do we mean a rule or realm of supposedly dead material atoms? Do we mean one of simple and known laws? Do we include man within nature, even Shakespeare and especially Christ? Is there a dialectic or paradox in nature, or do we find that only in certain regions of theology? For every meaning of nature there is a corresponding one of supernature.

The Salvation religions of earth went beyond Judaism in making religion emphatically a religious experience. For great religious experience the Jews knew only conscience. That they knew as well as Immanuel Kant or anybody else. But the idea of being turned into a god so as to make you immortal; or of being possessed by a god to make an invention or write a poem, or to conceive some grand new revelation of truth, would have been and indeed was, a profanity to the Jews. No doubt, the whole Christian doctrine of the Incarnation, with its wide range of suggestion about God's being seen and known in a man, or visiting a man, was as offensive to old Judaism as it later was to Semitic kinsmen, the Arabs and their Mohammed.

The Jewish Jahweh, when the prophets left off making his lineaments clear, was still above the heavens, transcendent. He never trod this earth in proper person, even if in ancient times he may have appeared in Abraham's tent as an angel. He was more of a king always than a father, more a law than a spirit. When he spoke too it was more often in anger than not. That is like our conscience; reproof or remorse is the stinging part of it. Symbolically at least, we can see that a Christ, and on the feminine side a Virgin Mary "Mother of God," and some of the saints, were needed if God was to be represented as goodness and love incarnate.

37

The reward most often mentioned for good conduct in Jewish religion is not salvation or eternal life, but something like peace under one's own vine and fig tree—among quiet and happy neighbors of course; or "length of life in the land which the Lord, thy God, giveth thee." These quoted words give an ancient form of the ideal; but they pinpoint the social and perhaps we may say the terrestrial character of Jewish vision. It all fits in with the common Jewish conception of the Messiah's mission as that of bringing in a Davidic kingdom and a millennium upon this earth. Shall we say that the Jewish religion was realistic and of this world where other religions have been more romantic and other-worldly? Let this question be postponed to other chapters.

* * * *

After taking notice of several dictionary definitions of religion and emphasizing the concept of devotion or "positive concern," we discussed the meaning of worship and the relation of religion to magic and morals. We traced some of the angles of human experience and developments which, from earliest times to the present, have left their mark on theology, including the contributions of Judaism and its holy book, the Old Testament.

Now we proceed to questions which involve the authority and use of certain Christian documents which have long been received and accepted by many as recitals of historical fact. For that purpose, a one-sided report is now offered on two dialogues with earnest and confident spokesmen for sects outside canonical circles.

VI. The Gospel Witness

ONCE WHEN WE LIVED in Amherst, Massachusetts, a pair of young Mormon "elders" came to the house for discussion of a paper on Mormon history into which I had put a little research and had sent to one of their predecessors with whom we had held pleasant social relations, and whom we had judged to be a very able youth. These two newcomers wanted to go over that paper with me and discuss it in detail. We had to admire their frank, simple-minded approach. And we had to start with respect for a religion which is able to send most of its young men into the mission field for a couple of years; and which also eschews tobacco, alcohol and coffee. We had been at a Christmas party with the previous elder and had noted his quiet restraint. And once in a Salt Lake City hotel I asked a nice little waitress who was serving us coffee something or other about it; and she responded, with simplicity, that she had never tasted coffee in her life.

These two young fellows had me read my paper, which had been put in their hands, while they listened until they wanted to break in with a comment or a question. The discussion soon turned on accepting Joseph Smith and the Book of Mormon as religious authorities. I had referred in the paper to some of the miracle stories in the Book of Mormon. There was the story about Jesus, long after his ascension into heaven, descending again from the skies and landing somewhere in America, out in our own West it seemed to be, perhaps just because of the deserts and open spaces. The story is in the book of Nephi 3, chapter 11.

Jesus was revisiting earth among his Jewish kinsmen. The Ten Lost Tribes, it seems, had migrated to this country from the Holy Land ages before he was born. They were at this time not too far from a fall from grace which would lead presently to their being overwhelmed in war and utterly destroyed. One of the very last of their scribes or prophets was to leave behind those bronze plates, with the historic records on them, plates which Joseph Smith was one day to discover and translate.

In the book of Nephi Jesus descends again to Earth, and preaches the Sermon on the Mount all over again and verbatim to a mighty congregation gathered outdoors in a wide place. No human being, it is safe to say, could have so repeated it after such a long time, without a manuscript, even if the Sermon of the Mount had been actually one sermon instead of excerpts from many. Do you imagine Jesus would have wished to repeat so meticulously? It seems as if he would have done as Russell A. Conwell did with the famous lecture, *Acres of Diamonds,* with which he earned between eight and nine million dollars, probably more than any other man ever earned in this country by purely personal services. Conwell gave it all away, like a sure-enough first-century Christian. He says he always tried to get to an overnight stand in time to visit the barber shop and a store or two, so as to acquire fresh background and possibly a local story or two to use.

Apart from this puzzle of the literal repetition, it seems that, whatever language Jesus may have spoken on a trip to this country, it would be another tremendous miracle to get it all translated and rendered into English so near the King James version of the Bible. But here it is that way in the book of Nephi, thanks to the courtesy of the bronze plates and Joseph Smith's reading thereof.

Nephi goes on to tell of Jesus appointing another Twelve Disciples for the New World, but we needn't go into that. The young Mormon elders appeared to accept all this literally, although one imagines that not all Mormons by any means are now as fundamentalist as that. They seemed to think that if I could accept some of the miracles in the Gospels, as they supposed I did, it was foolish to boggle over their particular Mormon miracles. When they found there was no agreement about the factuality of the Christian miracles and the authority behind those reports, the Amherst party broke up in friendly agreement that there was no use proceeding without any common ground to stand on.

One day a handsome young woman representing Jehovah's Witnesses dropped in at our home in the New Hampshire hills and presently began quoting the Bible to me text by text. She thought her texts settled many important questions of the hour for good and all, such questions as who and what is responsible for the recent World War, and where civilization is headed, and why. On the basis of texts she argued that disbelief in the Bible was the main obstacle and culprit. If men would only accept its authority, all would be well. Some of her texts were taken from the Hebrew prophets, and some from the New Testament. Most of the latter concerned Jesus' coming again on the clouds of heaven. One could see that if we ever get into an atomic war, the Adventists and Jehovah's Witnesses will be quick to say: "There! This proves we were right. Why didn't you listen to us and accept the Bible?" It is easy for them to show that Jesus warned of a coming "end of the world."

Of course, all Adventists have to admit past human mistakes in figuring out the date of the Second Coming. And, no doubt, the year 1000 A.D., when so many people became terribly excited, was a natural inference from things said in the New Testament about millenniums. It marked one millennium from Jesus' birth, a one thousand-year period. My interviewer said nothing about now pinning down the date to any given year and month. But she was sure the end was near. And half the road signs we see warning us with the words, "Prepare to meet your God," may not be referring to traffic accidents bringing us into the presence of God a few at a time. One often wonders whether they refer to a personal Judgment Day or to a general one.

There is no use in defending your outworks when engaged with a textualist, so after a little badinage I told the young lady I was sure the Bible was not originally meant to be literally believed. A lot of it was drama, likely made to be enacted at go-to-church time instead of having a modern service with sermon. In fact, sermons are a rather recent invention and drama an ancient one. Take for instance, I said, that story of Peter's forgetting one of the most important warnings anybody ever had and quite the most specific one Jesus ever gave him, and then remembering it all of a sudden a few minutes later at the crowing of a cock. Surely that is part of a play. Or take the story in John's Gospel about Jesus handing the sop to Judas, pointing him out as the traitor, and then and there telling him to get on with the business. Or the tale of just what Jesus said in his lonely prayer at the Garden of Gethsemane when even James, Peter and John had been left behind and there was no one on hand to hear what he said. Who is it reports all that? Why to be sure the author of the drama.

And what can you do with Jesus' lineage being traced from David through Joseph by two different lines and lengths of descent? How can you make anything of that unless you assume that the news of the miraculous Virgin Birth had not yet been received where these ancestral trees were first worked out, and that very likely people were celebrating Jesus' birthday and his descent from King David with a play, and wanted to make it realistic by bringing in a few familiar names—varying them a little in another locality or in next year's version?

Some years ago, a magazine called *Christianity Today* which reached me in the mail, sent perhaps for proselyting purposes, contained a passage dealing with the genealogy of Jesus: "The great difference between the genealogies in Matthew and Luke has, of course, created difficulty. There is an explanation which seems at least plausible, and it is that Joseph was the legal, not the natural, father, and that Matthew, the 'legalist,' gives us the legal genealogy while Luke, the physician, gives us the genealogy through the real mother. . . . The alternative is not one which ordinarily decent critics would lightly accept." Apart from the question how much blood inheritance can be founded on a "legal" descent instead of a real descent, the alternative the writer had in mind was, we may be sure, not that the gospel genealogies present a dramatic fiction.

Presently this Jehovah's Witness guest of ours said that unless we had the Bible for common ground, and of course she meant for proof-texts, there was no use arguing. So she left us, pleasantly enough.

The question of what kind of literature the "Gospel Witness" is takes its place above all other Biblical questions on which some understanding is necessary. One can surely raise this question without assuming that fundamentalists are wrong about everything in religion or in their devotions. There are too many friendly people among them for that. And somehow these two interviews, with two Mormons and with a Witness revived an old interest in theological studies.

VII. What the Gospels Are

In all strictness the Gospels are not historical documents. They are catechisms for use in common worship, containing the cult-legends of the Lord Jesus Christ. Of what the teaching of Jesus was in reality only an approximate idea can be formed from the teaching that has been attributed to him. It may be said without a trace of paradox that of the teaching he actually gave no collection was ever made. Neither the preacher nor his most faithful hearers dreamed of fixing the tenor of his preaching for the purpose of transmitting it to posterity; every purpose of that kind was thrust aside by the imminent prospect of the Kingdom of God, the near coming of which was continually announced by the first apostles after the death of Jesus.

Just as a legend has been built up for him (Jesus), so too there has been built up for him a body of teaching, and it has been done by borrowings from many quarters. One part of the sayings which constitute the synoptic tradition was taken from the teaching of the Rabbis, while the whole of it, even where the spirit is that of hellenic Christianity, has the tone of Jewish hellenism. It is safe to say that the teaching of the first three Gospels is conceived after the manner of Jesus and directly penetrated by his spirit.

—Alfred Loisy, in *The Birth
of the Christian Religion,*
translated by L. P. Jacks
(George Allen and Unwin,
Ltd., London, 1948)

I therefore stand and work in the world as one who aims at making men less shallow and morally better by making them think.
—Albert Schweitzer, in *Out of My Life
and Thought* (Mentor ed.)

TURNING FROM THE TESTIMONY of the two Mormon elders and the Adventist young lady, we may take something of a look at the field of fairly recent New Testament scholarship. We may recall presently two who were very prominent fifty years

43

ago: Alfred Loisy, Roman Catholic Modernist, and Albert
Schweitzer the medical missionary who worked in Lambaréné,
Africa. The latter had earned doctorates in theology and in
music as well as in medicine. His *The Quest of the Historical
Jesus,* written when he was quite a young man, had established
the central importance of the expectation shared by Jesus and
the early disciples of the imminent coming of a divine kingdom
foretold by ancient prophets of Israel.

But we want to speak first of two scholars of the present
day and hour, because we were referred to them when we asked
a professor at a well-known theological school the question of
who was bringing the latest news in New Testament criticism.
We were led to Oscar Cullmann and Rudolph Bultmann in particular. In successive generations orthodoxy has been challenged
by students possessing new techniques and means of investiga-
tion, though we must confess it seems the Church has slowly
and reluctantly, if at all, profited by their conclusions.

Oscar Cullmann says that if we are to see the evolution
which leads from the Old Testament to Christ, or from Christ
to the Church, we must be "both theologians and historians."
Of course, that disqualifies most of us though it also reminds
us of the fellow who built his house on the state line so that
he could escape a sheriff coming in either direction. A man might
conveniently poise his remarks or tenets between the two states
of theology and history. Cullmann further says: "The inter-
preter (of Scripture) must subject his own ideas to the severe
control of Scripture."[1] That implies we must start with the
assumption that the Scriptures are a strictly literal authority
instead of an imaginative guide, and perhaps it reveals another
assumption, that we can agree on just what in a given case the
words of Scripture say or mean.

Cullmann marks off "apostolic" and "post-apostolic" ages
very sharply and says that at the dividing point in time gospel
writing definitely decayed in quality. No actual date for this
decay is given, and one wonders if the date or dividing line does
not have to be drawn in accordance with what Cullmann judges
to have been the decay in quality. The reader may know that
there were from a dozen to twenty gospels written in the first
two centuries or so. The dating of them, though, or of the frag-

---

1. Oscar Cullmann. *The Early Church.* Westminster Press, p. 15.

ments of them which have survived, is by no means close or certain. They were spread about and used, some in one region and some in another, before a more or less official selection (the canon) was made, in which our four, Matthew, Mark, Luke and John were adopted and the rest left to be known as "apocryphal."

In another passage Cullmann says that there came a time when the period of direct revelation was ended. This also he fails to locate upon the calendar, and probably he thinks we should not ask him about it. But in any case he goes on to say that the four Gospels which were finally adopted are not biographies or memoirs but "testimonies of the faith." That might possibly suggest to you or me that their truth is given in a literary or dramatic form and is spiritual rather than literal. But one is confident the meaning, in Cullmann's thought, is that the Gospels belong primarily in the exclusive sphere of theology.

Speaking of St. Paul, Cullmann says: "The unique honor of this Apostle is that he has received a direct apocalypsis."[2] That big word "apocalypsis" certainly belongs to theology for Cullmann, although we easily gather that the immediate reference is to St. Paul's conversion experience on the Damascus road.

Cullmann looks straight at the fact that St. Paul's earliest writings show that he expected Christ's return to this earth within his own lifetime. In other words, St. Paul and his contemporaries were living in their present as a kind of interim. Cullmann even credits Jesus with a misapprehension upon the same point: "Certainly Jesus did not reckon on the period of waiting lasting more than a few decades."[3] Our theologian makes no further use of this recognition or concession and even seems to beat the bush a little to let it appear as if Jesus had not after all said anything so very plain when he sent out certain missionaries and told them they would not have time to go around the borders of Judea and return before Kingdom Come. There it stands though on this theologian's page, the plain accrediting of a theological error to Jesus himself.

At this point we may pause to note that neither Cullmann nor Bultmann finds any church father or apostle who did not make theological errors, and very often on the most important point or points.

2. *Op. cit.*, p. 72.
3. *Op. cit.*, p. 152.

Bultmann appears to be a good stout Lutheran in basic sympathies, although his critics make more of his attachment to existentialism. One finds him a much better reasoner than Cullmann. He stands pretty well alongside Cullmann though, in saying that the Gospels are not history or biography. If we were to express in our own language what Bultmann thinks the Gospels really are, we might say he thinks they are the utterance of a faith, an enthusiasm, a deep concern which is both for the individual and for all men. We bring our familiar vocabulary into use because Bultmann's own particular word for what the Gospels are seems unnecessarily unfamiliar and strange. He says the Gospels are "kerygma," a word derived from the Greek "keryx" meaning "herald." He seems to mean that they are a kind of heraldic proclamation, which may not after all be too far from what we suggested in more familiar terms. Nor is it too far from Cullmann's notion of the Gospels being testimonies of the faith. It is interesting though that Bultmann thinks the Christian proclamation is most clearly given in that one of the Gospels which he regards as both the last to be written and the least historical, namely St. John's. That fact he seems to account for on the ground that it took time for Christianity to get crystallized into theological expression, or perhaps we had better say to make a good start in that direction. For plainly, according to him, the crystallizing process is still going on.

No doubt our very first need as Bible students is for some kind of present-day analogy, or analogies, for the kind of thing the Gospels are; that is, if we are to break with the inherited preconception that they are to be approached as matter-of-fact history. We can all assume that they had the very highest of motives behind them, that of explaining the good news of the Gospel of Jesus, or of Christ. If we are not unalterably prejudiced against the word "propaganda," then perhaps we might say that both of these great theologians of our time are saying the Gospels are propaganda. Once you try to explain with a clear, fresh, voice the meaning of a religious message, then you are engaged in propaganda, sermonic propaganda. We would not say that the Gospels are even superficially like the political handbooks they get out for election campaigns of course, because that might suggest insincerity in the Gospel writers. There was no insincerity. They were in earnest. They believed they were dwelling upon the greatest matters. But, of course, they wanted

46

to be eloquent. They wanted to reach the people. All preachers do. They wanted to set fire to the word and spread it. They both understood and spoke out of a kind of fire and also in terms of popular and current ideas.

Readers approaching the Bible after reading real biographies have long supposed that when you saw the words, "Gospel according to Matthew," or the like, at the head of a work, it meant that it was composed by an actual disciple of Jesus who carried that name; or by the companion and amanuensis of one. But scholars now tell us that the phrase "according to" at the mast-head of a book was a common and proper enough literary device for recommending it. It was like either Democrats or Republicans of today labelling their platform "Jeffersonian Democracy" without having asked Mr. Jefferson about it. No doubt such interpreters of our day can be sincere. There seems to be no reason at all for doubting the sincerity of our gospel writers even in their most dramatic parts.

Alfred Loisy's view of what the Gospels are is in initial phrasing not very different from Bultmann's or Cullmann's. He says they are "catechesis," which is to say the kind of stuff catechisms are made of. He means they were constructed to answer questions raised in the early churches, the answers no doubt incorporating passages, parables, and maybe sermons in Jesus' own words as handed down by oral tradition. They are, as it were, handbooks for initiates or catechumens. Part of the material would almost inevitably have been dramatized, or handled in the most graphic language that was near at hand, in order to make the subject matter appealing. Something of this sort was the procedure in Gospel days, and it was sufficiently above board when it was done. When was there not a call for artists in expression?

One matter that was dramatized with interesting divergencies, only partly obscured by later editors and commentators, is the question who was leader among the disciples after Jesus' death and in the churches during their earliest development. John's Gospel makes John to be the "beloved disciple," which gives him a very high prominence in the group, as high as anybody's, one would think. Maybe John stood first where that Gospel was written. There is a tradition that James, the brother of Jesus, was leader of the Jerusalem group until his martyrdom. In one short sentence Jesus points to Peter and says:

47

"Upon this rock I build my church." The Roman Church has built up from that text the doctrine of Petrine supremacy. In St. Paul's letters, James, Peter, and John, in that order of naming, constitute the leadership. Paul also says that he is not sure whether any of them are as big as their reputation.[4] Paul is the nearest we get to solid historic evidence about earliest Christian leadership.

It would be easy to find differences between the Synoptic writers which reflect a psychological bent besides perhaps a local atmosphere. Mark's writing is more Jewish in point of view than Luke's or John's. And he is inclined to Spartan brevity by comparison with all the others. Luke has the most sympathy with underdogs or proletariat and perhaps a slight anti-Jewish bias.

Matthew is inclined, you might say he actually bent over, to show how certain Jewish prophecies have been fulfilled in Jesus. He manhandles a good many of them to make them fit into his drama; but no doubt does this with Jewish simplicity and faith.

John wrote his Gospel at a time and in a locality where Greek ideas, philosophies, and terms were in the air. Bultmann says John was affected by Gnosticism, which Adolph Harnack dubbed "the acute grecizing of Christianity." But, as we have seen, this does not keep John from being, according to Bultmann, righter than the others on the main point of the Christian religion. The same modern authority squarely says that Greek words and concepts helped to reinforce Christianity where it was coming into contact with Greek civilization—that is to say with the big world. Of course, according to Bultmann, John was not quite right in his theology, but then neither has anybody else ever been that. It is hard to satisfy a good theologian.

Alfred Loisy makes a comment on all our four Gospels together which is relevant to their total character in quite another way. He says that if the early Christians had been really interested in history and biography as some people now assume that they were, then we should not, all of us, including Matthew, Mark, Luke, and John, be as dependent as we are upon such a thin trickle of facts about the life of Jesus. Of course, Loisy is characterizing Mark's Gospel, the one which the others took

---

4. See Galatians 2.

over almost bodily because there was so little else to go by for data or events. We see that Loisy's statement does discount the miraculous legends about Jesus' birth which are found in Matthew and Luke, and such a story as that of the small boy putting in their place all the "doctors" in the temple and getting safely away with it. He, of course, recognizes that there existed somewhere, probably not just where Mark lived or travelled or he would have included them, a collection of sayings of Jesus containing the Sermon on the Mount and some of the parables that are missing in Mark. But even with these items included in the story of Jesus' preaching, Loisy thinks the paucity of biographical materials a striking fact.

There is a similar and, as we see it, perhaps a more acute mystery when we turn to St. Paul. Some of Paul's writings are the very oldest Christian scripts we have. He wrote while a Jew named James, brother of Jesus, was head or first-mentioned staff man of the Jewish sect, or Way, which sprang from Jesus. Paul met James, Peter and John, and conferred at some length with these three unquestionably leading disciples. They must have been full to the brim of reminiscences of Jesus. And yet it seems as if Jesus had remained for Paul almost a stranger in those aspects of his life we are most interested to dwell upon. Paul's voluminous writings refer to no events in Jesus' life except some of the very last in Jerusalem: the Lord's Supper, the crucifixion minus all details, and the resurrection. And how could he have written so many epistles of advice without ever quoting the Sermon on the Mount, or any of the parables, or any single word Jesus ever spoke save the traditional words that are spoken in celebration of the Lord's Supper: "This is my body and my blood . . . ?" Paul would have been forced to learn those words just by partaking in the formal meals of the brotherhood, or in the ritual of the church. Where are any words at all that he got from Jesus or from any direct reporter?

We have no wish to make a mystery more impenetrable than it is. No doubt Paul felt he had no need to look up Jesus' biography; because the Jesus who concerned him, who had raised him from the dead spiritually, and had been resurrected in spirit if not in the flesh, had met him in a mystical vision on the road to Damascus and demanded to know why he, Saul of Tarsus then, was "kicking against the pricks." St. Paul was an original man. His religion was an original experience. He did not need

49

to get the message of love, for example, from Jesus. He could state it himself, and he did in I Corinthians 13. His faith was that we all need to be renewed in the inner man, the Old Adam needs to be cast out, and all of us need to be resurrected or reborn of the spirit. With St. Paul everything is more first-hand than has been recognized.

Jesus' disciples were not scholars, if indeed they even knew how to make the characters or to write at all. Maybe they did not realize how important the story of Jesus' everyday life and the report of his sayings would some day be to some of the people who followed after his name. Maybe they felt there was not time nor any sense in writing books and finding ghost-writers to help out their awkwardness with a pen. According to all the Seventh Day Adventists, and to all the scholars we have been looking into in this chapter, everybody was then anticipating that Second Coming when Jesus would ride in again, this time on the clouds of heaven. That was their first great religious concern, the big item of the *kerygma,* the catechesis, the faith, the Word, the gospel. So near, too, was the expected event. It was to happen during the lifetime of some of them, John in particular. Jesus had said so. Somehow this strange prophecy has come down to us in spite of what looks like its utter confutation. Eugene Sue wrote a book about the Wandering Jew who was unable to die until Jesus got back to earth from the sky. This wanderer was the disciple John, though he travelled unknown and almost in hiding. Why bother about books or annals of a past career of Jesus when a new career was just around the corner? Even St. Paul started with that conviction, according to Bultmann, even if maybe he changed it.

The Gospel Witness is, then, not what it has been taken to be. It is something we ourselves have to look through or behind to gather what Jesus means to us and our times; to see what great concerns and faith are opened to us in the whole movement which runs from Jesus and his age clean to ours.

VIII. The Figure of Jesus

ONE CAN EASILY IMAGINE that recalling a few favorite passages from the Gospels gives many people the initial feeling of knowing all that anyone should ask to know about who and what was Jesus. And they might say to us something like this: "See here! Jesus spoke the Sermon on the Mount, whether all of it on the same day or not. In it he gives us the Beatitudes and the Lord's Prayer. He said the Sabbath was made for man and not man for the Sabbath. He said that discipleship to him consisted not of saying 'Lord, Lord,' over and over; but of works and fruits. He spoke the parable of the Good Samaritan. He advised that it should be left to the man who was himself without sin to cast the first stone at the woman taken in adultery. He put the humble Publican above the self-righteous Pharisee. He said: 'Suffer the little children to come unto me.' He taught that the law and the prophets are all summed up in the two commandments, to love God and to love one's brother-man or neighbor. On the cross he prayed: 'Father, forgive them for they know not what they do.' Now that is enough to know about Jesus. Why look further, probing into all the corners of the Gospels for little things to raise questions about? Why not halt right here and show your deep respect and reverence for the figure of Jesus?"

Of course the question is loaded a little, to make it appeal to liberals and humanists in the broad sense. No Fundamentalist would think the challenge adequate to the central purpose and aim of Jesus' gospel or message. But we did try to make the appeal universal so far as it went.

And truly this challenge is enough to halt practically everyone in his tracks long enough for him to show respect and reverence for the source of these teachings. In fact, the Sermon on the Mount, in spite of its not being found in the oldest of the Gospels and being some sort of a collection, has proven itself to be enough to win reverence from leaders of all the great

51

religions of the world. Great democrats like Abraham Lincoln and Leo Tolstoy have found the Great Sermon a landmark able to stand out by itself in human history, practically as if Jesus had said nothing else. Many liberal Christians quote the Sermon on the Mount as practically Bible enough, if not religion enough; although many of them would like to include the story of the Good Samaritan and perhaps Jesus' saying in Mark: "Why callest thou me good? There is none good save one, even God."

The most important fact to recognize is that while there are people who see in Jesus a simple figure to be identified with a few readily compassed teachings, and who challenge others to accept their view, very few of them are actually satisfied to know so little of Jesus or to let the matter go. They really do not find it enough to admire the Sermon on the Mount, or to see and know Jesus only in a few selected passages from the Gospels. Who would be satisfied to feel he knew Homer by reading only the Iliad and ignoring the Odyssey? Who ever stopped short with reading half the story of a great hero? Most people think of Jesus as the central figure of the four Gospels in their full length; and they try to find wholeness of outlook, of message, and of personality all the way through. Of course they never give up the hope of finding some ancient manuscript or other which gives further words from him. But as things stand they expect us all to find in the Gospels at least as realistic and living a presence as in the hero of any great novel—in fact they claim to find more than that. They speak of Jesus as their personal Master and Savior and go to him with their every problem, or they glory in the "living Word" with its personal impact upon all history.

The deep desire to know the founder of Christianity is a pointed continuation of that vital curiosity, that deep spiritual impulsion, which centuries ago demanded the translation of the New Testament out of Latin into English and the other modern tongues, so that any man could go to the sources for himself and get as close as he might to Jesus, the very headspring of it all; and incidentally to St. Paul and the apostles and evangelists.

Thomas Jefferson was pained when he found the image of Jesus confused in the usual presentation. He felt that the first step needed to clarify that image was to take manful hold of the New Testament and to cut out with scissors all the words there attributed to Jesus in person, and to paste these "direct sayings" together in parallel columns. There was a column each for Matthew, Mark, Luke and John, except of course where a story was not reported in all of them. In this way Jefferson pieced together what was given the name of Jefferson's Bible. But he himself was never quite satisfied with it. In the first place, the four columns did not fit together very well in many places; there were many variants and some contradictions, as you might expect, if they were thoroughly human documents; and Jefferson came to feel the heavy hand of ancient reporters, editors, translators, lying upon the texts, compelling one to look beyond all textuality to an extent. He could not feel that all the supposed sayings of Jesus were genuine.

His general conclusion was not unlike that of the great German New Testament scholar, Adolph Harnack, who came along in the next century and found two kinds of sayings attributed to Jesus. In the first place there were the great new truths which had never been uttered before, or at least not anything like so forcefully and well. These truly belonged to Jesus, thought Harnack. His disciples or biographers could never have thought up those things. Then there were other sayings attributed to Jesus as the result of misunderstanding and the usual earthiness of the human mind, or that had crept into the story of Jesus while his words were being passed around from mouth to mouth before they were written down.

In his book, *What Is Christianity?*, Harnack concluded that the whole of Jesus' teaching could be summed up under any one of three headings: the Kingdom of God and its coming as a spiritual event in the hearts of men; the Fatherhood of God and the infinite value of the human soul; the higher law of righteousness which is the law of love. Jesus' own teaching was not only always one and the same all over the Gospels; but it could be summed up about equally well under any one of these three heads. Of course then the things which Jesus never said, but which had crept into the Gospels in one way or another, would be the ones that countered, changed, or qualified this central teaching, threefold in name only. Harnack's kind of criticism suited many people at the time.

In people like Jefferson and Harnack, not to go any further for famous names, we see a conjunction of the deistic and liberal interpretation of Christianity which characterized the 18th and 19th centuries in important circles. It left out many of the

Messianic features, including the dogma which presents Jesus as a single savior sent from Heaven to save men from their sins, whose death upon the cross was part of a divine plan, and who was to act as Judge when the Kingdom of God miraculously appeared to the people waiting on the housetops to see it come. Of course the deistic and liberal teaching had never been accepted by the evangelistic churches at large, or by the Established churches except perhaps for what was called the Broad Church wing of the Church of England. There was a handful of Roman Catholic modernists who took practically the same ground, but they and the "higher critics" in Lutheran Germany stood only as individuals. Nowadays hardly any New Testament scholar follows that old liberal line.

Albert Schweitzer, he of Lambaréné, is perhaps our last earth-shaking New Testament critic. In his *Quest of the Historical Jesus* the discovery was that the historical Jesus insisted upon "returning to his own century." That is, Jesus was in no sense a modern liberal. In fact he was what we call an Adventist. And Schweitzer suggested the probability that some of the most strenuous requirements of the Gospels, such as turning the other cheek, giving your property to the poor, paying wages without work, living out of a common basket, leaving parents behind and the dead "to bury their own dead" were a kind of "interim's ethic." That is to say, these harsh-seeming rules were for a short and quick pull, which would be all. Not only was there a terrific hurry about spreading the word and getting a lot of evangelizing done, but if this world's clock was nearly ready to stop ticking, what was the sense in worrying about tomorrow or making any careful plans for the social and economic life of the earth?

We have seen that both Bultmann and Cullmann agree with Schweitzer that Jesus shared a lot of the Adventist outlook which was common to his times. We find Jesus quizzing the disciples about what other men think of him and his mission, and then he asks them what they personally think about who he is. Peter tells him he is the Messiah, and Jesus replies telling Peter to keep it dark. The Messianic faith at large involved to be sure a lot of unsettled questions, such as whether the Kingdom was coming by rebellion against earthly rulers or by the direct intervention of God; when and how the dead are to be raised up; rewards and punishments at Judgment day for the righteous folk and for the unrighteous; whether eternal punishment or no, a millennium; the individual's part in serving or preparing for the coming Kingdom. The clearest points in Jesus' teaching upon the whole subject were that the Kingdom of God was not to come by armed rebellion but unexpectedly, at God's own time and hour. And it is also clear in many of the discourses reported as from Jesus that the Son of Man, with angel escort, was to come riding through cloven skies to the great Day of Judgment.

It was a time of superheated religious imagination in a country and a spiritual climate which favored that kind of thing. The nation had always had more than its share of trying ordeals and anguished hours. In Jewish history there had been few long intervals of home-rule and peace to restore balance of mind and spirit. Recently the Jews had been kicked around like a football. Probably no modern religious revival, no Titus Oates conspiracy, no Communist scare, can give any sufficient idea of the common people's excitement about the Messianic hope in that generation. To Jesus, as to others, the popular Messianic faith and its interpretation was probably the focus of everyday concern.

Of course if Jesus was an Adventist, that does make a little difference in just how clearly he represents for us the heights and depths of religious leadership and sacrifice in his "going up to Jerusalem," daring all the opposition there and enduring crucifixion. If he was carrying out a pre-arranged divine plan, that makes some difference. If, as scholars hint, he looked for divine intervention which did not come off; or for a quick resurrection, with spectacular ascent into heaven, and an early return upon the clouds, then he had advantages over the ordinary dim-sighted and short-sighted human being called upon to bear witness or to stake his all. Socrates submitted to the law of the state, when it was putting him to death, without any heavenly vistas open and clear before him; and he did it with simple dignity. But we do not expect that of ordinary men, though it does reflect great honor on humanity. Probably the firm belief of any of the later martyrs of Christian history that they were passing through the flames to quick and ineffable rewards and glory detracts from the value of their example for us.

Against this Adventist background, there is something to be said for the person who wants to think of Jesus in terms of just a few great passages of the Sermon on the Mount and a few beautiful scenes or acts, even if that makes him a literary or dramatic figure instead of a realistic personality pervading the whole of the Gospels. And some people have no choice, for they never had any lively sense of Jesus as a total person. Of course, even they may have some suspicion that it is the fault of the tradition and build-up that the real Jesus is obscured.

One observes over and over how far every reader is from giving equal weight to everything Jesus is reported to have said or done. Whether we are thinking about ourselves or the ancients makes no difference. It seems as if nobody can, or ever did, form an image of Jesus without forgetting or rejecting some feature or features of his teaching. If we do not like a saying, we may make it mean something rather different from the obvious or we may suspect the dull ears, the dumb minds, or the narrow propagandists, who heard and reported, or edited, or translated him. We streamline the conception to suit us. One biographer after another gives his widely different interpretation of Jesus just as the painters have always made him a Nordic or pleased the home folk in their rendering of his complexion, hair, or beard. The virtues biographers have most feelingly ascribed to Jesus are either universal and such as the veriest heathen would echo, like love of little children, sympathy with the poor, benevolence; or else they are the kind most admired by the biographer himself and very likely of current style. For example, Jesus has been presented as a go-getter or as an apostle of the strenuous life.

In olden days St. Bernard of Clairvaux preached the Second Crusade with its goal of restoring Palestine, which was Jesus' home, to the Christian world; and others after Bernard preached that perhaps worst tragedy of human history, the Children's Crusade, which left youth from the West—England, France, Germany, Italy, stranded all over the Near East, many of them in slavery. Some of the children found slavery without going that far. Europe had racks and stakes, torture and secticide for heretics before we had genocide. The Ku Klux Klan of our day harangue their mobs with the printed evangel in their hands. Tolstoy and others are sure Jesus was a pacifist, in spite of all the consecrated military banners that have floated his name. Some leave out of their picture of Jesus everything that shows him an Adventist. Jehovah's Witnesses and many others stress that part very heavily. Revivalists have found their teaching of hell-fire in the parable of the Judgment, where the saints and the sinners are separated right and left, and waved into eternal blessedness or eternal gnashing of teeth. How could any great prophet have been melodramatic enough to divide humanity into black and white in that fashion? Of course it was an Old Testament contrast of righteous and unrighteous, unfortunately carried along into the New Testament, and of course we seem to be carrying it along into international politics ourselves. But great prophets are supposed to lead.

Perhaps Jesus' treatment of the Pharisees was also rather in black and white and wholesale, somewhat as if they were a whole class of people devoted to externals. It was otherwise when he met Zaccheus the publican and the thieves on the cross. These he treats as individuals, ignoring slogans and bad names.

There is a great deal of contradiction on the Gospel pages, a good deal of which we may indeed suspect is due to those who were even in those days constructing an image of Jesus to show to us. Once Jesus says: "He that is not for me is against me," and another time: "He that is not against me is for me." That is verbal of course, but it reminds us of other equally plain contraventions. Jesus tells the people he is not going to give them any "sign" save the "sign of Jonah"—which appears to mean troubles about to come. And then the story makes him multiply miracles, especially of course in John but plentifully everywhere. He turns water into wine. He heals instantaneously and casts out devils. He multiplies the loaves and fishes to feed a vast multitude. He gives fishermen a great draught of fishes. He walks on the water. He raises the dead. The name of his miracles, like that of the demons he casts out, is Legion.

He says: "Blessed are the meek (or the gentle)," and then he lashes the money changers out of the temple. He says in Mark that there are none good save God, himself no exception to the rule; and yet he accepts men's worship, and not only the dumb worship of the poor woman who kisses the hem of his garment or the other one who spreads all the costly nard in the alabaster cruse on his feet. The saying in Mark just quoted, startles us into wondering whether Jesus would not find it extremely discomposing to come back and find so many people saying "Lord, Lord" to him, instead of doing "the great things of the Law." But at times he seems to welcome recognition of his divinity.

Jesus implies in one of the parables, and in certain other

sayings, that the resurrection from the dead will not be of the body; and yet he reappears after the Resurrection and invites Doubting Thomas to prove who it is by putting his finger into the nail holes.

In that oldest Gospel, Mark's, James and John come to Jesus one day asking that they may sit on his right hand and his left in the Kingdom of Heaven. We are straightway reminded of another passage in Matthew (19:28), where, addressing the Twelve as a body, he says: "Ye which have followed me, in the regeneration when the Son of Man shall sit on the throne of his glory ye also shall sit on twelve thrones, judging the twelve tribes of Israel." In the Mark story of James and John, they are rebuked for their vain-glory in asking for the two greatest seats, if not exactly for asking a thing silly in itself. For Jesus goes on to preach a resounding sermon against pursuit of the earthly type of honors, and declares that the chief one among his disciples is that one who serves most and best. We love to quote that. We feel that it makes James and John look like the veriest of hypocrites as well as beggars. Shall we conclude that they were looking for the loaves and fishes? But then we recall the Matthew passage and have to acknowledge that Jesus himself has partly justified them in nominating themselves for dignities or running for the highest offices established for the Twelve. He was talking about twelve thrones, was he not? He had kindled their imagination with that perspective, had he not? When the Gospel pages are collated, it certainly leaves James and John looking less silly than they did in the first place. And the sermon about honor belonging most to those who serve best is threatened with tarnish, although this story is indeed not one that we find much difficulty in referring to the makers of tradition instead of to Jesus himself.

In fact it is a perfect instance in which to catch tradition either helping out or hindering Gospel stories by its interference. For in Matthew and Luke we find the story changed; now it is not the disciples themselves but their mother who comes to Jesus with this unseemly request. We can more readily forgive a fond mother asking such special favors for her sons, especially if she is on a visit and not familiar with Jesus' teaching about service making or marking the man. No doubt he had often made that point, we may think. From their point of view, Matthew and Luke were engaged in edification, improving and burnishing up, catechesis, *kerygma*, preaching. Maybe what the whole story does for us is to make it a bit easier to assign to tradition some more contradictions and things we do not like. In any case we may go on to greater matters of wonder. Jesus says, Matthew 11:27 and Luke 10:22, that nobody can know the Father unless the Son, that is to say Jesus himself, reveals God to them. We should have expected this saying to be in John's Gospel rather. For then the "Son" might mean some mystical figure or eternal actor only dramatically symbolized by Jesus himself. Then we should know and be glad to have it made clear that the saying was part of a literary build-up, like those long speeches in John ("I am the vine and my Father is the husbandman," "I am in my Father, and He is in Me.") which may very well represent an impression made by Jesus upon others but nothing a man could possibly say about himself. The claim to be the one and only revealer of the true God is too disrespectful of other religious founders to say nothing of other good people at large, for the Jesus we reverence ever to have made it. This one saying, taken seriously, seems enough to explain how Mr. Gandhi, who was familiar with the Bible, could say that he never had found his "guru," or his thoroughly satisfactory religious teacher. We may ask why Mr. Gandhi did not stop with the Sermon on the Mount. Well, he must have felt unable to do so. Either here, or in even more serious matters, he could not feel that he knew Jesus whole, or that he could fall back upon the Sermon on the Mount for adequate knowledge of Jesus.

Jesus sometimes, and not always in John, makes it a virtue to believe in him, and perhaps in his mission as Messiah. See for example Mark 16:16: "He that believeth and is baptized shall be saved." But surely too many people accept their religious as well as some of their political beliefs on the basis of mere authority, mere traditional faith. That is what is wrong over wide ranges of the human landscape: this believing without question what we are told. One of the things that divides the nations from one another and hinders peace is the variance in their sacred beliefs and revealers. And we must recall that in a generation taught to some extent by science there is nothing more sacred and less to be tampered with than facts and truth itself. How can we make a virtue of believing beyond or against or without the evidence? Mr. Gandhi even said once that there

59

is no God except Truth—not that we pretend to know just what he meant. Jesus in the Gospel of John says the Truth shall set the disciples free. Philosophy has sometimes at least seen Truth, Goodness, and Beauty as a Trinity in one. And as we said, here is science making a God of truth in a practical way of it. At least, just as there is a beauty of holiness and a divinity of love, there is also a sacredness of truth over against the lie that divides a man against himself.

There is another point in Jesus' reported teaching which is perhaps the most searching one of all for the modern student, or for any thoughtful people once they focus their eyes on it. Jesus claims the power to forgive sins. In the story of the man sick of a palsy, he tells the man his sins are forgiven, and the bystanders evidently think Jesus is exercising the power to forgive sins. He is either doing that or claiming the authority to speak for God. And the difference is not in the least to the point. For the basic assumption to be reckoned with is that God can forgive sins, not to speak of being able to deputize the power. That assumption involves a monarchical conception of God and a formalistic conception of sin. It turns our wrong-doing, selfishness, and meanness into a breach of covenant or a defiance of authority instead of leaving it a matter of diseased growth or corruption. The idea at work is that the monarch who made the law can forgive the breach.

Possibly we could make sense of such an idea in terms of human relationships, where a friend undertakes to overlook a wrong done him in the sense of foregoing penalties and taking the wrong-doer back into his circle of associates. But the main thing about our greater sins of commission and omission is and remains that we have perpetrated them. That is something which nobody on earth or in heaven can cause to cease being a fact for ever and ever. One cannot forgive himself for some of these things, and has no wish to do so. They are a part of himself. The only realistic thing to do about them, after repentance and waking up, is to weigh them down with better deeds and regain self-respect. If I cannot forgive myself, what is the sense in asking "God" to do it? God's forgiveness might make sense in that social way if we believed in that kind of a God and if we still believed in an old-fashioned hell after death and were being let off from that punishment. But what we feel an actual need of is not forgiveness but being born into the power to

60

do what is right and to rise into one's better self. Our vital concern is to achieve positive worth, character: something which we ourselves, the discerning among our neighbors, and God the Universal spirit can and will approve.

It may be only in a few homely scenes, where Jesus is dealing with troubled folk, like that woman with the alabaster cruse of ointment, that Jesus offers or affirms forgiveness of sins. But we may well wish that somewhere or other he had given forthright and affirmative recognition to the positive need of achieving manhood of our own.

In Mr. Gandhi's autobiography, he tells how the Christian missionaries tried to convert him when he was a young man in South Africa on a mission to his fellow-countrymen who had been imported there in numbers as cheap labor and were being treated as expendables on top of being thoroughly segregated. He says the missionaries, with whom in a spirit of inquiry he associated quite a while, wanted him to pray that his sins be forgiven for Christ's sake. What he wanted was to be reconstructed so that he would no longer commit those sins. He says he could not get the missionaries interested in his problem and he was not interested in theirs. They told him he wanted the impossible because all basic improvement in a man had to be through imputation of Christ's righteousness. In fact what he was offered and what he was urged to seek in religion was not goodness of his own, not achievement, not living a significant life. It was salvation.

If we could only interpret discipleship to Jesus in terms of the Sermon on the Mount and a few other sayings attributed to him, seeing it as a summons to seek the right facing the consequences, and to leave selfishness and littleness of outlook as far as possible behind! Even the Evangelicals teach that nobody can expect even a negative perfection. For those who regard religion as a positive activity it would be the persistent and honest pursuit that mattered. As Jesus tells one woman, it would be the love behind the sins. But taking the Gospels as a whole, we cannot safely be so positive. Somewhere, on the basis of the Gospels, there has arisen the belief that Jesus went up to Jerusalem and sacrificed his life not to settle his problem but to settle ours. And we still have to reckon here and there with the wide tradition which makes Jesus a gloriously divine scapegoat, but still a scapegoat. He gave his life for us in a different sense from that in which many stout men and boys, women and girls too, may be asked any moment to do the same.

It just might be that St. Paul started something for the future ages when he neglected to hunt up and repeat biographical facts and stories about Jesus and spoke (instead) of the mystical Christ he had met on Damascus Road. True, liberals have for a long time criticized Paul for theologizing Jesus and forgetting the simple Galilean figure of the man. But they could be wrong, or half-wrong. Some evangelicals too have awakened the echoes in their demand for "a return to the historical Jesus." In the first place maybe they asked an unrealistic and impossible thing. Perhaps Paul was, in a back-handed way, helping towards starting something more to the point. Perhaps, whether he quite meant it so or not, he may have been opening a way to make the Jesus of the Sermon on the Mount into a universal, timeless, figure whose name was not all-important. That is what Alfred Loisy wanted done and he pleaded with a pope or two to take the lead in doing it. He wanted the Church to stand on the ground that a living truth had been growing within the bosom of the Church and within the heart of the world's literature, and that this living Gospel only started from Jesus of Galilee; was written into our Gospels with other things besides; and that truly the Gospels need to be interpreted by the Spirit.

George Fox, the Quaker, taught that the Inner Light was above the Scriptures and was needed when we tried to interpret them. He also suggested the practice of sitting together in a quiet congregation to see if some fresh inspiration of the Holy Spirit would come to some one and lead him to speak acceptably, on the road to their Damascus or Jerusalem, in the midst of wars, facing the problems of their own times with the help of every saint they might know about.

Perhaps no other man has contributed as much to the continuation of this doctrine of the Inner Light as did the poet Whittier:

> A sweeter song shall then be heard,
> Confessing, in a world's accord,
> The Inward Christ, the living Word.

But it is Albert Schweitzer, neither Quaker nor poet but musician and mystic, who has given the world a famous paragraph about a universal leader, from Galilee first and from many other places since, alive and active in our times, classic in framing, humane and belonging to the whole earth: "As one unknown and nameless he comes to us just as on the shore of the lake he approached those who knew not who he was. His words are the same: 'Follow me,' and he puts us to the tasks which he has to carry out in our age. . . ." The revealing tasks Schweitzer has in mind are probably the kind to which he has devoted his life in Africa: medical missions, with now and then a broader perspective on questions of international justice.

Schweitzer uncovers the mystical roots of much Christian religious drama in a very suggestive way. The words to inspire many features of that drama were either in Jesus' teaching or they crept in fast from all sorts of sources. We see how features of the drama may have sprung from words: the crêche, the singing angels, the Magi from afar. "He came unto his own and his own received him not." "The foxes have holes and the birds of the air have their nests; but the Son of Man hath not where to lay his head." "A prophet is not without honor save in his own country." "The poor heard him gladly." "Things hidden from the wise and prudent are revealed unto babes." "Not many rich shall enter into the kingdom of heaven." That last sentence at least inspired the early adventures in Christian Communism from one angle, although "interim's ethic" may have worked from another. If we respect drama for what it is, there is in our Gospels a story good for wide humanity, based on facts and figures from one time of history but containing hints from far places and most distant times. A move towards making the story universal was certainly edged along on one side long ago, by St. Paul and St. John, who looked beyond the historical Jesus (in so far as they actually knew or knew about him) and reached in their theological fashion beyond history into the world of dramatic and literary imagination.

IX. The Apostolic Age

Recall those loved ones in whose lives you have "seen God's
excellent glory and beauty," whose exalted character has showed
your low aims, whose gentleness has rebuked your harsh judgments, whose integrity has quickened your conscience. . . .
Can you think of them and still believe that human life is a
mean thing, that it has a history but no future, that its significance is to be found in the lower orders of being which are
subject to death?

—HAROLD E. B. SPEIGHT

THE THEME of the Apostolic Age is the first assault of Christian
missions upon the wide world. In that age Christianity moved
mightily on its way towards "conquering" the Mediterranean
and Western World. The story is told chiefly in the Book of
Acts and in St. Paul's Epistles. The Book of Acts starts with
the Day of Pentecost, moves on into the doings of Peter and
John (reported to have been one of the earliest martyrs), tells
of their conflicts with the Jewish law, brings in the heroic martyrdom of Stephen, outlines some further travels of Peter. Then
comes the conversion of Saul of Tarsus and his making-over into
Paul the Apostle; and his wide travels. There are faint echoes
of Apollos, Barnabas, Titus, and others who did the same kind
of work as Apostles, whether they are entitled to the name or
not.

We have often heard preachers or orators declare that the
great unanswerable question which should put all infidels and
heretics out of countenance is the question about what mighty
force, what supernatural impulse and faith, it could have been
that launched the Apostolic Age. We may simply answer by
saying how this matter looks to us.

At Jesus' crucifixion all the men among his adherents seem
to have scattered for a time with only the faithful, die-hard,
feminine devotees left on the scene. The disciples felt themselves
defeated along with their master, who had been visibly confuted

in his teaching. So the group broke up. But presently they re-gathered at Jerusalem and went into that Upper Room; and anon they went out in a blaze of missionary enthusiasm. Such at least is the traditional picture. It is inevitable that we should ask what brought the followers of Jesus back to the mark, the starting-line; and what gave them that propulsion. And the traditional answer is in two major and complementary parts.

We are pointed first to the great miracle of the Resurrection and the manifestations of Jesus thereafter. We are told that Christianity is founded upon this greatest miracle of all the ages. And St. Paul is quoted in the lines: "If Christ be not raised from the dead, then is your faith vain."

It also appears, upon the pages of the Book of Acts, that soon after the disciples regathered they appointed twelve of their number and set them apart as "witnesses of the resurrec-tion." Of course we wonder just why the resurrection needed special or official witnesses if the event itself was overt and palpable; and not some kind of Mystery, or mystical event. That there may have been a problem about the nature of the resurrection is suggested by the variety of the reports of it that have come down, some of them with extraordinary details entirely lacking in or divergent from other accounts. The short-est resurrection story is in the oldest Gospel, that of Mark. This old story is somewhat confused for us by apparent addi-tions which have been made to the last chapter, so that scholars have long since been wondering about a lost conclusion of Mark's Gospel. In his final chapter, the two Marys go to the tomb on Sunday morning and see an angel, who tells them that Jesus is risen, that they are to go tell the disciples to proceed to Gali-lee, and that they shall see him there. Then follows a collection of surprisingly brief mentions (for so great an event)—bare references or echoes of reports we might almost call them. Per-haps these are addenda attached to Mark by some editor, derived from some other written source which itself had originated at a somewhat later time. This would have been in an effort to assimilate Mark's account to that of the other Synoptics, and to heal the bluntness and unsatisfactoriness of that "lost" end-ing which may have been cut off. These addenda lack the char-acter of first-hand accounts—the liveliness and the detail. The longer passages in Luke and Matthew and John have mystical features which look in various directions; and for graphic character these features rise to a peak in the picture of Jesus walking on the water to the disciples' boat, and of his inviting Doubting Thomas to put his finger into the nail-hole to prove that he is still with them in bodily presence. Doubting Thomas appears in John's Gospel, generally regarded as the latest to be written. Of course the Apocryphal writings go much further in miraculous details, but most of them are still later than St. John.

A reflection which these expanding resurrection stories raise is this: what after all can pious dramatic impulse do but strive by many expedients and by building out many dreams of the night to make a feeling, in this case a conviction of the continuation of the life and the spirit of Jesus, accessible to all classes of men? That is what "kerygma," gospellizing, and preaching seem to be for.

There is no need to forget, even if we could, that when these earliest Christian documents were being written Christians were living within a Roman world, in the reach and hearsay of many Mystery religions each of which had a god who dies, is resurrected, and becomes the "first fruits of them which slept." Osiris, Dionysus, and Mithras were such gods for their own respective cults. Even the native Greek Eleusinian Mysteries are also in some respects akin. These Greek Mysteries brought neophytes through trials and "death" into life or light eternal. Indeed, as St. John's Gospel itself suggests, in days of special trial eternal life may be a grand and life-giving discovery of the universal human heart when dedicated to high matters. For John says that to dwell in love is to dwell in God—in him who is eternal and in whose presence there is no death.

On the whole, our Gospel stories read like the literary presentation of a kind of story which might need official, ritualistic, witnesses. All the more so since St. Paul, the great Apostle, never refers to any of the details of any of the resurrection stories and plainly teaches that the resurrection of Christians at large, for which Jesus' own is the prototype, is not of the flesh. Paul had had his own personal experience of the resurrected Jesus. He had encountered Jesus in a vision on the road to Damascus. That event had been both his conversion and his personal Pentecost. Perhaps nothing could mean more to him than that experience.

Need we suppose that all the other disciples who came together presently in an Upper Room at Jerusalem understood precisely the same thing by the resurrection of Christ? Pretty certainly every one of them did have the feeling that Jesus lived on. We should all have had that. We have it in a degree when any great soul passes on. They felt that Jesus was still with and among them, and doubtless some of them heard his voice at times. But whatever knowledge of his resurrection they had as individuals or as a group, the fact is that it had not yet fired them with courage and enthusiasm to go out as burning brands ready for martyrdom. If some of them came to believe, like Doubting Thomas at the end of the story which had brought him to witness, that had not ended their hesitation—as one would think it might have. They had to wait for Pentecost.

Here comes in the other part of the usual explanation of the onset of the Apostolic Age. Pentecost itself is this other part. And it was either prepared for by foresight or else hindsight has found it way into the developed story. Tradition says that Jesus had foreseen his crucifixion and his defeat in men's eyes; and had warned his disciples in advance of the aspect of emblazoned failure due to fall upon his life and mission. If so, of course, they had forgotten it, like Peter forgetting he had been warned of his denial until the cock crowed. But we are told that in anticipation Jesus had bidden them await the coming of the Comforter, or the Holy Ghost.

And now, so the story goes on, here is Peter standing up day after day in that Upper Room before a group of a hundred and twenty followers, men and women. He calls the prophets to bear witness on the subject of Jesus' mission and his crucifixion. He proves a resurrection to have been anticipated in Old Testament days long ago by calling upon King David as a witness to it. Then he tells the hundred and twenty that they are all witnesses of the resurrection. He does this without describing any particular vision they may all share, or saying what part the official witnesses are to uphold. Then he recalls the special prophecies about the outpouring of the Holy Spirit in the "latter days of earth." This is eloquence suited to the hour and to the audience. It is the first major Christian revival. And even while Peter is speaking as perhaps few men ever spake before or since, down come the "tongues of fire." The disciples are all at once "speaking with tongues" and prophesying, and all the bystanders say: "These men are drunk with new wine." But Peter says, No,

67

we are witnessing the fulfilment of a prophecy. And so the Apostolic Age is begun.

In this way the Pentecost story comes to the support of the Resurrection faith as the story is popularly presented. No doubt Peter was an orator, the pattern of great modern revivalists. This is another explanatory element which does not come into the conventional explanation, but one feels confident that, on the basis of the report in Acts, it ought to be mentioned and heavily scored.

However, turning aside conventional explanation of the Apostolic Age, and allowing for Peter's oratory, there is yet another thing which almost certainly played a mighty part, if not the mightiest, which scholars like Albert Schweitzer and even Bultmann put at the very top, and which is pretty thoroughly covered up if not entirely disregarded in the conventional explanation of the coming of the Apostolic Age. In the first chapter of the Book of Acts is the story of the Ascension of Jesus, of his being taken up into the skies before the eyes of his disciples. Then and there an angel tells them "this same Jesus shall return in like manner." That is a prophecy of what is called the Second Coming of Christ. It combines with ideas of a Last Judgment and an End of the World. Perhaps this belief played a big part and maybe the decisive one in rallying the vagrant disciples a while after Jesus' crucifixion. A little time might have been required to ferment this Messianism, especially if there were really lively disappointment about failure of divine intervention at Jerusalem; and then the disciples would have consolidated as a group of Adventists looking intently for Kingdom Come. Such groups have revived many times since with less occasion. At the close of the year 999, end of the first millennium A.D., the near expectancy seems to have been very widespread indeed; but of course it was defeated and its adherents had to regather themselves.

Not only had Jesus himself foretold his return in this manner. St. Peter in his Pentecostal sermon had recalled the faith, or he now did so, and had declared that the days were short. In what Bultmann confidently refers to as some of the earliest chapters of St. Paul's writings the approaching end of the world hangs over the page like a great dark cloud, though to be sure with no zero-hour attached. Paul's urgency is like Jesus' own; he warns people not to be caught napping. In Thessalonians II he comforts them with the reminder that troubles and persecutions must come first (perhaps they find themselves already in the midst of these), before the day when the Lord Christ is to be revealed from heaven "with his mighty angels." What could be much more obvious than this ancient working of Adventism and its influence upon the scenes where Christianity was launched as a missionary movement?

In the later Pauline epistles, written when time has flown on, and also in John's Gospel and most of the remainder of the New Testament except the book of Revelations, the Christian movement has taken a rather more mystical or spiritual direction. Time and disappointment sober many men and educate the more teachable ones. Like the old Judaism, this new Christianity had to re-interpret itself. It based the new interpretation upon other ideas found in St. John and elsewhere.

So far as St. Paul is concerned, we can see in his later writings that he was merely driven back from the Messianism in which he had been immersed, upon his original experience of Christianity. After all, Christ had already come once upon the clouds of heaven to Saul of Tarsus, and that man had then and there been made over into the likeness of the New Adam and given an apostleship.

But the Adventism which was in Christianity from the beginning has never been fully conquered, although we may forget how old it is, when we meet it today and also when we try to explain the onset of the Apostolic Age. A new idea seldom or never kills an older one. It merely relegates the older one to what we might call a submerged group. In this case the Adventist faith retreated and lived a subdued life on the fringe of the Christian movement for a time, but always ready to emerge and be revived by new champions like the Millerites or Jehovah's Witnesses of our own day. Among neighbors of the day, it is chiefly Jehovah's Witnesses who scan the Scriptures with one eye and the horizon with the other. But indeed the most sober of us may feel that this time the expectation of an end of the world, in accordance with some of the intents, purposes, or meanings of that phrase, has more of a chance to be correct and prophetic. In fact the secular prophets of doom may just now be more numerous than those of religious ordination and pretensions. We hope not though, and that is a mighty point on which to differ.

Are we injuring the cause of growing religion or of improvement in humanity either by not accepting the conventional explanation of the Apostolic Age or, in the case of Adventist neighbors, by suggesting that their faith was once quite flatly defeated in the persons of both St. Paul and of Jesus?

No doubt both children and adults feel that the issues of life and the moral standards of today are dependent upon the familiar creeds and world pictures they have grown up with so far. But the best of us can be mistaken in such matters. Some of us have already discovered we are better off without certain beliefs to which we once clung tightly.

We can be thankful that the relation of a modern man to the religion of his forebears, and to those forebears themselves, is not what it would be if we had to assume that Christianity had ever been just a matter of what the first founders or any of their successors had believed about the Second Coming of Christ. No doubt ever since St. Paul wrote that famous chapter about love, the 13th chapter of First Corinthians, all Adventists worth counting and nearly everybody else has liked to hear it read in church. I suppose there has always been some store set by the parable of the Good Samaritan, on every sea and shore where our religion has gone. We know that when the Saracens, in the last Crusade, captured St. Francis of Assisi, they looked him over, stood him on a stump and told him to go on preaching. They wanted to keep him as their own holy man, but kindly let him go home after a while.

In what we call the Dark Ages, all through the persecutions of heretics and the Jewish pogroms (St. Bernard of Clairvaux, that great persecutor, halted one of those pogroms in its tracks), monks in the monasteries were copying and illuminating the manuscripts of the Gospels, containing the Beatitudes along with much other scripture of Old and New Testaments. We may suppose the parables were occasionally read in their chapels, alongside the fiery denunciations of sinner nations and individuals from the Old Testament and the dire prophecies of weeping and gnashing of teeth from the New. The gentler things were copied and kept, too, and for some purpose or reason.

Even so, gentle spirits of today can contemplate pictures of hell-fire everlasting, if it be at some distance and if the phrases which embalm the idea are sufficiently resonant. There is a story of an old-time Negro preacher dilating on these latter-day scenes. When he got to the weeping and gnashing of teeth, an elderly voice from the congregation interrupted with a question: "Parson, how about us which ain't got no teeth?" "Teeth will be provided, Brother, teeth will be provided."

Our appraisal of human behavior and character is nowadays complicated by a good many considerations, some of them introduced by the psychologists and sociologists. But one thinks our evaluation of humanity has risen a little. At least we have transcended the Calvinist doctrine of total depravity as applied to all or even most people. If we have seen or read Bernard Shaw's play, *Joan of Arc*, we probably saw the point that it was not sheer cruelty that led to the burning at the stake of that sublimely simple and heroic figure. Reasons of Church and State, held with inborn prejudice and deep tenacity, helped to make that possible. Lord Salisbury and the Feudal System were as harsh in their attitude to Joan as was the Church. The Feudal System was one kind of a God in which men lived and moved and had their being. Such ethics as many men held were draped upon the framework of that system. Men can and will with undisturbed conscience burn other men to serve their God. And no doubt in the case of church machinery built to save millions of people from hell, some churchmen could burn others and still sleep o' nights. We hope there were some tender-hearted people who never could have done so.

If we ourselves are less inclined than people of former ages to view other men's character, at least in the case of those who are not Communists, in black and white, and somewhat less inclined to persecute whole classes, the difference in our favor, in this age of so much more travel and mixing, may be due in part to a broader experience and a somewhat better educational system. If we are modest enough to admit that fact, we do not have to raise, let alone settle, the question of whether or not human nature has improved in strictly moral stature as time has gone on.

Everybody, through the Christian ages, has been offered the teaching that supernaturally imparted love (agape) is entirely different from any natural brotherly love; and has been told that human standards of right and wrong bear no resemblance to God's standards and are not enough for us to go by in passing judgment upon men and events. Such vacating of primary moral judgment in favor of religious doctrine may have helped

71

Adventists and others to look forward with equanimity to a separation at Kingdom Come of saints and sinners, "the sheep on the right hand, but the goats on the left." It seems clear that the impact of such preaching, such demotion of native human fellowship and regard, has decreased to some extent. But the main point is that our credos do not sit too close to our natural sense, which on the contrary has a tendency to grow in an expanding experience and even to reject the credo.

*　　*　　*　　*

We have been discussing how the Apostolic Age began. We gave a look at the traditional way of explaining it, on the basis of Resurrection and Pentecost. We have gone on to contemplate what scholars like Schweitzer, and many plain people like Jehovah's Witnesses, think was the biggest factor of all: belief in a Second Coming of miraculous nature. That was a form of the ancient Messianic expectation which was powerfully present upon the scenes, and which to this day dieth not.

But there is another great question about the Apostolic Age. What did it take to make an Apostle, as distinguished from any other kind of famous missionary? When and where did apostleship end, and with it end the Apostolic Age? Involved here is the question about the tenet of Apostolic Succession.

We have seen that one idea of an Apostle, or rather of the group of Apostles, is that they were elected to be witnesses of the Resurrection. Possibly they were the same group as the Twelve Disciples, filled out by an election to supply the place of Judas. Oscar Cullmann thus defines an Apostle in rather hard and fast terms: "an eye-witness, who saw the resurrected, and who received either from the incarnate Jesus or the resurrected Christ, the direct and unique command to testify to what he has seen and known."[1] This definition is very carefully worded so as not to exclude St. Paul, who never saw Jesus in the flesh or upon the earth, but only in the sky and in what was probably a kind of trance. Meanwhile, we may note that the same Greek word, "apostolos," which means "messenger," had sometimes been used by Jesus himself, or by whoever translated Jesus' speech from Aramaic into Greek, when in earlier days he had sent out some of the Disciples as missionaries to go around the coasts of Judea.

---

1. *Op. cit.,* p. 76.

What was St. Paul's idea of an Apostle, or of the Apostles? Well, in Galatians 1, he tells how after three years in the mission-field under his own steam-power or a separate impulsion from above, he made a trip to Jerusalem especially to see Peter. He says that on this trip he met none of the other "apostles" except James, brother of the Lord. If this James was ever one of the Twelve we are not told anywhere about when he was converted or drawn into the early group of the Disciples or into that of the Apostles. During this visit of Paul's there was no meeting of the Apostolic board, or if there was one Paul was not invited. Then, after fourteen years more in the missionary field, Paul says that he went up to Jerusalem again, to consult those who were represented "to be somewhat." Whether they really were official or very special leaders, in commanding position and recognition, he says made no difference to him. He had Titus with him, and Titus joined him in making a defense of their joint mission to the Gentiles. The two of them finally won the approval of the pillars of the Church, among whom Paul names three: James, Peter and John. The remainder of Galatians II is taken up with the story of a renege at Antioch by Peter, surnamed "the Rock," in the important matter that had been agreed upon at the conference mentioned. We are led to remark that Peter's nickname has as little foundation in his known character as was ever seen in the case of a nickname being given to a man. We seem almost justified in supposing that there was no fixed order of Apostles at this time.

It also seems legitimate to suspect that the terms "Apostle" and "Apostolic Age" developed in the process of the hierarchical build-up which occurs in all live religious movements. Practical functions and official responsibilities create titles which gather dignity as time moves on. Sacred title and rank attaches itself to certain early leaders, and in the end their personal name and fame bolster and support establishment and orthodoxy. They themselves in turn receive more official honor and dignity of position.

There was presently a very real need to justify special, circumscribed and channelled "apostolic succession" and authority. Others than St. Paul might claim to have visions and direct commission; and they did. But that was not permissible on the road which led to order and discipline in a movement, especially Roman-style. Uncanonized and irregular founders and new prophets led to division of authority, confusion, splinterization, less power for the clergy with which to influence mankind in that direction the clergy felt was right and good—and often it may have been so.

So it was felt by those in position of power that even men good enough to come down to us as Church Fathers, men like Irenaeus, Ignatius, Polycarp, and the Shepherd of Hermas, should be distinguished from the Apostolic group, or from the group of leaders in the first order of dignity, and prevented from acquiring too much recognition for their personal authority. They all had their individualities and minor heresies, their own lack of clearness on points where they should have stood fixed as ancient landmarks. Even their fresh words and personal names for things made a troublesome problem for those who would organize and consolidate. On top of all that, no doubt the older and more removed the authority, the better it is for an establishment. The Church Fathers could be witnesses to the prime authority of the Apostles, chiefly known to the world after a while in the two figures of St. Peter and St. Paul. They could be a part of the chain of authority from Christ through the Apostles and on down. But that was all. And in the same way presently the ranks of Church Fathers themselves were closed for the very same reason as that which ended apostleship: the purpose and end of supporting and enforcing the order and system of the Church.

In all of this, as in the first launching of the Apostolic Age, what was the place and part played by the Holy Ghost or the Holy Spirit?

X. The Trinity and the Holy Ghost

The answer to many problems would seem to be more humus —more of that which was once vital itself and now has power to give vitality. For a soil, this might be a load of leaf mould or a green crop turned under; for a mind, it might be a page of history or an example left by a hero. To have a sense of humus is to have an appreciation of the past, to realize that to discard the achievements and virtues slowly built up through long periods of human society and to attempt to live solely in this present is like throwing away humus and trying to exist in more or less inorganic hardpan. A young human plant needs mellowed soil deep enough to encourage his roots to go down and rich enough in stored energy to give vigor.

—BERTHA DAMON, *A Sense of Humus*
Simon and Schuster, New York (1943)

THE APOSTLE'S CREED, which is the oldest of the creeds and the foundation of them all, is itself the development of a baptismal formula dating back to the beginnings of the Church and containing the line: "in the name of the Father, and of the Son, and of the Holy Ghost."

The doctrine of the Trinity can be made one of the most mysterious of matters in religion. And the Holy Ghost can be made a very unique part of the "godhead," known only in religion and the Christian religion at that. Or the Trinity in all of its parts can be looked upon as a practical and somewhat loose, rather than definitive, way of recognizing quite divergent elements of religion and worship, as well as of theology. There have been quite a few efforts to so account for it. The simple basis of these attempts appears to be something like this. There is in religion always a recognition of natural powers about and over us, which, as the mind of man takes hold and thinks even a little, develops into a sense of dependence, awe, wonder, order and sometimes beauty. Again, there is in man a function of reverence for what is morally above and beyond us, or for what uplifts as does excellence or beauty of character. Thirdly, there is an inner enjoyment and participation in that spirit of God which is love or enthusiasm. All three of these aspects belong naturally within religion and have their reflection in theology.

"God the Father," with or without deeper religious overtones, is a phrase that has stood imaginatively and practically for the whole fact of something the mind finds over all, in all, primordial and ultimate. God has been called The Creator, the Cosmos, the Great I Am, the Eternal, the Infinite, the Universal, the Evolutionary Energy or just Evolution. He has even been called the Great Unknowable. As John Burroughs and Luther Burbank remind us, he has been worshipped under the name of "Mother Nature." Theodore Parker used to address his public prayers to "Our Father and Mother God." By almost any name since we became monotheists, "God the Father" stands for that which is both above and beneath all, both behind and before, and universally present. Without any question we are his dependent children. There is reason for saying "his" if we recognize at all that we ourselves, consciousness and all, are fragments of his inclusiveness. Once our worship has outgrown that curious notion of a universal power playing favorites among the tribes of man, at war with one another, it may consist chiefly of awe, wonder, sense of grandeur or order and beauty. The mood of such worship is sublime contemplation. It is either of the mind or of the aesthetic sense—as in the case of some of the mystics, and outstandingly of Spinoza, sublimest instance of worship as contemplation. What it does for us is to lift us out of ourselves and above the battle or whatever noises distract us.

"God the Son" is a phrase that, on the other hand, has really stood for something different: for the ideal and the holy, for moral purity and rightness, as we really sense these things in a man or a woman. That is where the need of an incarnation comes in. Emerson once said that the average man can sense a principle or a cause only when it is embodied in a person. No doubt great and good men often help us to form ideals of character more perfect even than what they illustrate in their own lives; but they have a necessary educational function in this aspect of worship, or of life itself. It is common for religions to claim that at least some one person was a perfect example of conduct for us to follow. We could indeed be surrounded by almost a vacuum in the way of stimulation to reverence and aspiration if we were brought up in a circle composed only of perverted human beings. We are the fortunate ones, we who have early found on the streets, at school, or in public life, people who have elicited the full sense of admiration or reverence.

George Foote Moore, teacher of religions at Harvard, once paused in the middle of a lecture to say he didn't see it mattered whether we worship God or Christ if we have previously ascribed all divine virtues to Jesus. His idea was that worship begins where we begin to profoundly admire and look up to something felt to be greatly above us. If we get from some person suggestions of the highest ideals of conduct, then he is symbolically playing the role of "God the Son." Perhaps we might here adapt and use a famous saying of Jesus, making it read: "Inasmuch as you have reverenced somebody who deserved it, then you have done it unto me and unto the Father."

It is true, as George Foote Moore had already said, that the ancient Jews ascribed moral virtues, as well as some vices, to Jahweh; and that Jesus said goodness belonged to the Father alone and not to the Son. That could be a confusion in the interpretation of the Trinity as we have been approaching that very high matter. It is also true that the Sermon on the Mount tells us in effect that God is tender-hearted and loves even the sparrows. And we have all been told many times and oft that the Father first loved us and sent his only Son as a martyr for our sinful sakes. The fact is that our imagination can put together any pleasing combination of attributes to be ascribed to "God the Father," any unrealistic mixture of power and goodness, or of a divine over-all control with blessing for all in every pocket or stitch of creation. The doctrine of the Trinity however grew out of a somewhat more realistic observation of facts than that, and rests upon a more hard-boiled intellectual approach. And one feels there may be something in or about it surviving for the use of our age. For the God who made the whole world and ordered the stars, the God who aloof from man is all the power there is instead of a pervasive and distributed power of which we ourselves are a small but responsible part, seems to need a better reason than we can think of to justify him in calling all creation good. The wastefulness, the plagues and the famines, the war-instincts and the wars, the human stupidities which are in part original furniture, the inequalities of equipment among individuals; yes, the mis-births and the idiots and all the things we hide away from the sight of men—these all are in the way.

The God who made and controls all nature and history from above, or without, is a God in whom our age finds it difficult to believe. A psychologist was talking this matter over with a Fundamentalist, and finally exclaimed: "Oh, I see now. You and I have the same religion; only your God is my devil."

The utility of the credal presentation of "God the Son," like the utility of that love of goodness which does not call itself religious, has always been that we do not find our summons to reverence in nature, or in some idea of a Creator of the whole, or within the field of any science, or in the irremediable evils in which life seems caught. The call for reverence we find in the heroes and saints. It is in an utterly practical sense the place for God the Son.

To extend the point we are speaking of more widely: Absence of principles, or the inability to recognize a principle until, as Emerson suggested, it becomes incarnated in a party or a man is probably necessary to the making of a good party wheel-horse, a 100% Democrat or Republican—perhaps even a 100% American. Recently, in reading the autobiography of William Allen White, valiant Kansas editor of only yesterday, it presently struck me that he would not have known a principle if he had met it in the middle of the road. His loyalty was to Theodore Roosevelt, or the good old party, or the right kind of people. He could not see a principle apart from some of that kind of clothing. And he is not unlike the people who toast "My country, right or wrong!" Jefferson believed in the right and duty of revolution upon proper occasion. *He* saw principles behind and beneath his and Washington's patriotism. But such ability is exceptional, and often at least we see principles at work in the forms of people we revere—and as a part of the total and personal picture which they make for us.

This part of theology was grafted on to simple Jewish mono-theism after a mighty struggle against it in the Semitic branches of the early Church. In later times it came to be the chief reproach of Mohammed and Islam against Christianity. To all the Semites the idea of God as incarnated in a man was as near blasphemy as possible; and with reason, in view of their traditional idea of God as transcendent, too holy to be even named aloud by his right name. With one accord, Semites all warded off graven images as an invitation to idolatry. As to the danger involved they were absolutely right. The only point is that, as in other matters, the dangerousness involved sometimes does not quite settle the question. We are not blaming the Semites, but it did limit their range of appeal. They rendered mankind a great service in warding off popular kinds of idolatry. But one wonders if perhaps their native bias, if we may call it that, in the length and breadth of the matter has not made it a little easier for some Jews of today, when they abandon Jahweh, to adopt Ethical Culture or even Atheism as their moral citadel.

We find two of the greatest Jews of modern times, Spinoza and Einstein, reserving the name of religion (so far as their own personal kind of it is concerned) for the kind of contemplative feelings they have about law and order on the scale of the Absolute Substance or of the Cosmos (what we have named God the Father); while both of them put their ideals of conduct and their gentleness of spirit into a separate pocket and call it Ethics. Spinoza gave that title to his great book about the one substance, with its "attributes," "modes" and "accidents"; but we hardly see why except that he was a noble soul and was devoted to that excellence which was the rarest and most difficult thing under the sun. This excellence itself, personified or not, might fill for some great men the same place that "God the Son" filled for enough people to win it a place in Christian tradition.

The third member of the Trinity, the Holy Ghost, or Holy Spirit, is surely the canonical name for inspiration channelled, or ready to be channelled, into the high and highest regions. Spirit means the very breath of inward life, the springing fountains of spontaneity. Spirit rises as man rises, to be the living energy of curiosity, or search, of invention, of art. It is ever the life-giving energy of all pursuits which do not belong under the heading of drudgery. To worship in spirit and in truth is humble offer of the Self to the More and the Better. It is the reach of life which is in us towards fuller life. Its revelations are always first-hand; they come to us one at a time and directly, and of course they come with a power and quality that depends upon our status and preparation.

The Holy Ghost is not mentioned in the Old Testament, or at least not in our translations of it; and the Holy Spirit, mentioned not too many times, is hardly personified. But this does not mean that Judaism missed this element of theology as completely as it did the Incarnate Son. In the Old Testament, "the spirit of prophecy" came as a coal of fire upon the tongue. We can adopt the language of vividness and energy for our own use and say that the spirit compelled Amos, Isaiah, Jeremiah, and the others, to speak out for the principles of the Law and to beard tyranny enthroned. The spirit of prophecy is the Old Testament name for the Holy Ghost. What from our point of view is lacking in this part of the Hebrew outlook is simple recognition that God himself is sometimes a spirit of our spirits, universal and over-all; that he has at least an appointed dwelling-place within every one of us as well as in the Holy of Holies or some place which only priests can approach; and that wherever he visits he is the bringer of new life and sometimes of salvation.

In the New Testament Book of the Acts of the Apostles we find a localized example of a belief very widely held in that era that the end or objective of religion was "salvation." No doubt the earliest Christians were looking for an end of the world and postponing some or most of their salvation until that came along. But even so, in those same times there must have been some recognition of this other matter of being made over into a new man. That note is strong in St. Paul. Somehow or other we find the Holy Ghost mentioned more often by name in the Book of Acts than in all the rest of the New Testament put together. The wide winds bring a suggestion that this represents a surge upon what we may call the wider Mediterranean Sea at the time in which the Gospel was spreading from land to land. There is a contagiousness of a kind about the Holy Ghost. We do in a sense catch fire from other people. In those days the Holy Ghost was handing out commissions from above and teaching people to speak as having authority. Of course he was saving them from their old selves and from the world. The early Christians no doubt started out as Adventists in the main; even St. Paul had his good share of that. But all the same the age, including the Christians in it, was engaged in a warfare between the Flesh and the Spirit; and after all St. Paul had his share of that too. He even worked it out in that wonderful sketch of love as well-nigh the whole duty of man, and as salvation in itself.

One thing none of the New Testament scholars we have been quoting: Loisy, Schweitzer, Cullmann, Bultmann, seem to have recognized as fully as they might have, is that Paul must have belonged to that class of men which William James described as "divided souls" and, after Paul's experience on the road to Damascus, to the class of twice-born men. In fact St. Paul and St. Augustine are the great prototypes of the twice-born men, and they set the pattern for the evangelistic or revivalistic form of Christianity, the form continued by George Whitefield, John Wesley, Jonathan Edwards, Dwight L. Moody, William Booth, Billy Sunday, and Billy Graham.

The evangelistic line of Christian preaching has always been the dramatically effective or meteoric line. Adolph Harnack says that this type has provided the "shock-troops" of the movement from the beginning through the ages.[1] Most of the martyrs and great missionaries belonged to it of course. Harnack makes a musing reflection to the effect that Jesus himself does not appear to have belonged to the type of erstwhile divided souls who later found themselves in an upheaving religious experience. Due to circumstances of history perhaps, so Harnack reasons, it may be that the "once-born" type have not yet had their innings. That might or might not be wishful thinking on Harnack's part. Powerful emotional reactions leading to radical decisions certainly have produced men of dynamic force. Russell A. Conwell once said that he would have liked to ask Abraham Lincoln just one question: what agency was it that "broke the chrysalis of his will?" Conwell belonged to the twice-born type and probably thought everybody else ought to belong. In his autobiography he tells how, on a battlefield of the Civil War, he decided once for all to lead two lives, one for himself and one for Johnny Ring—a boy slaughtered on the field.

However, the Holy Ghost is multifarious in its visitations, sometimes awakening or inspiring original pioneers and seers without too much explosion or tumult. After all, deep religious emotion or enthusiasm is one thing and the production-line methods and results of the typical revival are something else. Revivals probably have stirred in quantity more excitement than genuine inspiration, although much depends on the issues presented and the agencies, as well as the mental preparation of the individual. But some of the great mystics seem not to have belonged to the evangelistic type at all; and the great established churches, Roman Catholic, Eastern, Lutheran, Episcopal, incline

1. Adolph Harnack. *History of Dogma,* Vol. 5, p. 74 fol.

to make religion a matter of tutelage, growth, and confirmation instead of "conversion." That these represent the majority of Christians may indeed mean little, for prestige and the ruts are on that side. But they have their inspired preachers and saints, in highest quality if not in proportional quantity. And the suddenness of conversion may be more of a mysterious and also of a relative matter than is commonly recognized. It is partly a question of how things look to outsiders, and whether men's reports conform to a pattern.

The universal mark of the Holy Ghost is the awakening of inward life. Like real education from Mark Hopkins or others, it makes self-starters. It is due to the Holy Ghost that Christianity is renewed in some places in every generation, through men who speak as "having authority" and who are more vital and effective when they speak out of experience than when they quote someone else, no matter whom. It is the Holy Ghost that makes a religion, or a Church, into a jet-propulsion system or movement, renewed by fresh life in a new generation.

Before the time of St. Paul Christianity was a branch of Judaism. From his time on it was becoming one of the Salvation or Mystery religions which were competing for prominence within the Roman Empire. Rudolph Eucken, rather overlooking the Messianism which went with sects of Judaism, classifies that religion, along with Confucianism, as a religion of Law; and then points a contrast which may have something in it by calling Christianity, Buddhism, and the Mystery religions (Manicheeism, Mithraism, Orphism, and the others) religions of Salvation. He is contrasting on the one hand the regulation of life in this world as that is proposed in Jewish law, along with its dream of the nation protected and prospered by the Almighty, and the people enjoying length of days under their own vine and fig-tree, with on the other hand the effort to save individuals, one at a time, out of and from the world and into a Kingdom of Heaven.

But the important point is that when both of those ideas of religion are full-grown we need them both. It may well have been fortunate that Christianity, without irrecoverably losing the Old Testament and its social message and while bringing along the Sermon on the Mount within the lids of that Bible which the Church bound up and chained down with its canon, had nevertheless swerved into that current of the times which turned it into a Mystery Religion, or a Religion of Salvation. It discovered something Judaism did not represent to the world. It discovered the power of the Spirit which is in man at large, and which can take over the man and make him an original and living creature above and beyond all the laws on earth. In later times, Christianity had to recur to some of its Jewish and Galilean roots when it felt the need of making itself into a prophetic and social gospel. That made it more of an all-around religion for the whole of human need or for all occasions. But sometimes progress is a matter of one thing at a time.

If it is felt we do not need the substance of the Trinity today, with its many-sided appeal, there is a simple thing to be said. God is first of all and forever whatever men worship and are devoted to. That is the basic meaning of the word. Even if the mind can find no cosmic God except law and order in the skies, and pattern and organization beneath his feet and all around, that is still something, not only to Einstein and Eddington but to all the people who have been terrified by the concept of "dead matter," Bertrand Russell's "blind omnipotent matter" rolling relentlessly over our little day. And it seems that we need the substance contained in the doctrine of the Second Person of the Trinity. In plain words, we need all the modern examples of courage and love of humanity we can get, from Father Damien, Doctor Grenfell, Mr. Gandhi, Doctor Schweitzer on down. Of course we have to change something stiff in our theology and our ideas of God to bring in such men as partial incarnations of God. And we need to know God as a moving spirit of love and good will which we have not originated but far to the contrary have discovered, often by contagion from others. But the wind bloweth where it listeth, and such is the coming of the Holy Spirit.

It is the historic shift towards democratic government and the democratic spirit, this reliance upon common people for the capacity of learning to govern themselves, this necessity of faith in the divine possibilities which are in all men, that enables us to understand in modern terms what was perhaps the greatest problem the Christian religion had to face in its infancy. A religion which depends largely on internal combustion is from the beginning and at every period of renewal beset with dangers not at all unlike those of political democracy. It is hard to keep such a religion from running wild in places, or from degenerating into mob-rule and losing its own free spirit, especially when times are exciting and hectic.

Of course one contribution of the Second Principle of the Trinity, the aspect of God which appeared in Jesus, with the aura of the Sermon on the Mount and the great parables attached to him, was to give men some standards to go by, objective standards of moral excellence. We need to admire and to look up at the very same time that we need enthusiasm and the urge to express ourselves. It is also true that even men equipped with high moral standards need to go out under the stars at times and to contemplate Nature and the Overall. The truth that was formulated in the doctrine of the Trinity comes at us from all three angles of which we have spoken.

How are we going to be sure that the yeast which works in us is pure? What public tests are we going to hold out to spellbinders who usually see something which strikes them in a problematic situation but seldom see the whole problem? How shall we distinguish clearly between genuine religious inspiration and mere inflation of the preacher's ego? What do we do when a Joseph Smith discovers a book of "revelations" which teaches polygamy or something more taboo. It is unnecessary to assume that we are always right in our criticism either. The question is about public standards to apply. How shall we guard against those physiological exuberances and sex-excitements which at revivals have been known to be confused with religion?

Not very long ago I was down in the basement stoking the coal furnace and heard, through the floor, a priest intoning overhead, over the radio: "Love Jesus, and do what you desire." I halted the shovel in mid-air. "A Catholic priest of all people, I thought!" Later it occurred to me he was half-quoting St. Augustine, a man who learned to base religion on self-denial. Augustine thought and deeply felt that if you once truly come to love God with heart and soul and mind, you can be safely trusted to follow your inclinations. How true! With your heart centered right, you can't go wrong. But can we trust an ordinary preacher to intone that way in public, or trust the ordinary man's response to such churchly authority?

We do not answer all these questions with any ready-made certainty. It may be that we need first to be psycho-analyzed ourselves. We may need to wait until in a given case some of the fruits begin showing up. The cheapenings and perversions of religion can themselves quote all the precedents in the world, or at any rate enough for many purposes. As was said in a former chapter, primitive man had his own idea of what it was to be religiously inspired. And the world never loses an old idea just because some of its advanced members have found a new one. The old lingers on somewhere, we may be sure.

St. Paul certainly gave the world a helpful answer to the question how to distinguish the works of the spirit from those of the flesh, as he called them. He went back to his Jewish foundations and, without quoting Jesus, to the principle of judging by the fruits. He said the works of the flesh are fornications, enmities, jealousies, wraths, drunkenness, and the like; and the works of the spirit are love, joy, peace, long-suffering, kindness, and so on. Where the issue was not a moral one, he did not allow himself to wax hot against plain vagaries of the spirit. He did not concern himself about that "speaking with tongues" which was the way some enthusiasts had of uttering forth long strings of nonsense syllables not adding up to words and sentences. Virtuosos in this art were claiming to be divinely possessed, to be revealing the immediate and blessed presence of God. Paul was content to say merely that there was no edification in them. Might we not to our advantage follow his line in speaking up to some exhibits of modern paintings? In some cases perhaps we might acknowledge the great possibility of the artist's having expressed his inner self with enjoyment and gusto, without being ashamed to confess that he has no significance for us, or no more than if it were a child's daub. Of course there is danger of *our* being immodest. But there is also that other danger which overcame the king in Andersen's fairy tale who was so taken in by high pressure salesmen that he had to wait for a street urchin to tell him he was naked.

Considerably later than Paul's time, when Marcion, like some people of today, wanted to repudiate the Creator God, to leave the Old Testament behind, and to present Christianity to the world as a very new beginning, the Church gathered our Bible together the way we have it, and took that Bible into its custody. They were partly justified, whether or not they were launching a claim for too much authority vested in the Church. The establishment of the "canon" meant the padlocking of the Bible both to keep the Old Testament in and to keep fresh elements or numbers out. At the same time the Church was building the creed longer and longer, aiming at more and more exclusion of ideas, as it found more and newer heresies in circulation. And it made doctrine as airtight as two or three generations of church lawyers were able to do it. The cause of these doings was the liveliness of the question of when the motions of the spirit were inspirations of the Holy Spirit. In other words, it was felt that the democratic tendencies of the spirit must be curbed by authority.

Enthusiasm itself, except organizing enthusiasm, is necessarily a problem, in the first place to the organizational mind and the busy planner of social and religious institutions. There is nothing much worth organizing except inspiration; but there is nothing on earth so hard to organize while the kettle is still boiling. First hand conviction is hostile to stereotyped modes of expression and even has a grudge against organized authority. Original inspiration probably suffers somewhat in being organized at all; but sober men as well as schemers feel the need of law, school, and church, partly to support accepted moral standards, partly to help in the teaching and transmitting of whatever the fathers think is truth, partly because in organization there is impact and strength. This multiple need is what perplexed the ancient Church when Marcion, the Montanists, and others kept on hearing voices in the night or dreaming new dreams. So the Church announced that the days of revelation were over. It won in its stand on that and on other questions, partly because so many people had been trained in the faith and skills of organization by Rome, that city to which in those days all roads led. Presently when the Church claimed authority inherited from the founding fathers, and in a very special way from St. Peter, there was nobody this side of Constantinople to say them Nay. And that city was distant from the growing centers of civilization.

*   *   *   *

We have not been defending the Trinity as a doctrine or dogma. We have simply been pointing out that it rendered a pragmatic service. We are far from implying that the doctrine of the Trinity, or any particular part of it, should be a required belief for today. The three "kinds of Gods" which appear in the dogma that Episcopal Bishop James A. Pike, of California, has recently declared to be *no longer* necessary, has helped different people to approach divinity from three different and prominent

86

angles. And it may be that at least as many as three different approaches to religion are still useful, especially where the words "God" and "divinity" are not in use, but would disturb the minds of some people of our day. But the Church, in spite of a lot of the eternal politics involved, in spite of the fight for prestige among different great cities and individuals, did collect and establish a package of doctrines that was perhaps better than any of the more extreme alternatives would have proved to be.

So far we have not faced the whole doctrine of the Trinity, which insisted that the three members of the godhead were all One God. There is something to be said for stopping where we are without going into that. A certain separateness, if not an actual departmentalizing of life, seems in many cases if not most to feature our modern religion or devotion. Some men chiefly worship power or grandeur, some worship goodness or the Golden Rule (at least they say that is what they believe in); while others just sense sometimes a current of life, a larger energy than common, an enthusiasm, welling up in them. There is a religion of the mind, directed towards something that controls a part of our destiny, or, especially if we are determinists, all of it. Then we have a religion which is either a sense of duty we cannot be rid of, or else a devotion to something we look up to and admire. In reverse action, in this particular branch of worship, every half-decent man knows of something he cannot do, or at which he just has to draw the line. Then, in the third place, all of life except the bare matter of making a living (which we all heartily wish we could escape from), consists of ferment and glow that leads on in enjoyment, in education and in self-respect.

Of course some of us have never reckoned with religion's being so wide a thing as we are here describing, especially where it comes to letting in all the glow and the gusto; but in a former chapter we expressed the feeling and conviction that devotion, on each man's own actual level, is the inwardness and reality of all religion.

Some leave out all "theology" for themselves, and very likely claim that that is the conclusion of the whole subject. Some identify religion with superstition. Once in a philosophy class the writer was trying to teach, a boy wrote that, personally, he did not believe in the existence of any "cosmetic God." One knew what he meant anyhow, and it was an echo of the times. But as we are led to see our human situation of today, every man has his religion, although it is likely to be one-sided or departmentalized when it is not primitive. In a way the place for various kinds of one-sidedness is sketched in the doctrine of the Trinity. In fact that doctrine even suggests handling the topic of worship in a partly unpietistic or unchurchly way. The Trinity constitutes a sort of old-time map on which one can find a place for all the actual devotions we have. As a mere map, it gives that much unity to the central business of life, under whatever comprehensive name you may choose—religion or not.

But now we must ask if there is anything equally matter of fact to be said in favor of the Trinity, as pragmatic symbol, when it goes on to say in effect that our three kinds of God are not separate but all one God. And some of us do think there is a kind of natural matrix which threatens to draw all these kinds of Gods we have been talking about into a kind of vital connection. That matrix is the womb of space-time and of evolution. We are all creatures of nature in the becoming. With all our criticisms and indignations, with all our unaccepted and unpopular blueprints for having the cosmos get along better— or even for having human society get along better—we yet belong to the process of life on earth. It certainly took something bigger, more primordial, more perennial, than us Johnny-come-latelies to get the first beginnings of mankind on to this planet, not to go further and speak of geniuses like Shakespeare, Bach, Aristotle, and Bacon, that have appeared on the scenes since. There has always been an organizing principle at work, and seemingly more and more of it. We are not saying this principle has always been victorious. Whitehead said it surely has been there, but partly attended to and partly not. Theilhard de Chardin thinks it has always been in central control. We have said not a word on that point. It is our extreme solitariness and our attitude of self-made man that has been questioned here —or denied. We are not questioning the part played by society in making the great men; but where did society come from? We are ready to think with de Chardin that there has pretty obviously been one kind of progress through history as well as through the animal parade, the phyla, and the atomic buzz before history. There have come about wider and wider forms

88

of consciousness, capable of controlling or organizing, or trying to control or organize, more and more of the earth into one. We also think we see in men a capacity of acting for wider and wider ends—recognizing the importance of more than just this one fellow, sympathizing rather more with the various colors of our skins; also sympathizing a little with different points of view. This widening goes on far enough to point to some kind of a world-religion among men. We even have vegetarians like Tolstoy and Gandhi; and here is Schweitzer preaching a sympathy with life itself—with everything that lives. There is at least a threat in that for all of us, of having to mend our ways beyond present horizons. Honestly we are getting humans who are more conspicuously interested in life that lies beyond humanity. We might need some of that when we get to the first asteroid. There is a broadening tendency towards sympathy with conscious beings that can hardly be denied. It is a tendency too large and too old for men to claim the making of it. There is around us suggestion of more of the same to come, and also of more and fuller life to be revealed.

So the men who gave us that partly hard-boiled doctrine of the Trinity, and went on to say that it was all one God they were talking about, had behind them at least the idea that we are all growing on the same cosmic tree. That would make everything one at the root, even if separate above ground or after leaving the main bole of the tree, in a hundred important ways. The name of the tree might as well, for all of us, be Ygdrasil. But there is no need to argue about the matter here. We cheerfully admit and proclaim that separateness in men's theology is going to last on and on and to save us from a lot of the mushy piety which otherwise might have the field too much to itself.

The Holy Ghost, then, is the Christian name for the inwardness and spirituality of God. In the broadest sense "spirit" means inspiration. In older Judaism we find that the "Spirit of Prophecy" was the same expression of God as the Christian "Holy Ghost," speaking through chosen and inspired prophets.

Everywhere the first work of the Spirit is to create "rugged individualists," "self-starters," persons who on all the higher levels are themselves fountains of creative power—lovers of beauty, discoverers, searchers, truth-seekers. Within Judaism and Christianity the Spirit is the inner energy of righteousness, the love of the highest forms of beauty or excellence recognized at the time and place. In other words, these passionate stirrings are men's own God speaking within. Some readers will discern that this way of describing the Spirit shows that St. Paul was wise when he urged his converts not to make too much of a distinction between "Greek and Barbarian."

On the intellectual side, where men are inspired to think for themselves, the first result is differences of opinion and interpretation when a question arises as to which road to take to reach a given objective. Original minds are normally in debate with one another, and there is always divergence among them. That means schisms and sects. We have shown how the work of the Holy Spirit created a problem for the earliest Christians. As long as all Christians were subject to Roman persecution they did not persecute one another. Rome's scorn made them all heretics together. But soon after Christianity became the established religion of the Roman Empire, Christians began to find reason for serious disciplinary measures in the interest of harmony and effective organization. Presently Christians began to put other Christians to death as the many groups strove with one another for complete dominance. That gave to the word "heresy" a bad odor. Let us now ask what heresy is, and what orthodoxy is.

XI. Orthodoxy and Heresy

THERE IS AN OLD New England joke to the effect that orthodoxy is *my* doxy and heterodoxy is *your* doxy. This joke fails to recognize any kind of evolution or growth in religious doctrine. And of course there are those who claim there has never been any change in correct doctrine but that the truth was revealed once for all. The evidence though is against this claim.

The moment organization took effect and controls were put to work in the Christian movement, even locally or provincially, there arose claims and counter-claims about correct doctrine. The crossfire and mutual bombardment in ancient days was quite as lively and hot as it has ever been in modern Protestantism. In this respect, Protestantism is nearer than Romanism to the Apostolic Age and the times shortly after.

The two wings of the Apostolic leadership fought out the question whether to try to convert the Gentiles without making them Jews as well as Christians. A very pointed angle of that question was whether to require circumcision. But another sharp one concerned the eating of meats. And an important one was whether to observe the Sabbath on Saturday, in harmony with ancient Jewish custom; or to use Sunday, which would be in line with the habit and ideas of the Roman world. It was a little easier to win adherents if you used Sunday, because that much would be *à la mode* and would not raise any unnecessary social difficulties.

For a time after the Apostolic Age the whole East was Arian in theology, and the West largely Trinitarian. But the Trinitarian principle was more fertile than its rival. In fact, the Arians had no idea to lead them on except that stream-lined Semitic one of monarchy and monotheism, with God as absolute ruler as well as Creator. Arius, who denied the deity of Jesus, insisted that Jesus had first lived in heaven, occupying a subordinate throne, which he had left to come down to this earth. It was not as if Arius had been championing such really seminal ideas as Athanasius was advocating in his teaching of the Incarnation and the Holy Ghost. Athanasius was making room for more varieties of religious experience. Unitarians of today are sometimes associated with Arius, but at least one of their greatest American teachers, the late Francis A. Christie, has declared that the modern Unitarian's inheritance is from Athanasius, not Arius. That offers to make it unanimous.

There were from the beginning different views of baptism which started rival sects. The central point of that difference was whether babies and children should be baptized or whether the rite was for converts only. That difference of view abides with us still. Resurrection of the flesh continued to be a matter of dispute, as plainly it had been in the days of Doubting Thomas and St. Paul. The grandest bee-hive of all for heresies was probably Gnosticism. Anybody can see that some of the Gnostics, like Valentinian, were over-intellectual for teachers of a practical religion, perhaps suffered from an overdose of Greek philosophy. And yet Bultmann says that "Gnosticism offered a stock of terms that were familiar to a lot of people." It spoke the Greek language and used words that were practically slogans in the philosophy of the times, terms like "logos" for example, terms which were familiar to the ordinary man's ear and so not exactly repellent to his mind. Bultmann goes on to say that Christian theology was "formed on the pattern of a Gnostic Redeemer myth."[1] By general consent where the term "heretic" · is still used, the Gnostics are now classified under that head although it does seem as if the author of St. John's Gospel, who uses that term "logos" in his very first chapter, could be considered either a Gnostic or a fellow-traveller.

There were different opinions about celibacy for the clergy, about asceticism and self-denial in general, about the division of power between God and Satan. The Semitic East fought off the use of "graven images" in the form of statues, icons, pictures, in the churches. They said such things were an open door to let in idolatry. On the other hand, Pope Leo I, speaking presently out of the barbarian West, said that pictures and icons were the books of the people who could not read. Leo provided a possible slogan for the tabloids and graphics of today, not to speak of television programs.

---

1. Bultmann, *The Theology of the New Testament*, Vol. 2, p. 6.

Nestorius contested the worship of the Virgin Mary, which worship did something practically to counterbalance some of the male, Old Testament patriarchal, military and fierce aspects of deity. Nestorianism was quite prominent for a time and is said to still maintain itself in pockets of Asia. It was another case of East against West, and it looks as if Nestorius became a heretic merely because the center of the rising civilization or culture was Rome instead of a city of Asia.

At times the energy at work in streamlining Christian dogma was involved in both geographical and political influences as well as the prestige of different dioceses: Jerusalem, Antioch, Alexandria, Constantinople, Rome. And as for the grand point of centralized management, Rome had become skillful in that long before it became Christian. Many a time it held to the middle of the road in interpreting a doctrine, or bluntly affirmed a contradiction without attempting to explain or rationalize. Some leaders wanted for what were lively reasons to stress the divinity of Jesus to the limit; others wished to stress his humanity lest his example for us prove nothing worth and his suffering on the cross only apparent rather than real. Under Roman leadership the final answer was to affirm that he was equally divine and human. Rome was a center of rule, not of philosophy or reason. Of course it can be believed that divine wisdom put Rome in the right place, at the right time; because then all roads led to Rome.

So long as Rome hesitated, which it often did, there was no fixed heresy. Settling questions of dogma involved in the first place settling Rome's own position in the Church, and that took a long time. Even after that matter was in the way to be settled, it took the Roman mill a long time to grind. In fact it is still grinding. We are forced to note today the claim of Rome to the right of promulgating new doctrines which shall henceforth be orthodox. In recent decades there have been the dogmas of the Immaculate Conception and of Papal Infallibility. But of course the concern about heresy today is not more real among Romanists than among Protestants. It is interesting that all modern theologians seem to think there is still something for themselves to clear up in the field of Christian doctrine, and that clearing up is what papal encyclicals are supposed to be for.

Bultmann says[2] that what distinguished Christianity in the

2. Rudolph Bultmann, *The Theology of the New Testament,* Vol. 2, p. 135.

beginning was not orthodoxy, but the possession of faith. That is perhaps the good Lutheran line. He explains that this faith was not yet The Faith, not the creed, that is. He even says that when the Church was in danger of straying into "mere moralism," Jesus' personal teaching was of little help because that simply made love the highest requirement. Once again as in the matter of the Second Coming, we note that, according to a prominent theologian, "true doctrine" does not originate with Jesus. Also Bultmann seems to think that among the Apostles, only St. Paul and St. John attain to the central point of Christian truth, and express it. We shall name that point in a moment when we speak of Ignatius. St. Paul is credited by Bultmann with having found the right theological track for the first time when he left Adventism behind and began to teach a present and spiritual meaning of resurrection and new life. Right here John, it seems, was quite a bit less confused all along. He straightly taught that religion is being born of the spirit—something that happens in individual lives, one by one. But Bultmann finds neither Paul nor John to have been adequate theologians. Much work was left to be done, and apparently it remains undone. You might say the pursuit of theology is like following a star and that the Wise Men are still on the road.

Among the Fathers who were not Apostles, Ignatius is the one singled out by Bultmann as holding something like the correct doctrine on the all-important point. That was the point that Christianity had started with a unique "eschatological event," the appearance of Jesus Christ on earth. Here is where Bultmann shows his Existentialist philosophy. This event provides, he says, the "indicative" on which to base a Christian "imperative." But Ignatius was right on this point, only to have many foibles or many circumstances of his age stand in the way of clear vision in other matters. The meaning of this one greatest event of the past, or of all time, had to be worked out in history, and Bultmann is as clear as Oscar Cullmann in suggesting that some of this task is left to theologians of this present day.

When we turn to Alfred Loisy, the view of what is orthodoxy or correct doctrine is quite different because Loisy does not begin with the assumption of either a single and unique divine revelation or a unique eschatological event. Like Albert Schweitzer, he thinks Jesus was an Adventist possessed of an inheritance from the great Hebrew prophets, which inheritance he carried on and enriched, teaching that love of God and of one's neighbor is one and the same thing. Perhaps it is not clear whether Loisy credits the historic Jesus with the origination of all the early Galilean teachings that are ascribed to him. Rather he seems to leave open the possibility that some of the parables and some parts of the Sermon on the Mount were just the best words of the time, and that they gravitated to Jesus as good stories and sayings do sometimes gravitate to famous men and become accredited to them. Like Schweitzer, Loisy is not too much concerned about the historical Jesus. Christianity in his view has been improving itself on the whole, and in most important respects, down through the centuries. That was, in his eyes, the advantage of having a central Church like the Roman Catholic, living through the ages and able to assimilate improvements and preside over that human evolution whose tap-root was Jewish-Christian. He even urged the papacy, in the person of Leo XIII, to take this view and to lead the van in the religious evolution of mankind. Somehow Leo rather tolerated Loisy's views for a time, or found him useful enough in other respects than we have dwelt upon so that he did not really condemn him. But when Pius X came into Peter's seat, down fell the axe of major excommunication which the world had long anticipated. Pius felt he did not need to lead any van. He only needed to hold the fort. Truth was eternal, once-revealed; and it lay in his charge and care.

Loisy had the melting-pot idea of Christian progress. He saw old Jewish and original Christian elements combining with ideas and forces from Greece, Rome, and all sorts of places and traditions. The product had been a grand one because the agents of it were all the great influences at work on the Mediterranean scene. He regarded Christianity as beating at heart with the same pulse that stirs all modern civilization when it is moving towards freedom and fulfillment. In his last writings at least, after the pope had rejected him, he seems to have entertained no doubt that sacred and secular forces, taking these distinctions conventionally, the Church on the one hand and literature and the arts on the other hand, had reacted upon and helped to educate one another. When he died at the end of the first World War, he thought the tendency of the ages on the whole had been upward. What he would think today, in the aftermath of another World War and since democratic faith has been given many a rude public jolt, is not for us to say.

The symbol for understanding Christianity's place, so Loisy thought and felt, was not a single star or a single cradle. Light, coming originally from the same sun above but at various angles, had been collected by a mighty receptor of the Mediterranean world into a single beam and instrument for carrying it on. Jews, Christians, Greeks, Romans, and even other great traditions could take some pride in that.

But Loisy was more than a little afraid of the phrase "religion of humanity," as that phrase had been used by August Comte in particular; and doubtless he would have felt the same about "humanism" as that word is often used today. In a letter to a friend, Miss M. Petre, of February 9, 1917, he wrote that what was wrong with Comte and others like him was that they had no real respect for humanity of the past. They merely hoped for a humanity of the future made more in their own image. He felt that if you are unsympathetic with all the past, you cannot be really intelligent about the future. Loisy was a historian, and the typical historian does not incline to believe in absolutely new beginnings. History is certainly relevant somehow to the future. He thought it relevant for faith. Of course, it can show the general effect of certain causes. But he thought it could also show a certain amount of attraction to the light, and that the light itself is a cause.

We quote a passage from that letter to Miss Petre:

"In principle we pursue and serve an ideal of humanity on a line of light that broadens continually in its three elements of duty, sacrifice, and love. These elements seem to me to be the foundation of every religion; in the lower forms it may be barely discernible, being as much confused as religion itself and as rudimentary as the feeble civilization of the uncivilized; in the religions of the civilized it is, in one sense or another, more clearly marked and is definitely oriented in this sense by Christianity, with its mythical synthesis of the religions of the Mediterranean world."

The main reason for so much quoting in this chapter from two great New Testament scholars, Cullmann and Bultmann, is to emphasize the fact that Christian doctrine has been involved in some kind of evolution until now if such men in our day have to disparage one ancient authority after another and to disagree so much among themselves even at this age. And the reason for quoting also Schweitzer and Loisy was to emphasize the other point that some scholars have seen Christianity as a human development, attached to this whole globe on which we live.

XII. Monasticism

SOME OF THE GREAT religions have almost from the first beginning
recognized the necessity of two levels of teaching. Perhaps that
is implied in the way Jesus gathered a few disciples to travel
with him and now and then distinguished between things which
were said for them and what was offered to the multitudes.
But Gautama made a more forcible distinction than that. Whereas he had a rather easy rule or requirement for laymen within
his movement, for his inner group of disciples he laid down the
eight-fold path which led the way to Nirvana or the final goal
of all men. That road called for real hill-climbing, but some were
assumed to be not yet ready for it.

One unintended effect of organizing what begins as an inspiration into a movement is that as it expands in breadth the
height or quality is somewhat lowered. The first comers are
likely to be people who by nature, experience, and need are in
earnest with the subject-matter and the aspirations. But soon
the contagion picks up others less inwardly engaged but induced
by more vigorous and determined neighbors. You might say that
in any human movement there are likely to be those who hang
onto their neighbors' coat-tails.

In the second and third generation, of course, everyone has
inherited the name and fame of his religion, just as we today
inherit our special denomination or our political party brand.
In most cases that means some little diminution of active enthusiasm in the cause. Perhaps we have heard people speak of somebody as having "the enthusiasm of a convert," implying that
any kind of a first-hand move, like getting personally converted,
is marked by freshness of enthusiasm and energy. Newly made
citizens sometimes shame older ones who have come to take
their country for granted.

Once more, it is a fact that light fades in proportion as you
move further away from the sun or source. Christianity, based
upon first-hand contact with founder or founders, was unable,

we feel sure, to pass on to succeeding generations the full impact of the personalities of Jesus and St. Paul, or the full force of their teachings. If it were not for that jet-propulsion system which is always to some extent at work in religion, bringing other original and dynamic leaders like St. Augustine, St. Francis, Luther, George Fox, John Wesley, on to the scenes with detonating explosions of the inner energies that were in them, one suspects a possibility that the Christian religion would not at all have become the world movement that it did, or have survived until now. And the religious jet-propeller does not seem to work with any dependable regularity or system. We have to yearn and pine for new leaders. So that at best we have the phenomenon of fading light to reckon with ever anew.

There was something of original force in all the martyrs. There had to be. And persecution and martyrdom helped to keep up the earnestness of Christianity in a way that demands more than just a little formal recognition from us, even if we may think the early martyrs were zealots and crazy to get to heaven in a hurry. It still takes original courage to be a martyr; and most of us have plenty of reason to halt before we either patronize or criticize and to wonder if we could do half as much for any enthusiasm or faith of our day, or for any human heaven whose attainment for all depended upon our unyielding loyalty and courage.

When the Romans fed Christians to lions in the arena, a lot of chaffy material must have fallen away from the Church. In fact, we know enough people backslid to create a theological problem about the possibility of a second conversion. Only a hard-core of the martyr-minded was left out in the open to court attention. Some went underground and that was sensible. Yet others retreated to the wilds of Northern Africa and like places. Then when the Emperor Constantine adopted Christianity and the Church moved along under gentle breezes so far as public relations were concerned, and when it rather helped than hindered in business and social life to be a Christian along with the Imperial Court, the Christian movement began to illustrate Jesus' parable of the different kinds of soil. It sprouted on all kinds of ground: thin, thorny, rocky, bird-haunted, as well as fertile. The Emperor who succeeded Constantine and had the job of bringing up Julian who became "the Apostate" must have been a patch of the rocky kind of soil, judging by the way he brought up his young cousins, Julian and Gallus, and by what happened to them.

When it came Julian's turn to be Emperor, he broke away from the kind of Christianity he had met in the high places where he was cast, and no wonder. He yet showed a kind of Christian earnestness in trying to get the old Roman religion on its legs again with some adaptation and new vision for a new age. But alas, in the first place the altars of that old religion were out in the woods and not in the haunts of men. He tried to interest his people in taking care of the sick, the poor, the strangers within the gate; but it simply did not work. The Roman religion had never been a socially-minded religion. And he himself was not leading any grass-roots movement within it. He was trying to inflate it with a breeze that had come from Palestine, only he himself did not know whence it came. The only real fun he had as Emperor, if you leave out restoring ancient shrines which had been allowed to tumble over, was in collecting the Christian doctors and setting them at debating their points of doctrine, like the two views on the question of the Trinity, in his imperial presence. That was fun. It showed up Christians practically hating one another over the Creed instead of being actively busy about those things for which he would have liked to take the credit away from them. But his persecution of Christianity helped it to take hold with renewed grip after he had gone and the world had been in a way freshly converted to Christ. Sometimes having the opposition take office has the effect of consolidating both parties behind a policy which the opposition's slogans had roundly condemned.

But the Christian wave of the future kept on flowing outward and over the face of the earth. Presently it reached one of our collateral ancestors, Clovis the Frank. He became converted on a bet. Then he converted his whole army overnight, so to speak, with a red-hot iron pointed at the middle of any objector. Such a mass conversion of itself made it inevitable that Christianity should mix with barbarism very confusedly. Wholesale conversion was proved to be nine-tenths corruption. At least we fell into the Dark Ages. And the Dark Ages were given their name by Protestants inclined to blame the Roman Catholic Church more than their own ancestors for the darkness that obtained.

Perhaps we are moving ahead of our story. "Monastics" is a good general name for all those who, long before Clovis, began to retire, either singly or in groups, to some place where in their time and generation they could be more in earnest about an inner religious life than were people around them. The organization, rules and activities of the monasteries were often closely modelled on non-Christian, even pre-Christian, monastic establishments, which were common in the Eastern Mediterranean lands. The recently deciphered Dead Sea Scrolls have confirmed and amplified what was already known of sects like the Essenes, not to mention groups in Egypt, Mesopotamia and other countries. The first Christians to seek a religious retreat did it singly, and did not call themselves by any generic name, or mass-name. Later they were looked back upon as "anchorites," that is cave-dwellers, for the African caves that were so popular as domiciles with many of them.

The most famous anchorite who ever lived in a well-known part of our world was St. Anthony, who lived from 250 A.D. to 350. Anatole France has done his best in a novel to debunk or deflate this man by psychoanalyzing him at a very considerable distance. Anthony sold his own and his sister's comfortable inheritance and gave all the money away, turning his sister over to a sorority of good women. Whether he consulted her about this move or not is, apparently, unknown. But woman's hour had not then struck.

Anthony fled from civilization in two moves. After the first step into the back-sands of Northern Africa he found, in a short time, too much company around him. So, like Daniel Boone under similar circumstances, he pulled up stakes and moved on into the real uncharted wastes, without blazing or marking any trail by which to be easily found. He reached a spot where he saw nobody but a few wandering Bedouins, with whom he traded the baskets he wove and the vegetables he grew. There was a cave there which he used, but Anatole France does not know how many hours, or minutes, Anthony spent in his lonely cave, contemplating the walls and tortured by ghosts of the worldly pleasures he had left behind. Whatever we do, we probably now and then wish we had done something else; or are tempted to do so. The simple and known truth about Anthony is that he stuck to his guns and by his life-long example won many thousands, some of them almost equally earnest with

101

himself, to his general way of life. He reappeared in the great world just twice. The first time was when he was sixty-nine years old; and it was on purpose to defy a law banning Christians from appearing on the streets of Alexandria. He may have been courting martyrdom; but, if so, he was by this time too well known and too much admired to be given that honor. His other and final appearance was at the age of an even one hundred, and was to help Athanasius the Trinitarian make his point against Arius. His reputation was by this time quite something to conjure with.

The religious anchorites or hermits sought a hard life, starved their passions, abandoned the world and the pleasures thereof, and went through a round of religious exercises largely of their own kind and choosing. Each rang his own bell if there was any. Whether some of them enjoyed the wide open spaces and sometimes felt the familiar world of old well lost may not be for us to say. Possible moral criticism of them is that they did not seek to help or better the human race except in one particular way. That way was by being examples of what was deemed a higher way of life. This kind of service is in a general way what the famous philosopher Epicurus had thought that the gods really rendered. The gods were not here, that is to say they were not in heaven, to lend us a hand in our difficulties, still less to save us, as if they cared anything about such matters or even noticed the need; but to show us how to live "a life above the battle." Christians long slandered the Epicureans, as if they were loud champions of wine, women, and song; nowadays the motives of Christians like Anthony are unsympathetically approached and misrepresented by Epicureans like Anatole France. The Epicureans might content themselves with saying the martyrs had foolish beliefs about heaven to support them.

The monasteries and nunneries, the Benedictines and the other great orders, also the friars of different shades of cloth, appeared in Europe, where and when there was not so much open space for spreading out in or so suitable a climate for living in the open. Also they came after there had been more experience with the whole inspiration of retiring from the world. Vagaries of all sorts, such as for instance that of the famous Simeon Stylites, who sought merit by standing on one leg atop a column, suggested and convinced almost everybody of the need of some organized control of this concentration upon a devout religious life. Benedict and Basil of Caesarea were real statesmen, and they pointed out the advantages of monastic communities for mutual correction and teaching, for mutual support, and for arranging some humdrum and useful occupations. These men organized the retirement inspiration.

In the earlier centuries it was often the Church itself, and the low level of religious earnestness within it, that men were escaping from to live the life of hermits. But it came to be more and more just the "world" itself that men wanted to leave behind. In the Dark and Middle Ages Europe was full of unremitting carnage and turmoil. Nowhere but in the monasteries was there room for any quiet pursuits. Perhaps here and there a few guild-towns were already growing up, where some of the practical arts like weaving were developing and winning an uncertain protection, just as there were universities where you could disagree with Aristotle by paying a fine of one pound a crack. At least that was the fine at Oxford. But nowhere at all was there any secular territory protected from the continuous incursions of warring overlords or the constant pressure of tyrannical hands, or the dangers of being drafted for military service.

Even great warriors dreamed constantly of escape from the world. Pepin the Short, father of Charlemagne the Great, wanted all his life to become a monk, but never could find the moment to quit his responsibilities.

St. Bernard of Clairvaux is reported to have been converted to monkdom while taking a lonesome ride to join in the siege of a castle. Going on horse-back, he had plenty of time to think; and he turned around and went home. He converted his six brothers and an uncle, his sister, who became an abbess, and various other neighbors. Presently he led a procession of some thirty-odd men up to the door of a poor and discouraged monastery and was admitted. He outdid all others in earnestness. Before very long he was assigned the duty of founding a branch-abbey, which under him became the most famous abbey in Europe, Clairvaux. He was caught in the Crusade fever and preached the Second Crusade with such fiery eloquence that they say mothers hid their sons and wives got their husbands off on errands so that they would not hear Bernard and join up.

When that Crusade was a flat failure, Bernard told the Lord that while He, the Lord, might have some good purpose in mind in permitting this enterprise in His own name to fail so disastrously, it was "a judgment hard to understand, and blessed was the man who was not offended in it." That reminds us—and it illustrates the state of human development which made the problem for or of the Middle Ages—of Richard Coeur de Lion's prayer after he was defeated in the Third Crusade, as it is reported by Richard of Devizes: "Fie, Fie! . . . O how unwilling should I be to forsake thee in so forlorn a position, were I thy Lord and advocate as thou art mine. In sooth my standards will in future be despised, not through my faults but through thine; in sooth, not through the cowardice of my warfare, art thou, thyself, my King and my God, conquered this day, and not Richard, thy servant."[1]

After Bernard's own plain talk to the Lord, he went back to his cell in the monastery, whence he made many popes, some of them his own pupils. And he continued to talk to the popes, old pupils or not, in the same forthright language he had used to the Lord. Which shows that some mighty churchmen of the Middle Ages not only insisted upon making an appeal to human judgment in Church affairs, but anticipated the Protestant principle of the right of private judgment quite broadly. Stout hearts and minds of all ages are akin. Bernard was a man of his age and he persecuted for the Faith. He was the chief agent in that holocaust of those plain Gospel-Christians, the Petrobrusians, as well as in the harrowing of poor Abelard. But he halted a Jewish pogrom, that being in his eyes no defense of the Faith. Bernard was an original force, a veritable part of that jet-propulsion system of which we spoke.

Meanwhile the monasteries copied the Bible for us with the worst and best things in it, and also many Latin and Greek texts that we might have lost, while leaving others for the Arabs to save. They made tapestries, painted, encouraged architecture, and fed starving Apollo a few morsels. They developed some of the homely crafts of peace: farming and gardening, building fishponds, planting trees, studying herbs and medicines. They did this in between prayers and studies, but with more time for it than was possible in the outside world. Possibly we may ourselves at any time become conscious, in this world of lost privacy and where "Whirl is king," of a crying, impractical need of monasteries or retreats.

---

1. *Chronicles of the Crusades.* Bohn's Library, 1848, p. 62.

Some years ago I climbed Mt. Washington with Horace Williams, philosopher from Chapel Hill, and we met the usual bands of young people on the trails. He remarked that this mountain-climbing was "the modern form of monasticism." His remark would probably have been closer to the point if those climbers we met had been refugees from confused, high-speed business activities instead of young fledglings stretching their muscles and being initiated to far views. Perhaps a better illustration of the monastic ideal at work in our times and one more adjusted to our mentality is to be found in the training of athletes, who eschew cigarettes and whiskey and go in for physical training and regular hours.

During the Dark and Middle Ages, of course, the Church was rendering some disservice to the future. It was clamping creeds, like irons, on men's minds as far as possible. In persecuting people like Joan of Arc, it was promoting that most direful of illusions, that the end justifies any means at all. On that road the ends themselves are usually lost sight of, even in our times. The Church was heading off the beginnings of science as well as it could. That was probably covering too much ground, even if it might have spared us the hydrogen bomb. Such disservices go on in kind not only among sects but wherever organization at a center becomes stronger than freedom of ideas. But the monasteries brought down to us Bible teachings which would provide critics with materials for criticizing the monastic way of life itself. And the monasteries made room for a few mystics in quiet places, and saved some room for the inner life to develop, away from bloody warfare.

XIII. Organization, Its Necessity and Dangers

MANY OF THE HISTORICAL problems of both Judaism and Christianity have been problems of the Church, or of other organized forms of religion. And so it is in our personal experience nowadays. It is time to look directly at the relations of religion and the church, both in a more general or parallel way, and more directly as they are felt in our own day.

We have all heard people say that they believe in religion but not in the Church. Meantime most of us see and feel that the Church ought to be a more effective organization and social promotion of a humanly shared religious aspiration. Approach the church from that angle, define it in terms of our very disappointment in it, and it becomes clear that the Church has been and is our historical attempt to fill an imperative need.

Religion is not the only field in which we sometimes hear talk to the effect that organization, in existing forms, is a folly or crime in itself. This talk comes occasionally from anarchists who profess not to believe in organization at all, partly from rank individualists, but occasionally from people who are morally puzzled.

In Lincoln Steffens' *Autobiography,* he tells a dream of walking on the streets with the Devil, and telling the Devil about a wonderful new idea which has just come to him. He asks Satan if he is not frightened; and at once His Satanic Majesty replies, No, he is not frightened at all. Because people will organize that idea to death and kill it, in the way they ruin many good ideas. After we have enjoyed the humor of this story, we readily recognize that the Devil, along with all the critics of organization as such, is taking in too much ground. In fact he is up to his old tricks. He is trying to scare us away from all social pursuit of the better life. He is trying to divide us and win. He would gladly reduce mankind to individual units if he could, that is so far as their inspirations are concerned, and to conquer by means of that extreme fission and confusion. No doubt he would even like to suppress the devilishly dangerous inspirations themselves, that is to say those that would embarrass him; lest one or two new ideas or visions should break loose and have an effective human career. But that being impossible, he can attack the secondary stage of activity following upon an inspiration, the organizing and the social effort to widen and spread it. One particular move of grand strategy on his part is to show us the string of past failures in church, government, schools, or other idealistic enterprises. That is a good Satanic line. But in the meantime it is almost strange that Satan is not an organization himself, at least if he has no organization behind him or bound up in nature to help him out. For that is nearly all there is of power in such creatures as hornets, wasps, or honey-bees.

Of course we ought to take a straight look at the fact that the church is only one particular kind of an organization or of a promotional method for religion. One thing preachers have to contend with more than of old, and it may do them good, is the fact that many good men think they can better teach and propagate real religion or their devotion to human causes and to the improvement of men by some other method than by subscribing to a church and attending it. Let us at least consider respectfully the possibility that some of them could indeed do better in other ways. Books are not social organizations, but you can organize around them, perhaps in the first place for discussion or for that popular spiritual activity churchmen now call "dialogue." Think of the organization which has so largely owed its existence to *Das Kapital*. And you can put a version of a book upon the screen and send it where people gather together and, perhaps for extraneous reasons, are willing to pay for admission and therefore are interested in getting their dollar's worth. In this way ideas and scenes from books insidiously affect men's motives and their personal power-generators. When the playwright Maxwell Anderson died recently the newspapers noted that he was a Baptist minister's son but always maintained that the stage was all the "religion" he had. Of course he meant that the theater was his substitute for the church and the only church he attended. We should not merely scoff at what this son of a clergyman says. It is probably better to give him a straight look, even if we conclude that books must be supplementary because directly they affect mostly ideas and there is a bigger problem of directly organizing human lives.

It is an interesting fact that Judaeo-Christianity appears to be the only major religious tradition that ever developed the idea of the church (or the synagogue), at least until very recent times. This is an age of borrowings and interchange. Most religions of the past have got along with altars and temples, sometimes among Jews and Christians associated with congregations, services and sermons. The church or synagogue may have been invented at the particular time the Jews were just back from Babylonian captivity, and Ezra the Scribe stood up to read the Scriptures, and all the people wept with joy. From that time on, the Jewish religion was social or congregational; and it had a chance of becoming a democratic movement gathered and inspired from the grass-roots. There is more possibility for all kinds of give and take by means of congregations, if they are democratic, than just by means of books. In fact, the very greatest books of the ages have frequently suggested and led on to some further kind of organization.

Certainly we must never be led into thinking of the church as the only, or even as a full-grown ideal of religious organization. Mr. Gandhi and others in India made use of the ashram idea, and Kagawa much the same in Japan. Toynbee Hall in London, Jane Addams' Hull House, and others, have provided for people to live together much or all of the week instead of just going to church a time or two. There have been religious communistic experiments like Robert Owen's New Harmony, Brook Farm, or for that matter like early Christianity itself. Islam uses the state in some places where we would use the church. The Greeks and the Mystery religions made religion into theatrical business out-and-out. The Greeks had sacred groves for chancels and scenery, processions, incantations, masses, hymns, chanting choirs, plays of a kind. They did not have sermons, which have gradually become the central feature of the bigger half of Jewish and Protestant worship and prominent in all Western religion.

Churches inherited from temples such features as sacrifices, or the mass; and this kind of ritual lives on, appealing to the emotions. The synagogue, before the time of Christianity, added readings from the law and the prophets, also responsive readings like the Psalms, a literary form made for echo and much abused by people without real literary instincts. Real hymns have largely succeeded chants among "dissenters." Synagogue and church developed the sermon over the same road, whether near the same time or not. They both began with the idea of taking a verse of Scripture and expanding or applying it. Uncovering the evolutionary root of the matter, Christian Science "readers" of our day have so far left "preaching" mainly to Mrs. Eddy; but one rather expects them to start dilating on passages of *Science and Health* at any time, if they have not already done so. For evolution is truly involved and presses on towards making the democratic point and freeing the individual human voice for uttering whatever it can about the relations of God and man. Among liberals sermons can be informative lectures on great subjects, travelogues from embattled situations, appeals for action, challenges to the conscience. Of course the idea of a Scriptural background or base for the sermon hangs on with a most powerful grip. And almost everywhere there is still the limitation that to preach you have to be ordained. Otherwise only if you are well known for something that attracts attention of the right kind, can you expect to find entrance into the pulpit at all easy to achieve. But life goes on apace and there is clearly a movement towards making the free human voice the center of the worshipping universe, just as Mr. Einstein has made the individual observer center of the physical universe.

It is certainly right and to the point to say that no one can or should want to think of anything about the church as perfect from the democratic point of view. As to sermons in particular, one weight upon the best preaching is that the good preacher often does not feel he is good enough to deliver the sermon he has prepared. Mr. Gandhi used to feel that he needed to go off once in a while and begin a hunger-strike or undertake some practical program that would give weight to his words.

If we glance over the whole ground and purpose behind modern worship, we cannot forbid a man's putting his personal effort and force into some other form of organization, such as the theater, novels with a purpose, committees, boards, leagues, settlements, beloved communities of some new order. On the other hand, we must deplore all narrow-gauge or single-track minds, all those people who look in some entirely new direction for almost-ready human perfection, even all those who are in a terrific hurry to save the world—as if that could be done.

Probably each generation will always have to save itself, and perhaps that is a law of nature and the best way for men. We should save our highest admiration for those who determine that nothing human in the present shall be entirely foreign to them, nothing subject to utter scorn that has bulked greatly in the past of humanity.

Our major and preferred form of religious organization now centers around the church, and it seems that there are two attitudes towards the church which ought to be avoided. One is the common orthodox one which calls upon us to substitute loyalty to church, Bible, creed, or one set of founding fathers and one moment of history for all fresh approach to religion, declaring that reason is subordinate to fixed rules or paragraphs and that the great moral issues of the day are just exactly those for which the church has the answers and with which it is now chiefly concerning itself. The opposite mistake is the belligerent and unsympathetic attack which views the church and everything which takes the name of religion in our society in the same way that you note the hole in the doughnut. The first of these two approaches turns us over to one group of Fundamentalists or another, according to what continent or what neck of the woods we happen to have been born in, and heads us backwards. It makes all life second-hand, and of course it is deadly. The second stance is outside the human race, so to speak, and analogous to that of the citizen who finds government so corrupt and wrong-headed, politics so rotten and hopeless, that he has stopped both voting and studying the issues. On that line it is hard to see how one can really be of much use, even with some small vision or revelation all his own to contribute.

*   *   *   *

The justification of the existence of the church rests not upon anything it has so far done or failed to do. It rests upon a principle which it has to some extent represented and to a great or greater extent misrepresented as well—the principle of organization. This principle is no less valid among humans than among ants and bees. In fact, as society becomes free society the importance of organization ramifies and pervades more and more the whole texture. Every lively interest of free men requires to be organized in the interest of extending it, of education and improvement, of conservation and tradition, of transmission to posterity. The church, as a form of social organization, stands

110

alongside government, political parties, labor unions, art societies, societies for the prevention of cruelty to animals, civil liberties unions, golf clubs, sodalities, the Baseball Hall of Fame, insurance organizations of one sort or another, and even Sears Roebuck catalogues. The validity of the principle of organization will not be denied. And if the interest is a great one, then no matter how much and how far it has been misrepresented or insulted in the past, it still makes its compelling demand for improvement of social impact, for helpful criticism, for being sent on into a future of further social effort and groping. If we feel any loyalty to the human enterprise upon the earth, that sense of loyalty requires us to push on its organization in some effective form.

However the strength and authority which a closely-knit organization may give to a religious movement is purchased at a high price. By its very nature, organization involves some degree of centralization of power, controls, policies and initiative. Rigidity of doctrine, a cherished repetition of religious ceremonies, exaltation of a few individuals who jealously guard their prerogatives—these are among the commonest characteristics of large organizations. The cost is high because the local congregations and their constituent members are either not free to stray at all from the prescribed path of doctrine or action, or else they are under pressure of one kind or another to conform.

Among Protestants it is generally supposed that the Roman Catholic Church is outstandingly the exemplar of organizational rigidity, and it is assumed by some Protestants that they themselves are quite immune from such authoritarianism. Actually in the world-wide Roman Catholic organization there is flexibility of rule to meet some local conditions without repudiating central control, and today there are signs of democratic pressures in various fields including birth-control. Meanwhile presbyter as well as priest, Methodist bishop as well as cardinal, represents one kind of hierarchy or another. Some denominations that were originally notable for the freedom of their local congregations and accustomed to lay leadership are now organized into synods, conferences, and councils which maintain permanent staffs well-trained in the arts of management and provided with modern means of communication and persuasion. There is evidence that centralized organization can be a real peril to denominations owing their origin, ironically enough, to that wave of rebellious inspiration which we call the Protestant Reformation.

111

By contrast, the Society of Friends may be noticed for its standing by the principle of "the priesthood of all believers," the responsibility of every member to participate in spiritual "concerns" and in practical expressions of the conscience of the group. Decisions are reached by a process which recognizes that with adequate reflection the Inner Light is able to show the way to any member. Instead of imposing their own views, leaders encourage others to express theirs; and they help to maintain conditions for such worship as shall open the doors of opportunity for service. Such organization as exists among the Quakers is of the simplest. "The spirit bloweth where it listeth"—yet there sometimes develops out of such quiet worship and freedom of expression a unity of concern and a clear direction for action.

There is, therefore, a dilemma facing religious groups. Organization offers strength and some degree of shelter and support for the individual. But it endangers the individual's capacity and desire for freedom and initiative. Churches that inherit or adopt methods of central management, which we think of as especially modern, benefit outwardly, especially in the census tables, by maintaining recognized "headquarters," massive money-raising efforts, and effective propaganda; and these evidences of strength are sometimes detrimental to their spiritual testimony. Fortunately, religious dedication and inspired social action does appear, particularly in those religious churches and groupings in which policies and decisions rest upon a democratic base.

XIV. Mysticism

HORACE WILLIAMS, philosopher at Chapel Hill, used to dispose of the problem about the whatness of mysticism by saying that it was simply feeling. And he was sometimes very respectful to feeling, even in teaching psychology or philosophy. In this definition of mysticism I think he was principally concerned with warding off the notion of there being in some people any separate or additional faculty for arriving at truth. Such a faculty could get in the way of his beloved logic. He did not want to see anybody jumping the traces of logic. But his definition of mysticism seems to us too broad. Not to more than mention the possible identification of feeling with touch, one of the five senses, almost any other function of the mind except deductive reasoning from set premises can be included under the general concept of "feeling." Witness: desire, will, instinct, emotion, imagination, aesthetic appreciation, judgment, trance, intuition, hunch. "Feeling" can cover all this ground and we do use it as broadly as this. Moreover psychology has used "feeling" as a name for the vague matrix out of which all the other mental functions have developed in the process of evolution. It does seem as if my old teacher's definition of mysticism would have been more helpful in discussing the topic, as it appears in the history of religion, if he had stopped short at making mysticism a particular species of feeling instead of carrying it back to nearly the whole of mentality. It seems as if he might have said that mysticism is a normal kind of feeling that individuals share in very different degrees: aesthetic feeling, trance, contemplative awe. Or if he was willing to use at all such qualifying terms as "abnormal" or "supernormal," doing so would have left us more receptive while still it would not have taken the whole topic outside the range of ordinary people. But in his defense, if I am right about why he was probably unwilling to use such qualifying terms, I must say that the first of them is unnecessarily prejudicial and disrespectful, and the second one says nothing. "Supernormal" can function only in opposition to "normal," which is a vague conception. It is like "supernatural," which derives its meaning from opposition to some particular concept of nature or of what is natural. "Extraordinary" would surely be better than either of those terms, yet not too helpful.

Once I had a letter from a friend recently out of the university who had gone into teaching in a school where it seems they pay special attention to children's ideas, or experiences, along lines where they are customarily repressed. At this school they make notes of the mysterious voices the children hear in the night, the odd things they see, and the invisible playmates (invisible, that is, to adults) with whom they claim to have extended dialogue. My friend was interested in making the point that these experiences of children were not "imaginary." That brings in another term which one fears has no clear meaning. Among other meanings, there is the imagination of the creative artist and there is the imagined bogey of the frightened child or woman. I rather think my friend was ready to accept the children's evidence for the existence of objective realities which we all might see if we had not allowed certain inborn capacities to wither away. His idea was Wordsworth's: "Shades of the prison-house close about the growing boy."

I had to write something in reply, and could not completely dodge the subject this teacher had mostly written about. It happened that I had just finished reading a book from an armful picked up two months before at a second-hand book-sale: *The Bay Path*, by J. G. Holland. This book is a story of the founding of the town of Springfield, Massachusetts, in the early days of the 17th century and in the time of the witchcraft trials. In it, the minister and his wife are distraught people, terribly pious, worried to death lest they finally turn out to be not of the elect or saved, and led on to reassure themselves by interfering with other people's lives and opinions in defense of the strictest orthodoxy and of the religious hierarchy. You can imagine what the atmosphere of their home was like. The pair have two abnormal or unusual children, whether it is born or bred into them. The older girl is always seeing faces at the window and always getting "bewitched." She blames different people for a while but finally settles on one harmless, humorous, Natty Bumppo kind of woodsman. He is the chief local non-conformist and the chief center of resistance to the parson's plans for having

114

people walk in lock-step. At a conference, with Natty Bumppo sitting on the other side of the room, this girl claims that he is sticking pins into her, and falls down into a real enough fit. And there is no doubt at all that J. G. Holland got this sort of detail out of the town records of witchcraft days. For it is the kind of testimony on which people were actually convicted of witchcraft and put to death.

I wrote that it seems as if those who were studying nice children from good homes of today, who had invisible playmates and saw wild faces at the windows, or heard Jesus speak to them, probably ought to study also some of those ancient records from Puritan days in order to get a balanced picture. The first question was not of realism in this relativistic world; but of how to educate children's moral sense, higher affections, and intelligence. Right or wrong, I went on to guess that these extraordinary experiences they were recording would increase in number and intensity as adults paid respectful attention to them. But moral effects and fruits were more important than realism, more important than the question whether the children are really normal and it is we adults who have grown up to be abnormal. So I wrote. What would you have said?

Is this experience of disembodied voices an example of mysticism? Not in some of the important senses of that word, of course. But it seems as if one of the things we ought to be aware of when we use the term ourselves is that there is a kind of ladder from lower to higher conventional meanings.

Some think that only a few of the greatest figures in religious history should be called mystics, figures like Jacob Behmen, Meister Eckhardt, Saint John of the Cross, Santa Theresa; and, if we are willing to step outside Christianity for a moment, Plotinus. Of course, we should note that in other religions than Christianity, there have been mystics who had ecstatic visions of God, and moments of utter harmony and peace with all earthly riddles solved in one sweeping glance which they cannot describe.

If mysticism is to be defined and confined, some of us are not the people to do it. But we are all necessarily concerned with some of the more common experiences which have been frequently called by that name or else said to be tinged with mysticism.

The experiences of these school children recall the boy Samuel in the Old Testament, who heard a voice calling him in the middle of the night and thought at first it was Eli, the high priest. It turned out to be Jehovah, and after the third call they had a talk. Then there is Joan of Arc, who had visions and heard voices which finally made her the head of a great nationalistic movement and a rank danger to both Feudalism and the Church, with the result that they put her to death. And then there are Mohammed and Joseph Smith, each of whom had a big book miraculously dictated to him or given him to translate. All these have been referred to as mystics, and some of them are quite important in religious and secular history.

Emerson, in his "Representative Men," picked out Emanuel Swedenborg to represent the mystics. That man was both a great mathematician and a great religious leader. He claimed to have walked the streets of Heaven. He wrote a travel-book called *Heaven and Hell,* and described both places well enough to prove that some kind of trancelike or compelling vision was in play. He infused a lot of common sense into his books too. My favorite quotation from him has long been this: "A man's love is his life." A simple man once rephrased that: "A man lives just as much as he loves, and no more." It would merely be more commonplace to say that a man lives in and through his interests, and that when he loses these, or they quit him, then for all practical purposes he is dead. Swedenborg also reported that God sent nobody to Hell, which was heresy when he said it. Bad men simply went to Hell, he said, by a kind of gravitation which brings all of us to our own place. A bad man would be far more miserable in Heaven than in Hell, because so much more out of place. After encountering a certain amount of this common sense, we might wonder whether Swedenborg merely had an odd way of speaking in order to make or underscore his point. But the New Church is built on his peculiar visions as well as on his unique moral insights, and Emerson used him as the very type of the mystic.

Others, but not Emerson I believe, see Swedenborg's mysticism as particularly active in that ascription of esoteric meanings to certain Bible pages in which he joins Jacob Behmen and others. Most Scripture has at least a double meaning, according to Swedenborg. When Moses hits the rock and the water gushes forth, it is not really rock that he hits off the most, and it is not exactly water that the Bible is there really interested in.

I forget what it is, although I once had it explained by a Swedenborgian friend. The same friend found a highly allegorical meaning in the slaughtering of the Amalekites at Jehovah's command. Give the human imagination an inch and it will take an ell. Enthusiastic imaginative writers can be specious or esoteric in their interpretations, even if it is only in the Bacon-Shakespeare controversy. But some of this has never been called mysticism.

The Danish historian of philosophy, Harald Höffding, says that all philosophy ends in mysticism. So religious writers cannot claim all the mysticism for their own order without strong opposition. Another philosopher has said that all men tend to the mystical in old age. The meaning there may possibly be the simple one that philosophy, like science, raises more or deeper mysteries as it penetrates further and further into the depths of subjects. But the equating of mysticism with mystery, although we come upon it occasionally, seems making it too commonplace.

Certainly there is a possible deeper idea of mysticism coming to us through the philosophy of Plato in particular. For that great idealist supports the opinion that our final picture of things has to be imaginative or figurative; and that our minds are not built to reach any literal truth in greatest matters. "There are more things in heaven and earth, Horatio, than are dreamt of in your philosophy," says Hamlet. In spite of all his critics, Plato agrees with Hamlet about rationalism, or understanding. He himself follows a line of thought as far as he can, and then brings in Diotima or some seer or seeress to tell a story; and he concludes that the truth of the matter is something like what the story suggests. Of course, the story, or allegory, always comes on top of a reasoned argument, and leads in the general direction the argument has assumed.

Plato and Neo-Platonism are at the founain-head of most of the great mysticisms of the West. Is it because they are not too literal-minded or too proud of belonging to the intelligentsia? But we are in some danger of getting into the depths of the subject before we have looked over the whole ground.

There is surely a lot of valuable, unmapped, territory in the human mind. About the surest thing to be noted is that we do a great deal of our travelling with something else than square-cut facts or readily formalized deductive reasoning to guide us. You might say that we have to be guided over some of the road, to quite a large extent, by some kind of feeling. You could bring in the word "intuition" to cover some of the ground. For years that was a disreputable word, associated with hunches and race-track bets. It was allowed to excuse unintelligent procedures. But in the meantime we probably kept on noticing that mothers had good intuitions when they missed their small children and heard a noise in the jam closet. And that even fair mechanics sometimes have good quick guesses about what is wrong with our car. If we keep one car long enough, we may even begin to have pretty good intuitions ourselves about it. We observe in general that the more experience people have had in a certain field, the better their quick intuitions are likely to be. True, sometimes their prejudices, which also grow, get the better of them. But it is seldom that real idlers make great inventions, although the inventor may look like an idler because he is going over things in his mind and is preoccupied, and we do not happen to be present when he takes the step, or makes the jump, from puzzlement to intuition.

We also know that through a great deal of past history men have been occasionally waking up in the middle of the night with sudden illuminations or suggestions on subjects with which they have been struggling in vain throughout the day. We need some kind of name for this sudden pointing up of cumulative experience. Call it intuition. Call it scientific imagination. Call it inspiration. I am not really so much interested in making the word "inspiration," or any other word in the field, respectable. But perhaps I am turning over a point which may help to keep some of the humblest of us in touch with mysticism. And that might be worth-while.

There is one other use of the word "intuition" which recent philosophy has emphasized, which may have both value and connections with the topic of mysticism if we are not disposed to unduly limit that. The man who has most emphasized the word in the particular sense we have in mind is Benedetto Croce, although Henri Bergson is as much responsible and perhaps better known. Croce uses intuition to mean the tool by which we apprehend a unique situation or know an individual person. Like Bergson, he says that science gives us, deals with, the general concept, the type only. Science makes machine-production possible by ignoring all individual peculiarities. The whole business of science is with type, or class; never with an individual. That is the power of science.

118

My wife once took a sick baby to the doctor and came home in tears because he had hardly looked at the child. After listening to her opening remarks he had reached into a cubby-hole of his desk and pulled out a prescription. He had generalized that baby. But the prescription worked. That is the tremendous power of the generality, seized and operated with. As Bacon said, speaking of this tool: "Knowledge is power."

But, points out Croce, it is the artist who deals with the individual and unique. Every movement of the artist is aimed at catching something rare and uncommon. The artist in words dreams up unique situations, and makes individual characters to go with them. At least he does that in proportion as he is successful. Or rather, to do so is his aim; and sometimes he is credited with success even by the toughest critics. Of course, poet Joyce Kilmer says that only God can make a tree; and one suspects he is right and would be right if he extended his point and applied it to men. Only God can make a living human soul, and he smashes the mold after every individual. Novelists may only create a good illusion.

Furthermore, if God is One, as religion says, you could not possibly know him scientifically, because science has no tools except general concepts and God is not a species or kind of being. That is a part of the meaning of Hegel's saying that the Understanding has no God. So intuition, mysticism, feeling, art, will be called upon to help out. Be sure that if the Universe is a unique Whole, then in its wholeness it will miss something of being scientifically known. One recalls J. B. S. Haldane saying: "The world is not only queerer than we suppose, but queerer than we can suppose."

But knowledge of God or of the Universe is only one part of the subject of mysticism, although one with which the most famous mystics have been much concerned. Without calling the great mystics supernormal, they could still have little to do with us. We have more to do with ordinary kinds of mysticism or feeling.

Going back to where we were considering intuition as one name for the quick summarizing of experience and the quick grasp of present hints, it might follow that those who took life seriously and did not run away from it would be the ones to get the best or most worth-while notion of or feeling for the meaning of life. The cenobites who retired to a protected spot, the artists who have made themselves mere spectators of human concerns instead of playing some active part among men, the pessimists who have lost hope and quit trying, might be rather expected to miss the mark more widely in their estimate of it. The load-carriers and certain other artists might do better.

This may be what William James was saying in that famous and much-slandered essay "The Will to Believe." The title of that essay turned out to be a disservice to its real thought. James has been accused of teaching that what makes you feel good is likely to be true. And according to some of the critics that might justify a religion which is merely a grown-up kind of belief in Santa Claus. What James really said is that an hypothesis about life which calls our powers into action and develops them has some initial edge over one which quenches the smoking tinder or the fire under life's boiler. If there be no other evidence to decide the matter, as James thought was sometimes the case, or if the viable and the dead-end hypotheses were just exactly balanced, then the one which leaves life a going concern, that is to say which does not destroy life, is intellectually preferable as well as doubtless more acceptable in other ways. James was saying that at a real impasse life can be its own argument. He reminds us there of that other more romantic New Englander, Emerson, who says "nature does not send these great instincts on fool's errands." This sort of argument is indeed romantic; but not necessarily and always weak. Along this line of thought and feeling arise masters and leaders whether saints or scientists, virtuosos of the arts and builders of new prospects, poets and democrats. Where has there ever been a powerful man for the centuries who did not live by faith? This much of James' pragmatism is a practical form of mysticism which, as he said, helps to make itself true.

In his *Varieties of Religious Experience*, James discusses many kinds of strongly emotional religious fermentation, including conversion, and only reaches the topic of mysticism towards the end of the book. In his open-minded, inquiring way he is not at all above raising the question whether some of the great mystics had a special sense or sensibility unknown to ordinary mortals. This claim it is to which he largely devotes his chapter on mysticism, although he recognizes a lot of the common forms of religious experience which have been called mystical, and even says that all personal religious experience has its roots in mystical states of consciousness. Perhaps that is a way of tracing all religion back to the great mystics. And James describes himself as almost entirely lacking in mystical experience, which may mean that he has ruled out of his working definition everything except the top brackets of the subject, the direct knowledge of "God," the cosmic consciousness, the sense of unity with self and the world, harmony and peace overall. Or the opposite of these things, as we shall note in a moment. We are now emphasizing James' plunge into all the grandeurs of the subject, where he admits there is no thoroughfare and no contact, except a thin subterranean one, with the rest of us mortals.

James knew the great founders of modern psychiatry: Janet, Morton Prince, Freud, Putnam, Adler, Jung. He reminds us that the psychiatrists have become used to claims of absolute certainty on the part of patients who are certainly abnormal in the sense of unhealthy. One thinks he found some of the psychiatrists too certain or absolute themselves. Some of the Freudians have explained away all of the great mystics they have studied—to their own satisfaction and, of course, overlooking any uniqueness which was beyond their science. Also they have explained away most of our heroes, and most of our own sense of higher values—to our dissatisfaction. We have an intuition, or something, which says they are wrong. And we have a lot of company in that. We may recall with pleasure what Charles Lamb said after expressing his admiration for that materialist philosopher, the poet Swinburne: "Of course I am righter than he is. So are the lambs and the swallows. But I am no match for him." Jesus is reported to have found something to the point in simple people, and all the great religious leaders have followed him in that. Perhaps what he found is intuitions, especially about what is right, or about trying hard to do the very best thing we can see how to do. The simple things do confound the wise at times. Horace Williams admitted that his wife could get the answer to a moral question quicker than he could. And she was no philosopher.

James himself joins the debunkers of mysticism on an important point which may or may not be decisive. Christians and other good religious people have concentrated their attention upon great mystics who had a positive, morale-boosting, message. But among the men of grand cosmic vision there have been some with an outlook religiously black if not clinically so. They are less famous and fewer in number. James, however, says the predominance of the mystics who see divine glory overall and in all makes an impressive phalanx. He raises the point that our views of life may express the fundamental condition of the body, healthful or not. And the predominance of optimistic mystics may prove that health is more normal than sickness.

Walt Whitman was a rugged and rustic mystic, and he and Margaret Fuller accepted the universe with a good deal of enthusiasm. They have the additional interest for us, that they are closer to most of us than the grand mystics are.

The late Paul Tillich, candidate for the post of leading theologian in America, has spoken with enthusiasm of the "nature mysticism" of the German poets, and of his own early kindling to love of nature and the out-of-doors. Of course, this suggests at once that those German poets, must be kin to Wordsworth. And I recall how that old Positivist, John Morley, once wrote from a vacation spot that he was living and "feeding on" Wordsworth. In "Tintern Abbey" and in "The Prelude" there is music, whether of the spheres or of the humble earth; possibly to some extent of both. And for my part I do love the mystics who are available for everybody's use.

The thought of this chapter has been that we do not have to follow on to the very heights of the subject of mysticism before finding in it something of value, something humanly usable, for every one of us. Religion is largely feeling, and so is mysticism in one sense or another of that word. When we say religion is faith we are probably on the same grand beam of light.

One kind of feeling that we have said too little about is aesthetic perception. Mysticism is mixed up with that. Said Wordsworth:

> *We live by admiration, hope, and love;*
> *And even as these are well and wisely fixed,*
> *In dignity of being we ascend.*

Mysticism is also conversion, new life, and the visitation of the Holy Spirit. And there is no use at all in being ashamed that decent and proper emotions play a part in our religion. If they did not, we should have no religion worth speaking of.

XV. Religious Reformers

AS A GENERAL THING, when the monastics came along they did not try to reform either the Church or the World. Rather they tried to save a few of the like-minded and earnest ones from the slackness of the Church, and left the World to God, to be attended to at the final hour when He should triumph over Satan. Mystics of the classic type were, of course, individualists, and like the monastics were supposed to help mankind chiefly by being examples of the life with God. Many of the great mystics lived in the monasteries, though they were not often left in peace even there, because their highly personal assurance of having reached the truth itself could hardly fit into the discipline of any order which was managed from the top by abbot or general. At the same time, the mystics and monastics were hardly ever involved in any social reforms. Joan of Arc, who put on armor and led in battle, is an exception to prove the rule among the mystics; St. Bernard who preached the Second Crusade is an exception to prove the rule for the monastics.

Christianity has never been a social gospel in the same sense that Judaism has always been. On the popular and evangelical side, it has always been emphatically a Salvation religion, operating on people one at a time. That is why the monastics could leave the world and go apart. The business on hand was not to save the world by tribes and nations, as it had largely been for the Jews, even for the Essenes, a late Jewish Sect. To a salvation religion, tribes existed, as nowadays we say the state exists, for the individual people in them.

Nevertheless, after the Church stopped looking for the heavens to open up and the End of the World to come immediately, the question of social arrangements and of a social gospel was never entirely set at rest. The Church soon abandoned its communistic experiment of having everyone eat at a common table. It stopped discouraging people from looking out for tomorrow. It did not, of course, change its honest opinion that the real business of religion was saving human souls. When it presently began to have to deal with social evils of all kinds, with the state growing weaker and more corrupt all the time, the foremost part of its strategy was always to make more Christians and to expand the Church. That is still the case to a large extent. We all take a similar attitude every time we say that the solving of this or that social problem must wait upon the improving of human nature, so as to have better parents to bring up children, better officials to deal with teen-agers and those who got off to a wrong start, better citizens to obey the laws and to vote. But in general we tend to disagree more with the Church's claim that the improvement of human nature and the solving of social problems should be left solely in its hands. Some priests, deacons, and church stalwarts set rather too conventional a standard. If things were left to churchmen, we feel there would be danger of the little problems getting in front of the big ones. Protestant churches have spent too much time and energy fighting Sunday baseball and working for Prohibition. Catholics have fought off birth-control and have been strong on censoring books that presented mental challenge. All large church bodies have frowned on free inquiry, recognition of doubt as necessary in the process of mental growth, and the use of the scientific method when it comes at all close to the border of their preserves.

The Church soon came to feel the need of tightening up its own organization. You might say it first discovered the strong impact of the social question within its own inward parts. When Ananias and Sapphira kept back a part of the price of the goods they had sold, St. Peter evidently felt the necessity of making an example of them for the benefit of the whole Church. And he did.[1] He forgot how he had got his own start, too, his own utter disloyalty in the past. When country or provincial preachers got out of line in doctrine or practice, they had to be straightened out. After a while whole sects or points of view were cut out in the same way surgeons remove a cancer, with quite a little of the surrounding tissues. That is to say, "fellow travellers" were not spared. Some of this persecution of heresy was social action with a vengeance. The secular arm, as it was called, that is to say the state, was invoked or not according to cir-

1. Acts 5.

cumstances. This is the road which eventually led to Roman unity. Christian Rome did not exactly make a desert and call it peace; but it did use all the Roman genius and all the prestige of the Great City in organizing one "holy" and undisputed Church.

In the Church, as in older days of empire, what Rome contributed to the world was organizing efficiency, centralized management, dominion. This Roman genius was applied first on the local or regional level and was then extended over problems ever wider and more various. Roman theocrats found it necessary to put discipline and order into the tag-rag of anchorites and hermits. So it established the monastic orders for them. And it harried Saint Francis until he, or his idea about street-missions, was thoroughly organized.

Under the Feudal System, religious orders and the Church itself were caught in between rival kingships and lordships, or between candidates for such positions of authority. From the Old Testament the Church had derived the ready example of the Almighty appointing kings, as in the cases of Saul and David. In the course of time it worked up a doctrine of the divine right of kings, which implied the need of their being anointed by a proper priest. As the Empire decayed and the Church waxed, the Church began claiming the right to approve and crown kings or decide questions of title. It stood ready to anoint with holy oil the man of its choice, and also to ward off pretenders by excommunication. If it could appoint or confirm, it could stigmatize or remove. Of course, what it had at first was only a strong influence, affected by personal prestige and by circumstances. But that influence continued to grow for a long time. At the zenith of its secular power, say around the year 1300, the Church had more civil power than any state, without having in the least abandoned its teaching that the salvation of human souls was its primary business.

All this time, while the Christian movement was romanizing itself, you might say that, apart from the personal example of life and occupation set by the monastics, the Church was the principal center of whatever social "reform" was put forward to any effect. In fact, through all those ages reform mostly consisted in reducing chaos to order within the Church, and barbarism to intimidated respect for a few things in religion. But the wider issue of reform was bound to present itself before too long. The Italian historian Guglielmo Ferrero says that history is always involved in a fight between two great conscious human needs: on the one hand for order, on the other hand for freedom. When things are at loose ends, when freedom has degenerated into orgy or license, when fresh tribes of barbarians irrupt upon the scenes, when war turns every orderly pursuit into a blind alley, then the great conscious and overriding need is for law and order. On the other hand, when tyranny grinds down, when all spontaneity is crushed, when life is bound up in taboos, when blue laws or red tape hamstring human aspirations, then the need and longing of mankind is for freedom and fresh air. "Ship me somewhere East of Suez, where the best is like the worst; where there ain't no Ten Commandments and a man can raise a thirst." Either way of it, basic reform looms as order of the day.

What we have said about the year 1300 does not mean that no world-reforming spirit was spread widely in previous ages. Of course it appeared, here and there. But it was not the hour for free criticism within the Church or anywhere else. The wave of the future was still on the side of centralizing authority. Only after that time did reform begin to wear the air with which we are so familiar today: that of outstanding and often quite unconsecrated individuals exercising the claimed right of private judgment against any custom, tradition, or institution in sight. From that time on we see increasing challenge to what is established, even if more often than not the reformer himself seems to accomplish little in his lifetime and the idea may only after his death sprout and take root.

Reformers as we know them and give them fame, and the leaders of the Protestant Reformation in particular, had but one single principle among them all. They were not completely aware of that one, and may have appealed to something else. But the principle they were always assuming or acting upon was the right of private judgment, in themselves and also within the people they approached with new ideas.

It is a big question where the democratic tendency took hold and began to grow in stature in the Western world. It may, indeed, have appeared here and there all over the West. For democracy is nothing but the right of private judgment in action. The Church long suppressed the beginnings of it which concerned itself, under the name of suppressing heresy. It quite extirpated people very admirable from our point of view, for example the Sect known as the Petrobrusians. It used the honesty of old St. Bernard against those people as well as in combing Abelard's locks. It was caught nodding and allowed Ulfilas to translate the Bible into Gothic; but soon it saw the point about allowing the common people to have the Bible in their own hands, and in their own vernacular, to exercise and develop their own private judgment upon; and it called a halt and even dug up John Wycliffe's bones and burned them.

The new universities played their part. Whatever advances education ever so little, that much invites somebody to differ from somebody else, and to get the habit. The Crusades brought the West again into contact with the East, where there were still Greek scholars and teachers of the language, and books in Greek. Among the Moslem enemies Europeans met people who had kept Aristotle's works and kept alive some of the old scientific beginnings. The Enlightenment and the Renaissance brought Greek literature and art under Western eyes again.

The Protestant Reformation was certainly a product of a good turn of the tide in religion from centralized control to personal affirmation. Martin Luther early produced a book with the title of "The Priesthood of Every Believer." What title could better express democratic vistas than that? Or what could better underscore the same idea than Luther's famous words before the Diet: "Here I stand. I can no other. God help me!" There, cynosure of every eye, was an individual standing on his own legs and appealing directly to God his only judge, with no apology to men who would be his judges.

To be sure there was much more to Luther's history than this, and there were things which threaten confusion to anyone trying to draw his portrait. You do not kill an old idea when you bring out a new and needed one, often not even in your own bosom. A new principle has unsuspected ramifications. And as Luther grew older he grew conservative, which development reflects a recognized psychological principle. The radicals in his own following, coming to the front while he was in hiding at the Wartburg, gave him fright enough for one man's life. He became more and more disconcerted at what the wine of new doctrine which he had helped to ferment was stirring up in men's souls. And with reason. Democracy was at dayspring; many have not to this day ceased to fear it more than anything;

liberty and the spirit are still edged tools for innocents and untried souls to wield. The Anabaptists really gave Luther a terrific shock. The Peasants' War, born of starvation and rags, brought out the bitter persecutor in Luther's own breast and made him curse in the pulpit. Even that noble-minded Swiss, Zwingli, had to be shown that a few ideas from the past were still nailed to the masthead. Luther put his finger on the Bible page where it said, "Hoc est corpus meum" ("This is my body"), and used it as authority for the statement that the sacrament genuinely contains the body and blood of the Christ. Therein he gave the lead for some to say that the principle of Protestantism is rule of Bible, substituted for rule of Church. But implied in those ninety-five theses from the heart and conscience of one Martin Luther and nailed on a church door, and of his whole breach with the Church including his marriage to an ex-nun, was the principle of the right of personal judgment even in the citadel of religion. The Roman Church at least did not miss the central point of Lutheranism or of any form of Protestantism. It kept its eyes on the scandal of multiplying division that went on and on among Protestants. That dividing and subdividing was a product of an insistence within individuals and groups upon the right of thinking for themselves, as much in interpreting the Bible and reading church history as in anything else. Anabaptists, Calvinists, Socinians and Huguenots, to mention only a few of the early post-Reformation sects, expressed in varying ways the principle of reform which Luther had adopted and exalted.

There may be a superficial plausibility in what people often say, that the Reformation merely substituted one authority for another, the Bible for the Church. Evangelicals have long talked grandly about the "rule of Scripture"; and John Wesley tried hard, though in vain, to persuade Protestant leaders of his day to agree upon reforming all the creeds and doctrines by rewording them entirely in scriptural phraseology. But all this was felt to be not to the point. Men wanted an instrument to help them exclude others and to confirm their own personal or sectarian notions. You simply could not make the Bible, or any other book, into a blunt instrument of absolute authority or a scalpel of absolute division. Varying interpretations undermine Scriptural authority upon every page and in the middle of well-nigh every sentence. Practically speaking, the Bible has always been somebody's interpretation of it, just as Jesus has often, in practice, been somebody's picture of him. That is where democracy or the right of private judgment always comes in, uninvited and sometimes unrecognized. People dispute about words, choose their own favorite texts, call for either a literal or a figurative meaning of sentences, and in the end go on to appeal to "common sense" or their version of it. The Bible has founded more new sects than any attempt to harmonize it is likely ever to bring together.

John Calvin did not even hold the Bible in hand when he persecuted heretics and burned Servetus at the stake. He made a special tool called The Five Points, and operated with that. Others used the Thirty-Nine Articles instead of the Bible for similar purposes. Liberals and conservatives both quote the Bible on almost any point, and they say the devil can do the same.

The principle of Protestantism has never been more nakedly and unashamedly stated than by George Fox, the Quaker. Fox said the Inner Light is the principle of authority in religion. When somebody appealed to the Scriptures in his presence, citing them as supreme, Fox spoke up with an "Oh, No." He said it was the Inner Light, which is behind the Scriptures and is needed for interpreting them, that is supreme. It was for this that Fox was put in jail. It probably did not occur to him or to the other very early Friends that the Scriptures could possibly mean one thing and the Inner Light say another. And so, in the third generation or so of Quakerism in America, the movement split into Orthodox and Hicksite forms over the question of which to follow in case of conflict, the Inner Light or the Scriptures. The Hicksites stayed with the Inner Light and the Orthodox became Biblical Christians, hard in many places to distinguish from any other evangelicals. For there are plenty of people who think the Bible is somehow a principle, and fail to see how much the right of private judgment is involved in every appeal to its pages.

According to Lucretia Mott, at a meeting where Quakers were discussing the question of the resurrection with thoughts on the approach of Easter, Elias Hicks was called upon to ask the benediction. That was before the partition of the Quakers. He arose and said: "To the Christ who was never crucified, who was never dead or buried, and who had no need to rise from the dead, I commend you." Those are the words of a mystic, no Biblicist.

That Martin Luther led a successful reformation may be credited to the strength and vigor of his personality; but even more credit is due to the fact that the world was now with him and ready to go on the reverse track from that centralizing one which had carried on the impulse of Ancient Rome.

No matter whether it is religious or civic affairs on which reformers busy themselves, there seem to be two romantic tendencies always at work: one to idealize the past and the other to idealize the future. The Hebrew prophets looked back, possibly not to a Garden of Eden yet to the patriarchs who signed the Covenant and to Moses the great law giver, and to a time when the people had been loyal and law-abiding. Elijah looked back to a time when the people had not worshipped Baal, or fire, or idols—well, hardly ever. Perhaps Elijah forgot the time when Aaron, brother of Moses, had made a golden calf for the people to bow down before, and the time when they had just had to abolish the high places because idolatry was being practiced. Of course, conservatives looked back to David and Solomon, victorious kings, bringing glory to all the nation. Even if Solomon had been deposed and David had stolen another man's wife and murdered her husband, nevertheless the one had supposedly written the Proverbs and the other most of the Psalms. So reformers could idealize David, at least, and look for a divine Messiah to come of his stock.

Jesus attacked the Pharisees for corrupting the ancient law and reducing it to a matter of outward conduct or appearances. Martin Luther looked back to the Apostolic Fathers and the writers of the Epistles, except James. Protestant leaders have recalled the pristine purity of the Church and the simplicity of its organization, and in some cases its Galilean message. New sects frequently call the sum of their beliefs "original Christianity"; or dub their churches "of God," "of Christ," or "of the prophets." They do this with the same honesty that writers and painters have used in picturing the life or the face of Christ in terms of their own ideals and sense of beauty. Personal, racial, and economic prejudices refuse to be kept down.

An allied observation is that hardly any reformers begin with the intention of founding a new sect. Rather they would reform an old one. Jesus came not to destroy but to fulfill, and stayed by the practices of the Jewish religion as long as he lived. John Wesley never left the Church of England or suffered his followers to time their services of worship in competition with it. New sects are usually helped in attaining self-consciousness by being ejected from the parent churches they are trying to reform. The name of many a new denomination was forced upon it by opponents. So we got "Quakers," "Shakers," "Mormons," "Unitarians," "Baptists."

Only a handful of great reformers have ever dreamed of a future without idealizing some rather remote past age, or some group of founders. Among the few stand out Francis Bacon with his "House of Solomon," Auguste Comte with his "Religion of Humanity," and Karl Marx with his "dictatorship of the proletariat."

Ever and anon we hear the argument that it would be better to cut loose from the past altogether instead of clogging the wheels of progress with a dead weight of ancient prejudices. The name of "Christian" is today deemed a dead weight by some who were born to it. So is the word "God." The question is asked, Why not have fresh thoughts clothed in fresh words which belong to our own age and which cannot be misunderstood?

The answer is ready and forcible enough. It is that there are almost as few new words that cannot be misunderstood as old ones. It is not just old books that are difficult to apply in new situations. There are also still many things that are made clearer by actions or in a man's face and spirit than by words, and of course religion still needs to be incarnated more than talked about. And then the past is basis of good dreams as well as of bad ones. In fact, the past is our roots and our common starting point. There is value in traditions, be they religious, political or scientific.

Yet surely, no matter where we find our visions of a future that will be kinder to all that lives, the first thing of all is that we should get them and move with conviction towards realizing them. Surely our greatest need is for reformers who are willing to take the responsibility of exercising the right of private judgment in the face of all the difficulties, all the dangers, and all the personal sacrifice. The rarest and most precious thing of all is fire of conviction with strength of character and the spirit of a Nathan Hale. It matters a good deal less how much we owe, or think we owe, to any part of the past. It is for lack of vision that the people perish, vision and the courage to match it.

It has been excellently well said that there is nothing in any sacred tradition which was not first fought for, and place for it won, by some lonely thinker. In our modern society the price for being an outstanding individual or reformer may not be as great as it usually was in former days, or under autocrats. But it is still great enough, even if more World Wars do not bring further reactions and lead to greater restrictions of speech, conscience, and religion.

Justice Holmes was not talking of ancient times when he said: "Only when you have worked alone—when you have felt around you a black gulf of solitude more isolating than that which surrounds a dying man, and in hope and despair have trusted to your own unshaken will—then only will you have achieved."

I suppose a truly democratic religion will be at least as hard on us as any previous kind. Socrates had the grace not to be terribly surprised, or to extend blame, when the Athenians put him to death. So long as they looked at things the way they did, it was logical for them to kill him. Jesus said: "Father forgive them, for they know not what they do." Mahatma Gandhi found time to make the sign of forgiveness for his assassin. The road is hard and challenging enough, and depth of understanding is one of the things that is challenged most.

XVI. The Possibilities of Child and Man

Said the little Eohippus,
"I'm going to be a horse!"

Cried all, "Before such things can come,
You idiotic child,
You must first change human nature!"
And they all sat back and smiled.

—CHARLOTTE PERKINS GILMAN

I ONCE HAD for a parishioner a hard-headed New England tack manufacturer named Frank Maglathlin, who claimed he went to church to get one sermon in a year or so that was worth remembering. He told of such a sermon by a great English-American preacher, Robert Collier, on "The Overplus of Blossom." It was about how nature spreads promise everywhere in the springtime, with the most bountiful profusion, but never begins to live up to that promise. In fact, if all the blossoms of spring produced ripe fruit we should not know what to do with it. The preacher had gone on to speak of human babies as blossoms, so full of beauty, hope and promise. But it was well-known that most babies grow up into rather commonplace adults, some into real failures. Perhaps it was just as well that some of the mothers could not see ahead. The preacher had added that we ought to find all the springtime promise inspiring but should not be too shocked when fulfillment falls far behind.

My friend's reminiscence of Robert Collier has often come to mind in connection with Jesus' love of little children and various sayings in Isaiah and the Gospels about the leadership of the little child, or the prominence of little ones in the Kingdom of Heaven. It seems worthwhile to ask in just what consists the loveliness and the leadership of little children.

We love little children for things we see in them right now, like the beauty and freshness of the dewy morn. We can well exalt the teachableness of children and young people in contrast with the immunity to new ideas and the love of old ways which characterize middle-aged people. We can admire children for accepting some things they cannot fully understand. It is a nice kind of modesty, although there is always a danger of some of that particular capacity degenerating into mere dependence upon other people for ideas and leadership. We can admire young people for the fresh outlook and the new hope they bring to any and all enterprises that engage them, even though we know they are sometimes in too much of a hurry and their initial enthusiasm may be like the evanescent dew. An old war-worn Y.M.C.A. Secretary I knew used to say: "Young people are good beginners and poor finishers." After all, we can't have everything good in one package.

In spite of religious prophets being often led to turn their gaze aside from the spoiled possibilities of adults to the unspoiled or untried possibilities of children, it might be a kind of whistling to keep their courage up. So far as official religious spokesmen are concerned, they have never been happy with the idea of the leadership of the little child. The Church set to work, not too long after the death of Christ, to "convert" the little children—something that apparently Jesus never attempted. He loved them the way he found them and left them. Of course, the Church has never been unanimous about trying to convert anybody except the heathen; the older churches merely went through some form of "confirming" their youth. But the only perfectly clear and safe spot conventional religion has really found for child-leadership is where obedience is made the first religious duty and virtue. Children lead in that virtue. They have been until lately the best example of obedience to authority and accepting what they are told. But that is not leadership; it is followership.

The best leaders of the human race, if we can identify them, are the prophets and reformers in the fullness of their stature and growth. Of course, these may be the very same people who, for some special purpose, set us to observing the little children, or the ants and the bees, or uneducated and simple people—in Jesus' language "the simple things of earth which do confound the wise." It is easy to confound the self-nominated wise men who are ready with the answers to our greatest and most complex problems. But for moral leadership we look to people who have been tried, and that is not the children. Elsewhere than in morals we look to the greatest artists, statesmen, organizers, articulate thinkers. Youth are leaders mainly in enthusiasm, and there they certainly help to get things moving.

Someone has given a good enough definition of a pessimist as "a man who has just spent the morning with an optimist." Or perhaps a pessimist could be defined as a person who has just taken a good look at three of the major problems of our times, one behind the other: war; over-population of the earth; and that increasing speed-up of life which Henry Adams wrote about so searchingly. Henry Adams was a pessimist. We need the encouragement of every kind of spring promise there is, including the children with their starry eyes, as we face those problems. But we need even more the case-hardened wisdom of much-tried and experienced people who are willing to drop their own business, if called upon, and to give their time and zeal to attacking such problems. And we are reminded that we really ought to mention with praise all those salaried and unsalaried teachers who are working at our problem of ignorance, perhaps the biggest human problem of them all.

Thank God, human problems cannot be reduced to over-simple solutions. That would be the ruin and finish of us all. Every generation needs plenty to tax all its ingenuity in doing its part and in growing. Thank God, nobody can surely predict just what is going to happen or prove that the future is hopeless. We would not try to shut science out of any field whatever even if it keeps on handing us bigger and seemingly more insoluble problems than ever before. But we just do not believe that science can settle the greatest human issues or prove that our situation is hopeless. It can serve our possibilities by measuring IQ's and setting up aptitude tests, by providing us with historical parallels and with many kinds of statistics. But there are more things in heaven and earth than are dreamed of in anybody's science. The good psychologist is often overheard telling his patient: "You don't know what you can do until you try." So with all the other kinds of good doctors; they admit they do not know everything about our case. So with the best teachers and the best statesmen. George Washington said he did not know whether the kind of democratic experiment he was helping to launch could succeed or not but he was willing to give his life to trying it out.

Somebody has well said that every man is an impossibility until he is born, and great men seem to be even more impossible than little ones until they appear. When they do appear their mission has often been to help us deal with problems to which our common minds found no answer. And great men and prophets are good at finding the common causes to which all men can rally as their very own. In other words, when we have great men they lead us to the breach.

*   *   *   *

Our religion has talked with a forked tongue about not only the possibilities or leadership of the little child but also about the good and bad of human nature. On the positive side, religious prophets have given us in the first chapter of Genesis and elsewhere the teaching that man was created in the image of God. We might not want to make too much of that ancient mode of speech about human possibilities if there had not followed a development within the Jewish religion and in the teaching of Jesus about the Fatherhood of God. The same teaching was buttressed also by St. Paul, on a famous occasion at Athens, when he called attention to what certain Greek poets had said about men being the offspring of God. The teaching of the Fatherhood of God has served as a practical basis for that highest ethical principle, the Brotherhood of Man. And it is associated with the claim of "God-given" rights to life, liberty, and the pursuit of happiness, as belonging to all men. With this appealing claim, the whole earth, and especially the Assembly Room of the United Nations, resounds. These prophetically revealed rights are now rung out by a bell which is heard around the earth. The Church and its prophets can take some credit for their part in this spiritual internationalism.

Yet when it comes to viewing human nature in the negative or pessimistic light, Christian teaching has been emphatic enough. Very early the Church began to take shelter from its own childlike idealism about man, if that is what it was, by introducing Adam's Fall and the doctrine of Original Sin. At the present day, perhaps these doctrines are mostly "fundamentalism," relegated by the main lines of modern Christianity and the New Orthodoxy to the dim background of things outgrown or not to be taken literally. But they still have an underground role to play in the almost universal way of teaching Salvation. In that indoctrination the Old Adam and the New Christ are set in counterpoint. There are two proxies at stake, the second in better position if it is buttressed by the first. In Adam we all sinned, by proxy. In Christ, we may all be saved, by proxy. That is to say, in neither case does the individual son of man carry his weight in the boat of life. In neither sin nor salvation does man take any leading part. In both matters, or perhaps we had better say in the religious drama set up for presenting man's two greatest problems, the Church has found it necessary to foreclose on native human possibilities, including even the little child of Isaiah's and Jesus' dreams.

Along with this demotion of human nature goes, of course, that famous separation between "natural religion" and "revealed religion." And along with that separation has been lost to sight the real paradox of universal human nature: of human nature open at both ends, the higher end and the lower. That wide paradox is formally replaced by a theological paradox in one figure alone, Jesus the Christ. In him is the combination of highest and maybe lowest, of divine and human, of creative and creature. In Christ is all promise or prospect and in us none at all. In him is what is left of the dialectic or self-contradiction of both nature and man.

The depreciation of man's nature, in the name of religion, somewhat dampens our efforts in the social and international fields. It affects the whole mind and outlook of man. Take, for example, Oscar Cullmann as social prophet. He is talking about the human future on this planet and it hardly matters that he is thinking of a Kingdom of God instead of the democratic society that other people would be thinking about, at the United Nations or wherever democracy gets even ambiguous praise. In Cullmann's view, no matter what we plan and perhaps pray for, the Kingdom of God is the divine good that will be established by supernatural power in due time. He says: "Modern exegetes (Bible-scholars, that is to say) are almost unanimous on this point, that the Kingdom will come from God alone, quite independent of human desires and actions."[1] This way of looking to God makes a difference in what we pray for and how we pray, in what we work for first and foremost.

We can grasp the pragmatic reason for this demotion of nature, society, man. It all reflects the tremendous emotional force with which religion as the experience of salvation sometimes hits

1. *Op. cit.,* p. 149.

137

"twice-born" men. For we know that all great emotional experiences, inspirations, rebirths, feel miraculous, even supernatural at the time. And we also know that religion deals with crises in the very deepest parts of the inward man.

We have no disposition to question the practical value of the old theological drama to many. But someone must interpret more widely for humble by-standers who are estranged but still seek religion, and also for people of all the other non-Christian religions coming to meet us.

Maybe we are going to be unfair, but something like this is what the by-stander sometimes thinks in self-communion during Divine Service:

"If only men would take their paradoxes or contradictions where they lie, all over the map of our experience, rather than in some one favored spot! If theologians could only see how funny and preposterous they sometimes are! Why do they waste time preaching at such helpless men as they say we are? They must feel that advising men to get on their knees and pray for themselves is somehow mysteriously less self-contradictory than would be advising them to get on their feet and try to do something for themselves and for humanity.

"Historically theologians have made a distinction between two kinds of divine grace to help explain how men can be preached to with any hope at all. In the first place, there is a 'general grace' of God which comes to all men freely and everywhere. This makes them capable of responding a little, but it is negative. Then there is a 'special grace' that comes from just one single historical source, from one spot on the ancient map. This is the grace that saves *some* men. As far as general grace is concerned, men are allowed to keep the illusion that they are self-propelled far enough to take the first step or to seek God. But the special grace is sent by God to destroy, in the first place, this illusion that men can do anything of any significance at all for themselves. They must be made to see that it is God, meaning by God an outside force, who has to save them and save the world if that is to be done. At the same time, and this is a paradox the theologians say nothing about, men must be given the illusion that under the workings of conversion they become 'new men in Christ,' new creatures with a positive content, no longer second-hand but original vehicles of divine power.

"Meantime not this 'God' himself can give us what nine-tenths of the human race really feels the need of and craves from the bottom of its soul. God cannot give what we most need because it is not to be given; it must be earned, worked for, born of struggle. Rugged individualists ought to understand that right away. What we really want includes peace of mind based on unity of mind and spirit. It involves some humble feeling of creativity and originality. It includes finding ourselves and amounting to something under our own steam-power."

Of course the business of personal achievement is plentifully paradoxical itself when we pray, in Old Testament words, "O Lord, establish Thou the work of our hands upon us." But paradoxes are met everywhere. We face them at almost every point when we examine human nature and realistically observe the relations of the individual to the totality of things.

We come back to the total paradox of human nature and the realistic relations of the individual to the totality of things. Alfred N. Whitehead is making that paradox as obvious as obvious, if not as plain as plain, when he says that a man finds "he must fight with himself for himself, and knows that he himself must do the fighting." The philosopher has no thought of an isolated individual. There is the "principle of concretion" (his metaphysical phrase for God), which helps to originate as well as to fulfill all the individuals. He is saying that what brings about all the fighting which erupts within man is a universal spirit as much as it is a private one. It is as near as life itself but "cometh from afar," and its coming is often a revelation. One of its universal offices is to rebuke the individual sometimes, as everybody knows and experiences beyond all reason and argument. It is also known in restoration and recovery of the central aim. Vision comes in the midst of time but is eternal in character and can make a great stillness. It seems to us unconquerable when we feel and recognize it as a universal and eternal direction and lift.

The catechism of our grandparents used to ask what is the chief end of man. And it answered: "to glorify God and enjoy him forever." If that is a song of the open road, and of every creature seeking its own proper fulfillment, it may not be as far off from the truth as some of us have been thinking. It still takes imagination. But the vital fact is that we all live within a matrix, with hindrance and help coming from within and below, from all around and above. If that be paradox, critics must be invited to make the most of it. We do not at all have to judge how useful to himself is some other man's dramatic vocabulary when he thinks of these things. But paradox and dialectic concentrated upon one moment in time past, dramatic and significant as no doubt it was, is surely becoming everyday less and less indispensable to the human race.

XVII. Humanism, Ancient and Modern

A committee of the North Carolina legislature reported in 1828 "inability to discover any method of educational improvement except to unite in prayer that a kind Providence will hasten the time when literary, moral and religious instruction shall pervade our country."

THE OLDEST FORM of humanism in religion is today quite disreputable, not spoken of in philosophically humanistic circles, and frequently made a charge against popular religion. We are talking about anthropomorphism, which is a big word for man's way of making the gods in his own likeness. We refer to it here because we feel the need of saying something respectful about it.

Heathen idols, the graven images which are forbidden in the Ten Commandments, ikons, God in paintings, all forcibly remind us of the ancient and modern custom of using the human image for the divine. Even Michelangelo painted a picture of God for the Sistine Chapel; and a man it was, with noble features and beard. The intention there was to do religion a service, and it was a great man at work on it. In fact, to have the human imagination kindled to the impression of lofty or divine qualities and aspects may be a powerful service of the arts on one side, even while it opens the dangerous possibility of making God all too human. It makes it possible to think of God as subject to human passions, and weaknesses, such as anger and favoritism.

The same point and counterpoint might apply to theriomorphism in its rendering of gods in animal form or likeness. The animals, or some of them, are the most striking representatives or symbols of certain noble qualities: perseverance, industriousness, loyalty. Robert the Bruce is said to have watched the spider fail sixty-nine times in rebuilding its web across the mouth of the cave where he was hiding, and to have taken heart when he saw the creature succeed at the seventieth try. The bees and ants are our conventional symbols of industriousness. And what shows devotion more appealingly and forcibly than a dog? It is uncertain whether the Egyptians ever had any symbolism of this sort in mind in making their animal or part-animal gods. But when a tribe chooses a totem-animal for itself, it would be safe to wager that there is some imaginative symbolism in the choice of bear, fox, snake.

It certainly seems worth noting that the anthropomorphic representation of gods can hardly have done us more harm than the opposite theological line. That begins with the proclamation that God's judgments are deeper and more final than our human judgments, and that his thoughts are not as our thoughts; then goes on to say that his standards of right and wrong do not bear the least resemblance to ours, and that, on the contrary, things which are utterly wrong and cruel in our eyes may be right in his. We know that men can be taught in church to forget their native moral sense when it conflicts with some need of promoting what is assumed to be religion. Such anti-humanism of the spirit is a rock on which religion and morality, religion and our higher nature, can split wide apart. It seems as if theologians needed to catch reproof on two accounts under this head of anthropomorphism.

It happens, however, that modern humanism poses fresh questions. It long ago centered on the questions of leaving God out of religion, of human responsibility for the future as well as the present, and of accepting the down-to-earth practical welfare of humans as the religious aim. Whether it has regarded itself as religious or anti-religious, the humanistic enterprise as conceived in recent debate has thought of its end and objective as attainable, if attainable at all, only upon this earth and in social arrangements which are men's sole and unescapable responsibility.

Let us look at three kinds of current humanism, and begin with the one which, in its claims, is most remote from any kind of theology and equally remote from any conventional religious interest.

(1) We may use the general name of Materialism for this first kind. Indeed materialism cannot be any simple or perfectly clear subject, since it rests upon the concept of "matter," which has suffered many sea-changes and has hardly come to rest. Men still debate, even if ignorantly, whether matter be dead or alive. But there are many well-recognized, accepted, labelled, movements or schools of thought which stand forth under the

name of materialism and yet at the same time strongly champion human betterment. Their leaders all come pretty near to calling themselves humanists, and they associate with other humanists. For example there is Marxian materialism. Communist leaders proudly call themselves materialists and of course welcome the charge of atheism which popes and many others are not backward in levelling at them. Marx is supposed to have set forth a materialistic interpretation of history for background. A few years ago an American university was getting ready to offer evening classes in history for working-men, as they are called, and a labor leader who must have been a Communist, demanded to be told whether or not the history would be taught from the materialistic point of view. If not, he said, it would be a waste of time. And at the same time that Marxists use the name of Materialists, they claim, as in Russia, to be leading the way in the grandest of human adventures, and one for all mankind. So they represent an important kind of humanism.

A kind of materialism is associated with Freud, and still more with some of the Freudians. Freud himself reduced love to sex, or made it hard to see any difference. His disciples have been busily engaged in deflating our human heroes one after another and sparing none. They have certainly promoted an earthy interpretation of greatness. It seems that most of them would not object at all to the name of "materialists," which has been freely thrown at them. They have also presented the idea of God as a wish-fulfillment, or pipe-dream, which formally entitles them to be called atheists. Meantime, the Freudians have worked practically to promote human health and maturity, and that clearly makes them humanists.

A very eloquent and effective combination of the same kind of herbs, to make a materialistic-humanistic broth, appears in that essay of Mr. Bertrand Russell, "A Free Man's Worship," which has found its way into so many collections of literary essays for college students. A man who was editing one of these collections for the English department of his University once asked me to help him find an equally effective and compendious counter-blast on the side of "idealism," to match a quotation from this essay of Mr. Russell's. It was not easy to do. Mr. Russell has a graphic and pointed eloquence all his own. My friend gave up.

Mr. Russell says in tones of deepest pathos: "The loneliness of humanity amid hostile forces is concentrated upon the individual soul, which must struggle alone, with what of courage it can command, against the whole weight of a universe that cares nothing for its hopes and fears. . . . Blind to good and evil, reckless of destruction, omnipotent matter rolls on its relentless way. . . ." We easily recognize this doctrine as materialism, whether in this "matter" Mr. Russell knows his onions or not. It invites the appellation of atheism just as much. And it fits in with a humanistic gospel or sermon, for Russell goes on to say: "It remains only to cherish, ere yet the blow falls, the lofty thoughts that ennoble his (man's) little day." We assume that he would have us not only think lofty thoughts, but spread them and act upon them.

Although Mr. Russell leaves us helpless and hopeless before "matter," he does not spend as much time actually reducing us to "the beggarly elements" as the Freudians and some others. There have been some who explained history in terms of economic forces and rolled us all up together into "the economic man." Some have explained us in terms of geography or food. The Behaviorists in psychology exalted the power of conditioned reflexes, which is reducing the human being to physiology. But Freudianism has gone further and often sounded like a regular campaign to reduce all human motivation to physiological complexes and all morals to moonshine.

(2) In opposition to this materialistic tendency to reduce us to some kind of a least common denominator, comes the philosophy of Creative Evolution. The central idea of this philosophy is that you cannot reduce "higher" phenomena to "lower" ones without having a remainder, or something left over and unexplained. For example, they say, you cannot fully explain biological phenomena in terms of chemistry, or chemical ones in terms of physics. On the contrary, there is a real novelty at every step of evolution as it rises from electrons to atoms, to molecules; goes on to cell, to vegetable, to animal, to man; and even from basic man to "Lord Christ's heart and Shakespeare's strain." The humanism which goes with the philosophic concept of creative evolution is often atheistic, or at least nontheistic; but never materialistic in intent.

Critics have sometimes called this creative evolution philosophy a kind of disguised materialism, noting that the steps, or "levels," of evolution suggest causal explanation to be achieved by science in the future. But some of us prefer to think of it as struggling with the difficulties of language, and possibly with almost hopeless mazes of ideation, to make a valid practical point: namely that the process of reducing, deflating, explaining in terms of rudiments, does not really work or serve intelligence very well at any single major turning point or joint of the evolutionary process.

The drama, and especially comedy, is frequently the most useful critic of mores and manners; and it seems as if a good joke might be good enough criticism of a philosophy. One fellow is supposed to have said to another: "We are all sprung from the monkeys." The other replied: "Well, I'm glad we sprang." With almost every evolutionary term containing an ambiguity to be ironed out in its use, if it is to be of any use, it seems likely that the metaphysics of evolution will remain a maze and matter of controversy for a long time yet.

(3) In the third place, there is Greek humanism from of old. This derived from the Attic emphasis upon a wide-ranging conflict, variously pointed up but all along the same line from Hesiod to Plato. There was the conflict between chaos and order, which led on into the conflict between the ordered and proportioned on the one hand and the disordered and disharmonious on the other. There was the one between Greeks and Barbarians, which, roughly taken, could signify that between the combed and the uncombed. There was the one between the rational and the passional, which could be pictured in terms of a fight going on between the rational principle and the animal instincts within a man. We know that reason was the human principle according to Aristotle and the Stoics, although the Epicureans thought that this was nonsense and said that feeling, or pleasure in their peculiar sense of the word, was the sole moral principle. Plato had forerun Aristotle with that famous picture of the soul as a charioteer driving two horses, one pulling upward toward the skies and the other downward to earth and into the dirt. In philosophy, the Greek conflict was that between idealism and materialism.

In art, in Plato's ideal republic as well as his ethics, and in religion, the Greek emphasis was upon order, harmony, beauty, and generalized types or ideals as opposed to ebullitions of mere self-expression or anything that can be ugly or uncouth. From the Greeks we get the ideal of aristocracy in government, and the classical ideal of art. With the Stoics in particular, religion was a matter of living rationally. And so the whole Greek outlook upon life worked together pretty closely to give us our notion of "the Humanities" as a field for college students to major in. We might say that we owe it equally to their prejudices and to their philosophy.

*　　*　　*　　*

It is time to go back and recall the broader and non-philosophical meaning of humanism which is akin to anthropomorphism and yet lies quite apart in its broader base. That broader meaning is at work wherever the more or less ideal, human image, even the more or less typical, is used in religion, or elsewhere, as in some degree a standard leading to a more desirable and approvable kind of living.

Certainly such humanism was at work in the deification of Jesus. It was present in the worship of the Virgin as ideal Mother, among other ascriptions of less universal appeal. In our own day, we find Father Pierre LeRoy, in his account of his famous friend Pierre Teilhard de Chardin, saying that Chardin "was to assign to the Virgin Mother a dominant role in his concept of generative evolution." That is an ancient story brought up to date and connected with a great teacher and person.

The same general kind of use has been made of great saints, the Buddhas, the Boddhisattvas, the avatars and national heroes and founders. It is useless to subject the broad human tendency to our own personal moral judgment—so far as making the present point is concerned. The point is the one Emerson was making when he said that the average man is incapable of seeing a principle or responding to it until he sees it illustrated in a person. We need to have our ideals embodied where we can see them in the flesh.

When scientists venerate and emulate Hippocrates, Galen, Pasteur, Darwin, Einstein, that is not an altogether different kind of thing from what the churches do. Maybe the only question these scientists, or their admirers, leave for us in theology is the big question whether there is any chance at all of finding or founding some kind of scientific Hall of Fame, or of heroism incarnate, to help promote humane and human ideals in every last one of us.

It has more than once been remarked of Aristotle, who is

146

philosophy incarnate, that his Unmoved Mover made a very poor God for most people to worship. But worship or aspiration needs to begin where we live. No doubt some of the philosophers, like some of the scientists and artists, need for working hours a church of their own kind to worship in. For that matter we need some kind of a church, or fellowship, or ideal bond, for base-ball enthusiasts, polar explorers, plant-breeders, medicine-mixers, lawyers and politicians, and all the rest. This is akin to saying we need some kind of group morale to follow us in our daily pursuits, our trades, our busy-hour occupations.

Somehow none of our most celebrated people, and none of the great main body of us, is backward in getting what ideal stimulus he can out of nature or outdoors scenes. Kipling's Tommy Atkins said, "For to admire and for to see, for to behold this world so wide." Emerson went to kirk one Sunday and wrote in his journal that the snow-storm against the window had preached a better sermon than Parson. Shakespeare spoke of "sermons in stones, books in the running brooks." When vacation time comes, we all run full speed, almost hell-bent, for the wilds of Mother Nature. Philosophers and scientists are as bad as anybody in wanting to *see* something good for the eyes. It is an indication of one kind of basic human unity. It also reminds us of St. Augustine's saying that not to know God is not to *see* him. It would be odd if we could not get further in human unity than enjoyment of outdoor nature, if we could not find a cynosure for all eyes in something which is distinctly human as well as in things of the good earth. And of course we do all see such a "God" together, though we do not every one call it "God." What we call the object of our highest reverence, what name we use is surely a minor question. The bigger question, as the angel told Abou Ben Adhem, is what we do about our human admirations and our highest reverences, which may of course come in flashes that are allowed to pass. "Inasmuch as you have done it into one of the least of these, you have done it unto me," says Jesus about such things as sharing crusts and visiting those in prison, and he might have applied the same principle to our admirations. God is in some of them.

Whenever Gautama, Mahatma Gandhi, Pasteur, Darwin, or any one of a dozen famous scientists in this very scientific age, reveals a spirit of sympathy and good will at work among human beings, between races, and galloping across national fron-

147

tiers, there is something which operates in the same way and to some extent as any universal God should work. In certain fine human or merely scientific contacts, we get an impulse more stirring than any we can possibly get from outdoor natural scenes. We need the human touch to make us more human. In great human beings whom we meet and have the grace to recognize, our own native possibilities or latent energies are summoned and called up. We feel it as a kind of revelation. Nobody can afford to live without a good man or a good book within reach.

If Gandhi, or good Dr. Grenfell, or any scientific hero who is victimized by the adulation of his followers, should strenuously object to being called anything as resonant as a "Boddhisattva," or an "incarnation of God," as we should expect them one and all to do, that would be a credit to their humility. If any one of the scientists should object even to being called a perfect exemplar of his own science or its procedures, we should sympathize with him in that. And we should admire him all the more. The disgust of good men at being idolized or deified may very well have deep overtones or undertones arising from the fact that in their personal vocabulary the word "God" stands for something altogether transcendent instead of an activating, immanent, spirit. In general, great heroes are set upon pedestals by their followers without being asked for their consent. And often it happens without anticipation, after their death, when they can do nothing at all about it. It may possibly be that this is what happened in Jesus' case.

All the same, the highest energy we know and meet anywhere must be universal God emerging or at least energizing in the evolutionary process. Of course it is also *not* God in full, because it suggests an infinite beyond. If theologians would only accept paradoxes where we all find them instead of going all out for one great find, or a single symbol!

There are many and various humanisms, then, all of them having some bearing on religion. Sometimes the term is used as part of an offensive against "God"; and may be justified in a way as a reaction to popular forms of theology. But as for humanism, broadly speaking, surely the first thing to be said is that for the ordinary uses of human nature symbols of God or of the highest virtues are needed as a focus of reverence, aspiration, stimulation.

Religion ought to use all necessary means of making its aspiration real and contagious among human beings. It is essential that God attract worship, immature worship perhaps, from all kinds and ages of people. Let us recognize, and with sympathy, that much of the Church's ceremonial, incense, millinery and icons were made for people who were not exactly intellectual. There is a High Church sanctuary in Boston, where they swing the censers up the aisle, and where a blind and deaf old lady attendant once explained to a questioner that with her two grand limitations of sense, she did love to go where she "could smell religion." Why not let God be in all his works, in evolution as a whole? Why not let his revelation begin at the bottom of creation and burn more brightly with the ascending series? There is need of a wide variety of churches too, some quite radical.

Who has not responded to the words of the familiar hymn:

O Thou in all thy might so far,
In all thy love so near,
Beyond the range of sun and star
And yet beside us here:

What heart can comprehend thy name
Or searching find thee out;
Who art within a quickening flame,
A presence round about?

It seems that we need to object to anthropomorphism in religion from two angles if at all: for not seeing God in animals and for making too much of a God out of any one particular human being. We do not at all know whether the highest is not better revealed on some other planet than on this one, in some better creature than man. We certainly need not make the totalitarian claim that he is perfectly revealed or incarnated anywhere.

It seems extremely important to note that men can incarnate forces too great to be identified with them. Somebody once saw Napoleon riding up the street on a horse, and went off to report that he had just seen the "Zeitgeist" ("Spirit of the Age") on horseback. That was an imaginative report and a kind of *bon mot*. If religion reaches so far in the direction of imaginative truth in its Saviors, Sons of God, Boddhisattvas, Saints, it is almost certainly a service, humanistically speaking. When an

149

incarnation represents unselfish love, the service is a great one but, of course, in no way final.

There is a humanistic value present in or absent from the typical act of organized worship. The other day after service I suggested to the minister an idea for an improvement in worship. When it came to the hymns, if the choir leader, who did such a good job in leading the choir, would only turn around, face the congregation, and lead them in singing the hymns, the singing would be better and the service improved. The preacher said he had made the same suggestion himself and been turned down. He said the choir-master wanted to keep the dignity of the service.

Is God more up in the chancel where the dignity centers, along with all the appointments of historical and sacramental worship? Or is he actually more in the congregation and the pews? Beautiful sanctuaries and cathedrals can and do sometimes foster a way of thinking of God as enthroned in dignity, receiving adoration, possessing qualities that affect the worshipper somewhat like a beautiful art-gallery or a star-spangled firmament. They can even help make you think of God as monarch, creator, wonder-worker, miraculous answerer to prayers— the more so as the front end of the church is more emphasized. But in all that dignification there is less of the sense of sharing a divine spirit than there is in some of the other features of a religious service. God is in the people, too. And the more that is made of congregational singing, of readings to the point and sermons addressed directly to the people, and of meditation and personal prayer at work in the pews, the more we can think of God as in the people themselves and "waiting to be known."

No doubt there are opposite experiences of God, both of which need to be dramatized and enforced in perhaps every possible way. The distance of God from us as ideal goodness, rebuking our pusillanimity, needs to be presented with convicting and condemning power. But his nearness, in kinship and in touch, responsive to earnest search, also needs to be dramatized and enforced.

If we overemphasize the truth that God is in the congregation we are in danger of making him too near and commonplace. If we emphasize his presence in the chancel and the high vaults we are in danger of making him distant and foreign, outside of instant and vital contact. It is no use saying one

150

or the other emphasis is dangerous, because both of them are that, while each is necessary in its place or turn.

Our notion of worship itself tends to divide on the same rock as our theology. Goodness rebukes us, beauty uplifts, and the aweful humbles us; and we need all these effects somewhere. Sometimes we need conviction of sin as powerful as can be brewed and administered. But if worship is regarded as having necessarily to do with a sanctuary, then it is less necessarily concerned with the inner man. That is probably why George Fox called the churches steeple-houses and set up homelier surroundings where the Spirit could move people with its presence.

It seems as if Emerson had half an idea when he said that "worship," among other terms, did not seem to be just the right name for our regular and constant communion with God. He suggested instead "glad and conspiring receptivity." That is a long phrase, covering aspiration, reverence, invocation, consecration. It would not work perfectly for every special occasion; but what would? Emerson, I admit, seems to be leaving out what much of the Church has long considered the first thing about approach to God: abject humility. He also omits what evangelicals sometimes make the only important thing about worship: conviction of sin. But he does not leave out plain humility or deep reverence.

A simplified humanism, one penetrating into theology, of course, calls for a less regal setting of worship. Posturing and folding of hands before humanity, its saints even, its dreams, would be foolish business. Perhaps Comte, and Rousseau before him, committed the mistake of putting a bucolic picture of human nature up for men to kneel before. We cannot rightly idealize humanity at large, of any age; or spare the thought of fulfillment yet to come. We cannot take that last away from even the saints.

* * * *

Humanism, in one form or another, has always existed since the earth produced man. At times, both in antiquity and in modern ages, thinkers have taken man's creative or constructive powers not only to be resident and inherent in him, but to be his own property, as if he had created these powers himself, or as if they had first come to the planet with the coming of the human race. At large, of course, men long lacked intimate knowledge of that principle of evolution which has so

151

deeply affected our age. And when ancient or modern humanists have accredited to man alone the power of seeking ideal objectives or sensible goals, this has seemed to the majority of religious people to be unreligious. To them it has appeared a cynical way of denying all credit to the power or powers that brought man, with his strange desires and longings, to birth upon the planet. The scientific unveiling of evolution in all the planetary, physical and biological aspects of evolution has only intensified this feeling with some religious people, who have still felt that a kind of cynicism is involved in making man, instead of God, the Creator. Further, the glorification of man and his possibilities has seemed unrealistic in the face of those depths of degradation into which individuals and whole nations have been seen to descend or fall.

But when humanism has not over-exalted mankind, past or future, it has brought thoughtful people to a reverence for the possibilities before mankind, man being a part of that evolutionary process in which his times are concerned. Men share, and can share sacrificially, in the long struggle for progress, for growth in knowledge, for democratic government, and for the brotherhood of man. Religion feels man to be a son of the sun and of light—in short a son of God. Such humanism calls to mankind for ardent but humble participation in the search for truth, in the creation and love of beauty, and in the improvement of the lot of all God's children. Such humanism puts a deep feeling into men's struggle for forms of religion meaningful to a generation which has abandoned the idea of God as king, dictator, or grandparent.

XVIII. Religious Idea of Democracy

Of all wit's uses
The main one
Is to live well
With who has none.
　　　—EMERSON

　　The question of good or bad, fit or not fit for self-government, is not to the point. It is a question of fundamental justice, and the just is always the expedient, as well as the right. It is a crime against humanity for one nation to govern another against its will. The master always says his slaves are not *fit* for freedom; the tyrant, that subjects are not *fit* to govern themselves. America deserves the gratitude of all upholders of liberty by founding her own freedom on the principle of the immutable *right* to self-government—that governments derive their just powers from the consent of the governed.
　　　—ALFRED RUSSELL WALLACE

THE OLDEST and most famous slogan of democracy is probably the one about governments being based on "the consent of the governed." That dates back at least as far as Marsiglio of Padua, at the beginning of the fourteenth century. It denies any right of anybody to tyrannize over the minds or bodies of the people. It reminds us that there must have been some freedom in the mediaeval universities, perhaps resting in part on their remoteness from life and their being confined to Latin as a language into which to put ideas. That was putting the ideas on a high shelf and making them less dangerous so far as the common people were concerned.

　　But this slogan has two limitations. One is that it is too passive. A man can submit to being bossed or henpecked; or he can appoint some agent to attend to all his business for him and pass over all the attendant responsibility. Until recent days, the women of the freest countries in the world consented to let the men run the whole business of government. The other limitation is that consent of the governed is somewhat ambiguous.

153

It can be taken collectively, the meaning of the slogan being understood to be that the majority has an unqualified right to rule. It leaves open the possibility of the majority tyrannizing over the minority. It does not speak expressly of individual freedoms as does our Bill of Rights.

This lack in the statement about consent of the governed is remedied to a considerable degree in the ringing motto we got from Theodore Parker and Abraham Lincoln, "government *of* the people, *by* the people, and *for* the people." To be sure there was one thing in Lincoln's soul, and doubtless in Parker's before him, and in Lincoln's voice at Gettysburg, which the motto does not put into explicit words. That is, enthusiasm. But government can be of and by and for the people in so far as there is no outer constraint and no wholesale delegation of responsibility, while still many of us do not go to the polls and vote. That is a lack of enthusiasm. And democracy is not very democratic without a great deal of initiative and enthusiasm on the part of the voter or the church-member. Enthusiasm made this country and its Constitution, and is needed today to fight city bosses, special interests, partisanship, arthritis in official knees, and pervasive ignorance about our greatest problems. Like anything else much worthwhile, democracy is at bottom an inspiration. The organization follows the inspiration. Putting the matter so, as it seems we must, calls for at most a merely tolerant view of some things that go on in the best democratic families and shows that democracy could rise much higher than it ever has done on this earth.

It may very well be that at the bottom of that sacredness of a few personal rights which all Americans are brought up to believe in, at least formally, lies a sacredness of humanity itself, as made up of "children of God," or as the center of our profoundest values. For this we really have to be enthusiastic. I suggest that such is the case. I suggest that the reason, probably the only basic reason, for our having these grand human rights, which it is the duty of everybody else to respect, is that it is deeply in the interest of everybody else that we should have them. We must not boggle over that word "interest." I might have said "religious concern," perhaps. If humanity is itself in any sense a divine or "sacred" enterprise, then the conditions by which it can really live and grow up are sacred. And the sacredness of the whole enterprise extends itself to the means by which each and every one of us can realize himself. That is why so many of these rights, if not all of them, are concerned with freedom, and why freedom of opportunity lies at the bottom of most of the other freedoms. If this is the true view of the matter of rights, then none of them are what ought to be called "gifts of God," if you mean handouts. They are tools to work with, under God and with God-given might and inspiration. When one of Dr. Franklin's correspondents complained in a letter to him that the Federal government was not providing the people with the "happiness" that was "guaranteed in the Constitution," the Doctor reminded him that what the Constitution guaranteed was the right to pursue happiness, but that each man must catch up with it for himself.

Shortly before the First World War or in the early stages of it I was one of those who heard Catherine Breshkovsky, then called "the little grandmother of the Russian Revolution," speak in Boston. She was not too long out of a Czarist prison and still had troubles when at home. She voiced a deep enthusiasm for something she found in this country, and the phrase she used for it was memorable: "the opportunity for developed activity." Women could gather audiences anywhere, to agitate for woman suffrage; and they could get on the train and move wherever they willed, to start the fire going in other regions, and all without any kind of governmental interference whatever. No prison, no Siberia, before their eyes!

Her phrase seems worth saving. Space for developed activity is the main gift which civilization has been increasing for Europe and America, through nearly twenty-five hundred years if you start with Greece. And it is the main gift the rest of the world is demanding now as a kind of divine right. Western civilization has in all these years multiplied for us the number of learned professions, starting originally from just three: ministry, law and medicine. It has brought women at last into all of them. It has proliferated arts, skilled occupations, trades and schools. Today anybody can make a brand-new kind of job for himself and many are doing it. Civilization has also ended for us many kinds of slavery, serfdoms, and caste systems. There are fewer little taboos to look out for in the sun of this Twentieth century. There are, God save the mark, more books of one kind or another, and probably more ideas of everyday kind, afloat. On the whole there is less confinement to the one ancient business

155

of nine-tenths of the people, that of ekeing out a living; and there is more social life and contact.

May we not, must we not, view democracy as first a spirit making a religious principle of this widening of life? May we not say democracy is that rule of the "kingdom of God," which opens space for creative imagination and individual attainment on all sides and in all the corners of earth? We certainly cannot ask room for ourselves, in anything, in any place, where in any serious measure it lessens the open space every other man has for living his life. That is the limitation. The extension of opportunity is sacred, and so is the mutuality of it.

On some of the sub-heads of getting civilized, practically everybody has to be a democrat up to a point which nears real enthusiasm. Did you ever meet a teacher who did not say that he was more interested in leading pupils to use their minds, or to think, than he was in "stuffing them with facts"? Or did you ever meet one who did not admit that you can't make a boy good by taking a stick to him? Perhaps this attitude is not universal, but we are constantly told that we have to appeal to something inside the boy. Nearly all teachers and all propagandists try to kindle interest and to make "self-starters." When a youth takes hold of some book in an interested way, most teachers smile and warm up. Many of them offer prizes, showing they are willing to use almost any gas that will fire an internal-combustion engine. Most of them prefer to awaken a higher curiosity if possible. Surely this is true of all the good and really successful teachers.

Social workers the world over have gone democratic to an enormous extent in the past half-century. They have discovered that "charity" is practically a "cuss-word." Nobody wants charity and hardly anybody, we are told, ought to have it thrust upon him. We should clearly accept the truth that a great deal of failure is not the individual's own fault, and we should stress the obligations of society to all. We should help people to help themselves. We should bolster and strengthen every particle of self-respect. Even psychiatrists should not let people lean on them. Every family should be given another and yet another chance to hold together as a going concern. Social service should be socialism in the form of encouraging rugged individualism. That is one more paradox!

One hardly knows what has happened in the last half-century

to all the orphanages where children were crowded together and taken care of by drill and mass-methods, because in that setting only such methods would preserve order. Those "homes" bristled with authority and necessary restrictions. Now the effort is all to find real private homes for children, not more than two in a family and if possible with born sons and daughters of the family alongside, so they can grow up as normal human beings and not as slaveys or machine-products. How often we are told that the first need of children is to be loved! This major-shift in social operations cannot be thought to have nothing to do with what it is that gives life a religious character.

If the spirit of democracy is initiative, ambition, energy, enthusiasm in the people's breast, then the democratic system of government or of the church is the one which offers a width of future prospects.

The makers of our Constitution had much human idealism and quite a good deal of the democratic spirit in them in matters close at home like local government in town-meeting for example, without being in the least favorably taken by the name of "democracy" for the national government they founded. They proclaimed belief in government based upon consent of the governed; but we cannot truthfully say that they believed in government by and of all the people. They started off with a property qualification upon the vote in many places. The President and the Senate were not to be elected directly by the people. Most of the founders feared the ignorance and passions of what John Adams called the "Many," or the "Mob"; and Adams continued to justify himself for that in his letters to Jefferson towards the end of his life. The sage of Monticello, who of course was head of the popular party for a long time, simply wrote back that he was more afraid of the selfishness of the Few.

The French Revolution sent the words "enthusiasm" and "democracy" equally and completely under a dark cloud for a long time. Until about 1840, the wealthier part of the North and East thought of Democracy as a perversion of the citizenry worked by Jefferson and Andrew Jackson, who, with the mob behind them, had taken the lid off a second Pandora's box and freed all the winged gulls and screaming eagles of the untamed frontier.

Democracy is ideal only when it is nothing else but an ideal. No human system of government is ideal. Democracy is a dangerous kind of government, though it is not alone in that. Those systems, like those individuals, which do the most promising and pledging of quick good results are often the most deceitful. Our world is simply full of disillusioned idealists, many of them gone conservative in old age. If there is anything great about democratic government it is its prospect, its facing the sunrise, its unlimited possibilities, its love of God and dissatisfaction with actualities. We can even quote St. Augustine on that: "Our heart is restless until we find rest in thee." We are not denying the deepest personal applications, but merely extending the idea to the whole of life.

Our modern aristocratic fears of the Many and of life have drifted more into what is accepted as the sphere of the church— at least as much as of government. We are frightened over increased disrespect for the law, even while forced to make more and more laws and thus increase the territory over which disrespect may spread and fester. We are dismayed to see popular religion losing its hold upon masses of the people, becoming less able to give solid support to law and order. We are disturbed to see large features of the public mores coming into question and debate: the permanence of marriage, the sacredness of property rights, perhaps for some of us the holiness of the Sabbath. An Episcopal clergyman said to me: "The only thing that is worse than divorce is no divorce." Some of these current changes of outlook seem almost treasonable. The individual is exercising his right of private judgment far and wide, and without due equipment for judging.

Some of us are now coming to believe in the church for the benefit of other people instead of for ourselves, and to contribute to its support as a bulwark of all traditional moralities. If so, of course, we choose the more conservative kind of churches for our support. Not thinking in terms of the Bible themselves, some citizens wish that others would listen to it and obey some of the familiar precepts taken from it. Honestly, we cannot do this and be free of spiritual kinship to Lenin and Marx, who claimed that "religion" is something to help manage the people. They said religion offers "pie in the sky" to take the worker's thoughts off his being exploited by Capitalists in this life.

There is something of a Liberal distrust of democracy, to be measured against the Conservative one. Where Conservatives distrust reason in the best of its works, and fear the right of private judgment turned loose in our world, Liberals often distrust the dominance of prejudice over reason in the great majority. And they can themselves get too far out of sympathy with dramatic and symbolic approaches to truth. They can be too pessimistic about the intellectual equipment, the training, the possibilities of the ordinary human, to really live in the democratic faith themselves, or in anything very much like it. After all we should miss General William Booth and his Army, Father Taylor of East Boston, and some of the Fundamentalist preachers of the backwoods. The like of some of these may still be needed for bringing up the rear-guard and for what reference they make to the Sermon on the Mount. Debits of any kind do not abolish credits and uses of other kinds than rational, in backward places, are not to be despised. What some Liberals need, it seems, is readiness for co-existence with ignorance and with minds indurated by traditional beliefs, while Liberals exercise their opportunity of gradually making themselves a majority. Willingness to coexist, with all snobbery and some of the haste that we get into discarded, is one of the attitudes needed for the great common prospect and hope of a growing mankind.

When Carl Schurz had been in this country two months, in the autumn of 1842, he wrote back to a former associate in the widespread European revolution of 1848, Malwida von Meissenbug. Schurz gave the most faithful, freshly percipient, rightly humble, impression of incipient democracy in action which I think I ever met. In the paragraphs we shall quote, he tells the German lady friend, apparently with inward enthusiasm, what is the relation of democratic faith to its problem.

"It is true, indeed, that the first sight of this country fills one with dumb astonishment. Here you see the principle of individual freedom carried to its ultimate consequences: voluntarily made laws treated with contempt; in another place you notice the crassest religious fanaticism venting itself in brutal acts; on the one hand you see the great mass of the laboring people in complete freedom striving for emancipation, and by their side the speculative spirit of capital plunging into unheard of enterprises; here is a party that calls itself Democratic and is at times the mainstay of the institution of slavery; there another party thunders against slavery but bases all its arguments on the authority of the Bible and mentally is incredibly abject in its dependence—at one time it displays an impetuous impulse for emancipation, while at another it has an active lust for oppression;—all these in complete liberty, moving in a confused tumult, one with the other, one by the side of the other. The democrat just arrived from Europe, who has so far lived in a world of ideas and has had no opportunity to see these ideas put into actual, sound practice, will ask himself, hesitatingly, Is this, indeed, a free people? Is this real democracy? Is democracy a fact if it shelters under one cloak such conflicting principles? Is this my idea? Thus he will doubtingly question himself, as he steps into this new, really *new* world. He observes and reflects, gradually casting aside, one after the other, the prejudices with which Europe has burdened him and finally he will arrive at the solution of the problem. Yes, this is humanity when it is free. Liberty breaks the chain of development. All strength, all weakness, all that is good, all that is bad, is here in full view and free activity. The struggle of principles goes on unimpeded; outward freedom shows us which enemies have to be overcome before we can gain inner freedom. He who wishes liberty must not be surprised if men do not appear better than they really are. It is true the ideal is not necessarily arrived at, but it would be an unhappy thought to force the ideal in spite of humanity."

Here follows a passage about the Jesuits being left free in America. Then Schurz goes on:

"Every glance into the political life of America strengthens my conviction that the aim of a revolution can be nothing less than to make room for the will of the people—in other words to break every authority which has its organization in the life of the state, as far as possible, to overturn the barriers to individual liberty. The will of the people will have its fling and indulge in all kinds of foolishness—but that is its way; if you want to show it the way and then give it liberty of action, it will, nevertheless, commit its own follies. Each of these follies clears away something, while the wisest thing that is done for the people accomplishes nothing until the popular judgment has progressed far enough to be able to do it for itself. . . .

"Here in America you can see every day how slightly a people needs to be governed. In fact, the thing that is not named in Europe without a shudder, anarchy, exists here in full bloom. Here are governments but no rulers—governors, but they are clerks. All the great educational establishments, the churches, the great means of transportation, etc., that are being organized here—almost all of these things owe their existence not to official authority but to the spontaneous cooperation of private individuals. One has glimpses into the productivity of liberty."[1]

Schurz certainly did not see us in 1852 as anything to be exactly admired from the artistic point of view; it was only from the farmer's, the cultivator's, angle that we scored. The people may be the source of their every prophet, of their own and the prophets' every dream, and even (under God) of sacred rights; but we are not beautiful in presence or noble in expression. Not classical art but modern is what is fit to draw our portrait. Much of what is good about us comes, as Schurz afterwards saw in Abraham Lincoln, out of what is supposed to be the bottom of the pile. But he did not miss seeing the fertile prairies and the fertile nation. The surge of life was over the land, and it was springtime. This new surge begins in freedom from restraint, the bursting of outer shells, so that we can move on to inner freedom and fruit. Schurz had the lively advantage, if we consent that it is one, of measuring the American adventure over against the Europe from which he had just escaped. Thence comes much of his warm sympathy; for the evils and dangers of the new world do not erase memory of the greater disadvantages and suppressions of that tyranny or hereditary aristocracy which would keep us either slaves or children. So he faces the uncertainties without losing heart.

His reaction was nothing momentary, to be later repented and expunged from the record. His was the eloquent voice in the Senate a few years later, pointing out with brilliant clarity and unfailing humor the corruptions and feebleness of the Grant administration. We have seldom had such political oratory in this country, before or since. Before that, he had got into politics in time to be one of the strong promoters of Abraham Lincoln; and no one at the end of the Civil War more represented Lincoln's principle of "malice towards none and charity for all." Years afterwards, he was one of those Mugwumps who brought Grover Cleveland, that honest and rugged man, onto the scene in the midst of the Gilded Age and the heyday of city bosses. He could see the American experiment (some of the founders had called it that) almost as a choice of the Leaden Casket; but yet it remained mankind's brightest and best hope. When

1. *The Letters and Speeches of Carl Schurz*, Vol. I, p. 5.

in this letter almost from the landing-dock of the ship that brought him, he uses that terrible word "anarchy"; the root idea of that is positive, human beings being allowed to make their own way without old-fashioned bosses or leading strings. That is to say, anarchy as he sees it does not mean chaos, at least not for more than an hour or so, but the gradual victory of common sense and kindness among men. His heart and his judgment abode in one and the same place. For it is the prospective and hopeful view of man's possibilities in whose service we are able to go all out. What else is there that is worth a fight for, forever and a day?

Of course water has gone over the dam since Schurz's time, and this day of ours is not exactly an easy one for believing in democracy. Many nations, like the Russians, agree with Abraham Lincoln that government ought to be *for,* or *in* the interest of the people; but insist that it must be *of* and *by* dictators. They leave out any individual freedom and initiative at the bottom of their whole system. At least that is the way they began, although they may be weakening a little. They have denied Marsiglio of Padua's dictum that government ought to rest upon consent of the governed. They distrust the common man. Perhaps they distrust the common man more than those Americans who do not go to church themselves but contribute their money because they think traditional authorities or literal belief in the Bible, and perhaps literal belief in hell, is needed to keep people's morals straight—especially the young people's. The Russians are more frank and adopt "atheism" as their slogan because the popular Christianity within Russia was, and is, a hindrance instead of a help in applying Marxist ideas to both government and business. We can see that they may be as honest in adopting "atheism" as some men of wealth among us are in supporting, at second hand, conservative religious beliefs. These last do not trust the young people to think things out as much as they trust themselves, without conservative beliefs, to be honest and fair. But when it comes to questions which involve the "haves" and the "have nots," there are always interested parties.

I suggest that putting religion into the idea of democracy means having enough of the spirit, hope, and faith of the matter to come out for it with some personal loyalty and some active belligerence. A real democrat cannot be concerned in maintaining the church just for the sake of having other people managed or pastured out under pastors. He must swell with the faith or the hope himself, even if in situations as trying as Winston Churchill's when he made for Britain that speech about "blood, sweat, and tears." You can have pieties, forms, religiosities, with ulterior and selfish motives behind, based on your fears. You can try to justify Cicero for implying that it is fear which makes religion. But religion in a world which talks about democracy as much as our world talks about it needs to be a first-hand religion.

To say the same thing in other language: Religion cannot consist of sitting on the lid while something else moves things around us and makes the world that is to be. It is not passive, not defensive, not a search for security. It is an active search for education and self-fulfillment. We get enough passivity in tired hours from television. We need a democratic principle which is also a main-spring. Who does not know what all the "rugged individualists" tell us, that the real fun of life is in doing things for yourself, winning your own way under difficulties, making new discoveries, making a new tool, getting grass to grow where it didn't, stretching your own mind, building for the future? There is only one thing that needs to be added to what the "rugged individualists" say about it. Here it is in a story. Two men were talking and they got on the subject of human nature. One of them said "You can't change it." The other replied, "I tell you, there is nothing worth doing except changing human nature." That is to say, the human adventure is the whole thing in the end. And that is the religion of the matter. If we expected religion to be anything less than that, the joke is on us.

John Dewey once defined a good man as "one who is getting better." That is at least a prospective and yeasty definition, with settling on our lees plainly left out. If he had stopped with saying we are always degenerating when we are not improving, that would have been a truism, heard so often that it strikes not a spark. Dewey improved on the truism. We might follow him further and say that a good society is one which is seeking improvement of the man in it, rather than one that is merely preserving law and order.

The word "God" is only a mere and short word for the convenience of simple people and for quick and common prayer.

163

But surely there is a universal spirit in man, encouraging us when we do a good piece of work or even when we try hard and fail, helping us not to accept failure, radiating approval somewhere from out the blue when we do the best thing we can think of to do for self and neighbors, undergirding us in an unanticipated way when we are thoroughly confident of our own motives. "His strength was as the strength of ten because his heart was pure." That is not broadside commendation for future reference; it is on the spot and of the moment. This universal spirit also rebukes us when we make snap judgment, or act or speak in too much of a hurry. Socrates was certainly right about one curious fact: remorse, that back-lash of conscience, is about the strongest and most terrible passion we have. He called it a divine visitation. It will continue to visit us as long as we really live. But we can have some hope that some of our positive propulsion is both human and universal or divine.

No individual can expect to be left to himself for lonely and uncontroverted judgment of what is good and valuable, or right; or the contrary. Adults must judge for little children and society must judge us all from the collective point of view. Parents and nurses must save infants from eating poisonous mushrooms. Society has the responsibility of protecting, through laws of decency, or laws against noises and miasmas, the freedom and life of all the rest of us from the license of the one, or the few, or the minority, or the majority. As Socrates freely admitted, the Athenians had their own responsibility to face in judging him from their point of view and not from his; and in passing upon the main objectives of the state and even the means of reaching towards them. There is personal judgment and there is social judgment, and each of them is absolute without equivocation. As a pacifist minister said when they burned him in effigy upon his own New England church green: "Every man has the right to be a prophet; but no man has the right to be a prophet and expect the rewards of a popular priest." The thing that is sacred in such a situation is judgment, at all the appropriate centers of it. The democratic point is that we cannot afford to lose the enthusiasm for individual freedom and initiative over any of the broad scenery, whether or not we like some of the reverberations of it brought by the morning paper.

*   *   *   *

I confess that instead of having a low estimate of human nature as a whole, for some reason I have always been goggle-eyed at the amount of unexpected kindness met with in ordinary people. I know that consciousness of low or selfish motives often present in myself has a bearing on that. But I was born to wonder, and the distant roll of pogroms and genocides, while it has sobered, has not overcome the near or the total impression of good in man. Why should there be so much sympathy in a world that has so much of tooth and claw in its history and its evolution? Possibly my admiration for humanity is due to having a deaf ear, or to not reading the right paper, or to leading a sheltered life. Perhaps! But some of those who see differently from me have been conditioned by a terrible sample of life on their side. Is it all a matter of local conditioning? Is faith in and hope for one's kind the normal thing; or is it something we ought to have outgrown? Probably we all ought to think over just where we have lived and with what advantages for getting at the widest truth. Democracy itself says that we must let others judge for themselves whether or not to believe that humanity has something of the divine in it. But it seems that even the critics should have some idea to give forth about what their criticism comes out of, and whence, and why they expect or hope to be heard.

XIX. Christian and World Unity

An eye-witness of the World's Parliament of Religions, at the Chicago World's Fair of 1893, described it in the following language:

> At the head of that procession walked a Swedenborgian layman, Mr. Charles C. Bonney, arm in arm with scarlet robed Cardinal Gibbons, the highest dignitary of the Roman Catholic Church in the United States. And behind them walked Greek and Jew, Confucian and Christian, Mohammedan and Parsee, all marching in one grand, triumphal procession of brotherhood. Would that some painter had been present to put on canvass that memorable scene, symbolic as it was of the death-knell of sectarian exclusiveness, prophetic as it was of the coming peace among the conflicting faiths of mankind . . .
>
> Yet at the very Parliament of Religions . . . there was witnessed the spectacle of representatives of each of the seven great religions claiming that his is the universal religion, destined to win the world to its side. The fervent Buddhist pictured the universal sway of Gautama's gospel. The enthusiastic Mohammedan made a corresponding claim for the certain victory of Islam over all its rivals. The Zoroastrian, the Confucian, the Jew, each in turn, sketched his own religion in terms of universal religion. The devout Christian prayed for "the redemption of all the world through our Lord and Savior Jesus Christ."
>
> —ALFRED W. MARTIN,
> *The World's Great Religions,* 1893

IN SPITE OF ALL the religious teaching of humility and meekness, when we get together as a sect or a cult, there is a kind of arrogance that attaches itself to us. Not only the Jews have been led by their religion to think of themselves as "a peculiar people." Every historic religion thinks of itself as possessing the most important point of truth, lacking to all others. Each religion thinks it has the greatest founder of all: Moses, Zoroaster, Gautama, Jesus, Mohammed. Each thinks it has the greatest religious book: the Old Testament, the New Testament, the

Sutras, the Upanishads, the Koran. Most of them have a specially sacred city or two, like Jerusalem or Mecca, which for one reason or another is practically necessary to the religion. It is of the nature of religions and in fact a part of their appeal to our human nature to regard their own beginnings in very sacred focus.

Happily, recent years have seen honest moves in the direction of a friendly rapprochement between Christian Churches, and between Christians and Jews. It has been found possible and gratifying to develop various forms of cooperative action, and even to recognize in a friendly way what might be called a "unity of intent." Ancient barriers have been pushed aside to allow sincere friendships to be enjoyed between Christian pastor and Jewish rabbi, Protestant minister and Catholic priest. And laymen have been even more ready to welcome the new atmosphere.

However, the climate of mutual appreciation, admirable as it is wherever it exists, does not mean that dogmatic positions on theological matters have been surrendered. A theologian like Rudolph Bultmann seems ready to concede about anything to philosophy and breadth except what indeed he shares with all fully orthodox Christians, belief in "one eschatological event," which was the coming of Christ at a point of historic and calendared time. But it is this one fact which reduces all other religions to an inferior and less sacred position which it is hard to imagine them, with their emphasis upon their own founders and beginnings, ever accepting.

All of those who base Christianity on a unique event, whether or not they add the word "eschatological" to it, hold back from in any degree tracing either Christianity's "conquest" of the West, or such improvements in social order and civilized ways of living as have come about in Europe in the Christian era, to the fact that Christianity inherited, affiliated, and mixed with a variety of religions and cultures. They have only a minor recognition ready for even the great Hebrew contribution of ethical feeling and the ethical principles worked out in Judea. They have no humble confession to make of obligations to the glory that was Greece and the organizing skill that was Rome. They make little of the Mediterranean melting-pot or mixing-bowl, that is so important to ordinary historians. This single-track type of historical view is characteristic of religions, so far as one knows. But it becomes a part of the religious problem, because others play the same game or the same high drama. It explains why "ecumenicism" and world-religion are neither of them practical politics at this hour.

Of course, the historical religions have all been greatly occupied in discussing what is the true or Catholic form of their own religion, and with healing some of their own inner divisions.

Within Christianity, for example, there have always been groups claiming to be the "one true Church." Roman Catholics have been outstanding in making this claim, but they have never been alone in doing so. There are Nestorian, Armenian, and Greek Orthodox or Eastern Orthodox groups, which from the beginning, or near it, have made such a claim. And since the Protestant Reformation, there has been no lack of Protestant sects claiming to represent true and original Christianity, to the exclusion or rejection of all others.

The Romanists have carried the word "Catholic" in their name. Their claim, thereby made, is that Christ founded the Church upon St. Peter, and that Peter has been followed by a succession of bishops of Rome, or popes, constituting through the ages a continuing headship of the "living church," one in order and doctrine, *semper, ubique, ab omnibus*. The Latin phrase, of course, means "always, everywhere, and acknowledged by all." It would frown upon or ignore sects and splinters of sects which did not matter. Once you grant the major premise of Jesus' having given Peter dominion, the Romanist claim is better in logic than it is in history. How it can be maintained against the Eastern Orthodox Church, for example, may well puzzle us. That one is just as old, and it has never acknowledged the rule of Rome.

But there is more point in noting that the claim of being truly Catholic has within the past century come to be made by churches which have associated themselves in the past with Protestantism, at least in the matter of rejecting Roman claims. High Church Episcopalians may reject the name of Protestant while calling themselves Catholic and pushing their claims of lineage back of the Protestant Reformation all the way to the Twelve Apostles as a group. So they emphasize "Apostolic Succession" but deny the "Petrine Supremacy."

"Ecumenicism" is the move for Christian unity, the effort to repair what is often referred to as the scandalous "rent in the seamless robe of Christ." The hope for Christian unity, or Church unity at least, rests, of course, upon agreement about Christian essentials of order and belief. At Ecumenical conferences so far, the Lutherans and the Church of England have not been more backward than Rome in insisting upon the Apostolic Succession as the first essential. And the acceptance of that basis would certainly increase the importance and status of all the "established" churches.

But a great many Protestants since Luther's own age have never made anything of the Apostolic Succession. In England the general name for all of these has been Dissenters; in the New World, of course, they are the vast majority. Most of these non-conformists have fallen back upon the Bible for enough authority to support them against any claims based upon streamlined historic connections with the other ancient source of authority—namely, the Apostles. Their attitudes toward the Bible have varied greatly. Some of them have been literalists or Fundamentalists, taking the letter of the Bible as complete and final authority. Some have stood upon what they conceive as the central message of the Bible, acknowledging it to be in origin or transmission a human document. Some affirm the necessity of the symbolic or mythical expression of religious truth, applying that to the Bible, but go on to claim that there is a central system of religious truth taught within it. Appeal to the Bible has usually been in the interest of founding another kind of claim to historicity or even catholicity, to purity of doctrine or order or both. Under historicity, some have emphasized getting back to origins or the teachings of Jesus.

At Ecumenical conferences there is as strong a group as any, and probably as important, consisting of "evangelical Christians." These usually present as the cardinal principle for uniting Christianity "the acceptance of Jesus Christ as our only personal Savior and Redeemer." They, at least, find this a very simple and obvious basis of union, and do not see why Christians cannot all subscribe to as much as that, and as little; and be content therewith. The spirit of evangelicalism is a mighty one, and its voice is strong.

There are many other important groups at ecumenical conferences. There are, of course, broad-church liberals who find the essential and abiding teaching of Jesus in the Sermon on the Mount, and feel that all Christians should accept that as

169

the foundation and go on to their specialties from there. But the great bodies of Christians feel that this is turning religion into "mere moralism." And these liberals are themselves embarrassed by a radical like Tolstoy, who nails the Great Sermon to the masthead of his ship but finds in it the teachings of pacifism, of Christian Communism, vegetarianism, and sex for procreation purposes only.

Why do we keep on having these ecumenical conferences? Agreement does indeed appear hopeless. Of course, we know the churches would all like more power and influence, and would have more of these things if they could pool their strength. If the churches could be one in something common, as in South American countries they are all Roman Catholic, their power would indeed be mighty. They would merely have to agree at church conferences instead of at the polls, where now they stand even-footed with the unorganized and unled masses on such questions as birth-control, divorce, prohibition, peace moves.

Church division has always been a scandal to many and especially to Roman Catholics. But it is not so to all. An old friend, Ralph Harper, used to declare that diversity in churches has as great value as unity. He said that God knew what he was doing when instead of making plain fruit he made apples, peaches, plums, grapes, melons and varieties of all these. Even so, God would likely enrich religion by making a variety of different churches. In fact, it would be necessary, to meet human needs.

Horace Williams, at Chapel Hill, used to say that the Methodists have always represented the valid point that religion is an experience of an epoch-making sort. You *get* religion. Of course, there have been others beside the Methodists to help make this point, but it was John Wesley who publicized it widely. Episcopalians and Roman Catholics, Williams said, stress church-attendance, conformity, confirmation, all these without too much revivalism. They stress beauty and historicity of worship. These are values denied only by those who would put all the emphasis elsewhere. The Presbyterians, Williams said, were early, strong, and persistent in demanding an educated ministry. The Baptists stood for informality, directness, and democracy in organization as well as worship.

There is a psychological problem for us all in human differences and conditionings, since we have to live together. We get adapted, body and mind, to different kinds of food. The problem of Christian unity is complicated by a fact which is older and broader than Christianity. The Jews probably need their Moses and the prophets in a special way. You lose momentum in quoting Jesus to them. Christians need Jesus, of course. Christian Scientists may need Mrs. Eddy, and Mormons Joseph Smith or his own Book. Methodists, it seems to us anyhow, could bring John Wesley more to the fore than they do, to their great advantage. For he was one of the really great men.

We need simple things learned at a mother's knee and remembered as from there. Heaven help us, we need, and nobody knows how much, some of us more than others, some of the popular elements in our religion. If this be treason to liberal religion, make the most of it! We need, from more than one point of view, to be reminded that it was not the religion of Jesus which conquered the world, but a popularized one based upon him. The adaptation of Christianity to popular understanding may after all not have constituted total failure if it made Christianity more approachable for many people and for many ages. After all that looks like a question on which idealists and realists may debate. As Henry Ward Beecher once said, what we call the "outer husks of religion" were back in springtime the tender breast of the mother nurturing the grain. No doubt there is a question of badness in religion; but there is also a question of immaturity, of child beginnings for child minds.

Certainly we ourselves need to grow up. And we need a balanced diet, not just one familiar food. I once asked a nice old Quaker lady from Indiana why her local Quaker church, like so many others, had given up the old Quaker custom of silent meeting or waiting for the Spirit to move to utterance. She said that her church got a minister because one man talked too much, Holy Spirit or not, every time they held meeting. And my friend whom I quoted on God's making fruits in variety used to say also that if a man was going to repeat phrases, lines, and sentiments in his "extempore" prayers from the pulpit, and so turn the service into a one-man ritual, then we might as well get the prayers set down in a book in the language of somebody who had the real gift of utterance. My friend who said this was an Episcopalian. His remark helps to explain, one thinks, why so many churches of congregational order print more and more of their order of service, including prayers. Meantime

Episcopalians are borrowing new prayers, and sometimes they use home-made ones. There is something to be said for a balanced diet. If the Quakers are abandoning silent worship, the other churches are putting it in, on some special days and occasions. Both paradox and satiation point tend to defeat us in streamlining religious worship. We have to give some recognition to psychological needs, conscious ones that is, as well as to "final truth."

This humble concession to psychology may leave some liberals dissatisfied and sticking to their question why Christians cannot unite upon the Great Sermon (as they see that), or upon the Galilean teaching of Jesus, for at least that much unity in the all-important field of practical endeavors of religion. Let others build their own porches, ells, annexes, narthexes, and gingerbread work, for their less widely and humanly important values. This question however is the same one that evangelicals and others have asked from their angles. To give the answer once more: the reason is that we cannot agree upon what are the very first human values. Some will think the first thing is learning obedience and becoming as little children in all spiritual affairs. Some will think it is becoming conscious of Sin. Some will think freedom to grow is the first human value. Some will think the first point in religion is to teach the moral law in society at large, and to bring in justice among men. This last is a social gospel.

One suspects that the really operative reason in keeping these Ecumenical conferences going in the face of what looks like hopelessness, is that in the present world churchmen are beginning to be faced with straight anti-religious opponents like the Marxists. These make the cleavages among Christians look less important to almost everybody by comparison. The word "heretic" is slowly becoming retired in our times, and being replaced, it seems, by "atheist."

Materialism and "atheism," between them, constitute a foreign enemy in one extension of that term, strong enough to bring together or unite in a degree of broad and close sympathy all the religious traditions of the world. But so far nine-tenths of the discussion of religious unity in this country, at least that part of it which occupies official bodies of Christians, concerns what is often referred to as restoration of "the seamless robe of Christ." Only among a few ex-Catholic Modernists like Alfred

Loisy, a few students of the future of world religions like Stanton Coit, Max Müller and Aldous Huxley (author of *The Perennial Philosophy*), a few great souls like Mahatma Gandhi, a few rebels against all established religions, and a handful of not very representative Christian liberals with probably counterparts in other religious sects, has the question of unity-in-difference among all the great religions, with deep mutual respect for all, really come to the fore.

XX. Immortal or Eternal Life

We are created moment by moment and the present is holy
ground.

—WILLIAM ERNEST HOCKING

THE SECRET

What are the secret springs of happiness?
—Loving and being loved—God's life in man begun;
—Work, with sure power, done with pains and grace;
—A mind at peace, fearless through time to run
From early dawn far past the setting sun.

These none need lack—free gifts to all the race
Like Beauty's mystery flashed from Nature's face,
Yet—hidden deep, beyond the eye's access
When men count Fortune more, and the Heart less.
—(*An unpublished poem by* W. E. HOCKING)

I ONCE WAS INVITED by the president of a certain university to
an interview concerning possible employment as a professor of
philosophy. After a few minutes the president asked about belief in personal immortality. He was answered with what was
then the plain and simple truth, that his visitor wobbled on
the subject. It is certainly possible to be very slow in coming
out of a bewilderment in that field, particularly if one has grown
up in a certain kind of environment. The president said he
wished I was as confident of personal endurance as he himself
was. But he did not withhold offer of the job.

If a sense of mystery is a wobble, I confess that I still wobble
on important aspects of the subject of immortality. But I could
not now answer the question with the same simplicity and
brevity, nor, probably, satisfy him even as well as at that time.
Perhaps one's answer would now naturally partake more of
the college professor's habit of bounding a topic on the North
and the South, and dividing it up under sub-heads.

However that might be, it seems that today the discussion

174

of the question should begin with emphasizing a point which somehow often gets entirely overlooked. And yet it must be the most practical and important point of all. I mean the point that there simply must be a fitness in these matters for which we ought to be profoundly grateful. There must be a structural correspondence between man as he is made and his ultimate destiny. If we are blue-printed for a certain kind of immortality, then it is most logical to suppose we shall have that kind of immortality, or a good chance at it. But on the other hand, the mere fact that anyone might possibly feel a craving for riding around on clouds, and singing all day long, does not prove that any of us could really stand up to that kind of life. It would presently be hell—if not on earth, then up in the clouds. As Socrates said, what we want or basically require is one thing; and what we crave, or at the moment think we want, is another.

The famous Congregational preacher, Dr. Washington Gladden, wrote once that he remembered figuring out as a boy that he would like to go to heaven and sing—I think it was for sixty-nine years that Dr. Gladden settled. It occurred to him that after that much time he would want something different to do.

It is the fundamental, built-in, structure of a man, the cosmic blue-print of his kind, that seems both to lay nature under an obligation and to provide a real promise. The fundamental question for our present theme is what a man is built to attempt, to achieve, to educate himself for, and to expect. If we can get started really thinking about this question of native adaptation, the answers ought to be at least of strong suggestive value. A mortal creature craving the life of angels would be something to make the angels weep. On the other hand, a mortal who is concerned merely with having a good time can hardly feel that nature is under any obligation to single him out and keep the good times and the delectabilities coming. Nor can such a man be for others a good judge or witness on what immortality might be or mean to people who take life seriously and face the problem of life as a matter of getting educated. Emerson once risked saying there is no mystery about whether one is due to survive this life or not: he has only to observe whether his interest is all centered in things of the moment and passing hour, or in things that last.

The seeming contradiction in supposing a natural balance between a man's basic construction and his prospects or fate, on the one hand, and the fact that some men take life seriously and some do not, on the other hand, is only apparent. The question whether life is a serious business or not is such a comprehensive question, and it has been adumbrated, illuminated, and sharpened by so many fine people and so many artists of one kind or another, that it seems as if there must be a right and a wrong to it—at least so far as concerns people not totally composed of instincts or lacking the powers of reason and choice. Certainly there is no more universal religious conviction than that life should be an earnest matter, to be respectfully faced and planned in so far as we have power and room for planning. Some people wake up at a late hour to discover that they have been wrong on the question, or at least that they have wasted their lives. Some wastrels brazen it out to the limits of our present scope and horizon; but they are quite a minority. The Church has even allowed a meaning and value to death-bed repentance, which may be puzzling to the simple-minded and a matter of scorn to others. There is too the doctrine of Purgatory, which is a way of supposing continued choice and eventual recovery beyond death. But when we speak of the blue-print of a human being laying both him and nature under obligations, we mean something simple and which begins to be justified if we are pretty well agreed that selfish pleasure-seeking, as a life aim, is something to be condemned. Of course, we shall have to expect religion to go on affirming more than that about the pattern of a man and even that he was made "in the image of God." But if anyone, while wishing for authority, prefers one that is more universal than the train of Jewish and Christian religion, we do truly suppose that the human race as a whole is on the side of those who believe in justice and kindness, in beauty, in truth and truthfulness, as universal values in human living.

Starting out from the principle of native adaptation, it seems as if there were certain clarities which can be developed for all people who have abandoned Biblical literalism and special texts as an approach to the question of immortality.

The first two clarities I have in mind must be stated negatively, and the first of them concerns the idea of a mortal putting on immortality at death. It is sometimes expressed as the hope of becoming new creatures, resurrected after the pattern of Christ's resurrection, and so made into fit citizens of heaven. "Even as in Adam all die, even so in Christ shall all be made alive!" But if we are unable to believe that God has the power to wash out our sins, or, in the more natural language of our day, the power to take away our meannesses and imperfections, then this idea of immortality is clearly impossible to hold by. Besides, of course, we are hardly interested in that kind of thing, but only in some kind of immortality for exactly such mortal and imperfect creatures as we are and expect to remain so long as we exist at all.

The situation is somewhat similar when we come, secondly, to contemplate heaven as a place of perfect peace or bliss, "where the wicked cease from troubling and the weary are at rest." Here comes our second negative clarity. Some of us were not very old before it occurred to us that this picture of heaven is a portrayal of sure-enough death, not of life. Perfect peace and perfect bliss, in fact perfect anything almost, are just other names for being totally out of the fight where all life and interest lies. Life is known only as effort, struggle, endurance, hope, a little daily attainment or improvement and a longing for a whole lot more.

Robert Louis Stevenson, in his *Vailima Letters,* wrote feelingly about these two notions, of becoming miraculously new creatures at death and of heaven as a place of rest and no problems. He said that if one could believe "this fairy-tale of an eternal tea-party, at which our friends all met us with their imperfections washed and ironed out," life would simply be too good to be true—or words to that effect. The exact words do not matter, for he goes on to make his personal view clear by adding that even while we are telling ourselves this fairy story, we know underneath all the time that it is a foolish fable, and that our real interest and our heart are concerned with sterner matters than that. From his South Seas isle, Stevenson viewed real life as a matter of eternal struggle.

The existence of such heavens and such scenes in religious pictures undoubtedly reflects the hardships of life, and the fact that people do get terribly tired sometimes. We all need respites now and then, if we deserve the name of workers at all; and some much more than others. This is true in the case of many men who look forward to retirement from business and perhaps going to Florida to live on the loose. All the good ones who have any strength left are presently again engaged in some kind of business, or art, or pursuit, that makes demands upon them. If they engage in real, self-rewarding, creative labor, making useful or beautiful things, instead of being content to make fire-crackers, gin, or some new kind of tonic or to accept drudgery in making anything, the change to retirement status may be a satisfactory and never-repented change. But you cannot take pursuit and all the climbing out of life and have much left.

* * * *

There are at least two positive ideas that are brought into the discussion of immortality and that admit of reasonably perfect clarity as well as acceptance of the value they carry. The first of these is the social idea of it. We live on socially in our works, our giving, our charities, the foundations we help to rear, above and through all else in our contribution to and influence upon the lives of others.

Patriotism is a part of the social idea in terms of which we carry on. There has probably never been a time when men were not called upon to risk life for tribe, for country, or for public cause. Internationalism, in its varied forms of helping backward peoples to a place in the sun, restoring cities destroyed by war, sending medical and friendly missions all over the earth, thinking of all our problems with some reference to their international setting—these international concerns are beginning to provide a motive in which men can live widely and more lastingly. Perhaps the central word for all this social idealism is "humanity." We are merely touching upon a grand motive that indeed has always to some extent wrought in men as a great incentive, and that in the future is sure to concern them more and more to their own good. So much of our vitality, particularly that of fathers, mothers, teachers, doctors, is a stirring of the blood with interest in new lives and in promoting their growth, opening doors for them and sending them out into the fray. In terms of this motive we all constantly reckon on living on after we are "gone," in the lives of others. It would not be day, but darkness, when this was not the case.

True enough, there is an immortality of all influence, good and bad. Our good and our bad deeds survive us as a part of what drives on, or else clogs all the human wheels. It would be nice if it happened earlier in many cases, but whenever and

178

if ever we decide that we would really like the world to be a little better off for our having lived, we have driven down a stake in something that can be, and is, called social immortality.

It may be said that this outgoing and ongoing of life is not strictly immortality, at least if it be true, as religion has generally taught, that God has "set eternity in the hearts of man," or even if he "has made us for himself"—in the sense both times of "eternity" as meaning everlastingness. In this day of the exploding atom, all human societies, adventures, dreams of the human future, memorials of the past, do lead a precarious existence. It is not too difficult to imagine ashes piled deep on every single book or tablet even, in or on which there remains any mention or relic of Plato, Shakespeare, Bach, or Jesus. No doubt we could still have faith, one means in the face of that prospect, in life's beginning somewhere again, on some planet or other, in some universe. But where might be the living tendrils of hope that went out from any hearts we knew of? Perhaps gone past all recovery! Still, brave men will never falter just because of such a possibility. Even under threat of such possible extinction of our world, blossom and root, there is some clarity in the social idea. Who builds on certainty alone?

When we turn to speak of another positive idea of immortality which possesses considerable clarity, we are turning towards something for which the phrase "eternal life" is often used in preference. It is frequently introduced by saying that quality is more important than quantity in life, and that significance and inner meaning are to be preferred to mere length of days. Eternal life, in the sense understood, is something we can possess now and that is not in the least doubtful. The Jesus of St. John is suggesting something of the sort when he says: "This is life eternal, to know thee, the only true God, and Jesus Christ whom thou has sent." In fact, where there is influence from the great period of Greece, or from the Greek Mysteries, the idea behind the phrase is in operation. Plato allowed only the shadows to time, reality being above the shifting scenes, and eternal. Spinoza was talking about eternal life when he urged seeing things "*sub specie aeternitatis.*" Great artists and others are affirming something of the sort when they identify themselves with the effort to construct something perfect, and perhaps suggest that they will be ready to die when they have pulled down that dream from heaven and made it live in a great hour.

Simeon, the prophet of old, could talk almost that language: "Now, O Lord, lettest thou thy servant depart in peace, for mine eyes have seen thy salvation." We are all expressing a very great feeling for this sentiment of eternal life when we magnify those great and high moments at which we complete some search, reach some long-sought goal, strike twelve.

That there is some possibility of self-deception in the feeling that we have attained immortality already in some high moment of existence may be recognized here by observing the humble fact that people sometimes fall in love and find it a divine experience; but presently fall out again and go to Reno or the divorce court.

But it has been well said that "a thing of beauty is a joy forever." There are achievements and attainments clear enough to be a joy forever in this relativistic world. A piece of scientific work so done that no one will have to follow after us and correct errors we have made, before they go on to attack some question still ahead, is a matter of complete and lasting enjoyment. We can even feel that a single day's work done up to the hilt possesses a kind of finality that carries on through. It can be strung on a kind of rosary of days and kept as something in a sense permanent. The fact that we can be mistaken in the first estimate of some of our efforts, or their consequences, proves nothing at all except that we can be mistaken.

We are reminded that it has been said that "an honest man is the noblest work of God," and if one could know himself to be that kind of a work of God, in the full range of connotation of the term "honest," no doubt he ought to have an artistic kind of pride in having arrived, once and for all. Unfortunately, that is impossible and even the thought of it is more than slightly ridiculous. That kind of human perfection is always for and in the eyes of others, if at all. We very much prefer to believe that even Jesus, or Gandhi, left it to others to make such claims for them and did what they could to head off praise. In one place in the Gospel of Mark, Jesus says: "There is none good save one, even God." There seems to be an invincible modesty in the best of men. They look far off and away to find a perfect son of God, if they find one anywhere.

In spite of the prejudice of certain artists that beauty and aesthetic value are to be found only in physical objects, one cannot help feeling that the highest kind of beauty, or aesthetic value, is to be found in human beings in the full range of what they are. We have all been forced to see that woman's beauty is not best found in doll-like features without intelligence and force of character behind them. We can hardly avoid the wider conclusion. There seems to be a kind of interchange or mixture in our highest conceptions, of beauty, of truth, of honesty, wholeness, humanity. But though there can be as much beauty of the kind that is a joy forever in human character as anywhere else, it is hardly anything that comes into anybody's calculations of eternal life, unless we take it piecemeal, fragmentarily, as of the moment, and quite modestly. Perhaps the closest we ever come to a sense of perfection in ourselves is in the confidence of having done the best thing we could see how to do at a certain time.

The notion of virtue being its own reward belongs to our topic. Henry Ward Beecher was giving Yale Divinity School students some lectures on preaching, and he was asked whether heaven was not unnecessary if virtue is its own reward. Beecher's reply was: "If there was enough of it to amount to anything it would be a great, an exceedingly great reward; but where it is a mere spark, a germ, where it is struggling for its own existence, where it bears but a few ripe fruits, the reward is hardly worth the culture." We were not there to ask him what heavenly rewards are supposed to be for, or what they consist of if not more work. Perhaps, though, his answer helps to show us why the conception of eternal life, clear and helpful as it is, does not satisfy those men whose approach to life is mainly moral, the kind of men who feel that character is the all-important thing. in life but that moral attainment here is so skimpy that life needs further scope and horizon.

* * * *

If there is any remaining mystery in the midst of all these clarities, perhaps we could say certainties, in the field of immortality, the probable root and ground of the mystery concerns the place of individuality in creation or the universe. How do individuals have value that does not end at all, under any circumstances, if that is a sensible question? Have we said enough to explain and confirm that there is such value when we say that a man is here to contribute his mote to society, as the coral insect contributes his mite to the ancestral halls, and then to perish, and that it lives on only in the sense of his having become an unconscious part of the family memorial, presently to be no more distinguished from anybody else's contribution? Or is the mystery of the individual's abiding value solved when we say that he is meant to be an artist of life, somehow and if he can, and that at his most abiding point he constructs something that is a little bit of a joy forever—to others? In either of these senses of it, the social and the artistic, there would be nothing in him that was not clear, nothing like being a thought in the mind of God, no real unsolved mystery.

To put the whole question again and with as little prejudice as possible: Is there something going on in the evolutionary scheme of things which is big enough to justify the individual in working for it and doing his part, with due sympathy or love for his peers, and then willingly ceasing to be? Many people feel that such a total giving-up of the ego, as something too small to worry about, is the answer. But the answer seems to border somewhat closely on materialism and to be in some danger of crossing the boundary. The difficulty some people have with the whole point of view is that, after all, individuals are the surest things we know, and in final estimate the most real or significant. It was the individual man, and not any tribe, that was supposed to be made in the image of God. And in metaphysics as well as religion, there is the view that not any mass, not any generality, not any type of thing, not any species of something, such as science is limited to dealing with and such as materialism is founded upon, can be the ultimate in our world. It really seems more hopeful that there should be final and everlasting victories, or roads open towards them, for individuals than that there are or can be any final and everlasting victories for societies or states.

There is a question about the universe in which we live that is parallel to an exceedingly prominent political question. In politics, we raise the question at every turn, or it is raised by others, whether the individual exists for the state or the state for the individual. And all Western democrats answer by claiming that the state exists for the individual citizens. Quite analogous and even more poignant is the philosophical question of which comes first in creation, the individual or the masses, the alone or the lump, the vital center or the stuff.

Even the individual atom is an embodied purpose, pattern, or organization. In a sense it is on its own. Take from it one electron, and if necessary it will spend all eternity trying to get that one electron back. So the molecule and the cell, too, are internally purposive, only more complex than the atom, holding to their form of organization, making and holding to their own ideal pattern. So it is with every other individual unit of a thing, all the way from vegetables and animals up to the most ambitious humans. The most significant thing about them from their own point of view is their inner purpose or aim. What are not purposive things are the mixed aggregates: the sticks and stones, the forests and mountains, the gases and the streams or pools of water, clouds and planets, rocks and strata, sand-piles and sky-scrapers. It matters not how much of the fore-ground they conspicuously occupy. These aggregates are all composed ultimately of real individual units, but are not themselves real units. To be an individual you must be organized around a center and in some degree self-made. Of course, while individuals are always on their own, in nature they usually do not dominate their masses. Alas, the same is true of individual humans in society! There are everywhere vast mass-effects, crowd-effects, which the sciences and the statisticians and the pollsters must deal with, and seek to discover the laws thereof.

This paramountcy or sole originality of the individuals is what Aristotle, Leibnitz, and others have meant by saying that all causation is at bottom teleological, or purposive, and goes back to individual units. This is one of the basic philosophies and it is easy to illustrate. Among us humans, as in nature, individuals can become quite lost to ordinary sight. They do that at election time, or in a mob, or under a war-fever. But nevertheless, in this philosophy, what we call the laws of nature are the summations of the wills of the individual units, or statistically calculable effects of the complex interactions of vast numbers of individuals.

The question is often asked whether there is any purpose in nature. And if you mean the kind of purpose I have for you, and you have for me; or in brief such purposes as people and groups have for other people and groups—for example, such purposes as we would have the Communists carry out for us, if only we could manage them—then probably there is no purpose in nature, of any visible kind at least, until you come to the higher orders of animals and men. We are here talking about what in philosophy is called external purpose. But what nature is chock full of, what you just cannot get rid of, is the internal purpose that is in all original units whatsoever. As we have just seen, in one philosophy of it all, all the other kinds of purpose ultimately go back to this kind.

It doesn't matter too much whether we can go along with Aristotle and project a central purpose which is in God, whom he called the Unmoved Mover. We can see that in order for that to be true God would have to be a "kind" of individual Himself, or else a spirit, like love let us say, genuinely constitutive of individuals. That is to say He must be Unique and One; as opposed to any number of laws (what we call the laws of nature). Perhaps that is what we think about God already, if we use the word at all in the deep places of our mind. God is no species or kind of a thing such as the sciences are solely capable of dealing with directly and to great effect. If he is at all, he is the kind of thing science could never discover in a million years. God's works, if we are to speak of God at all, are not blunderbuss or shot-gun effects. They fly straight toward a mark, even though they appear to meet resistance such as that offered by winds that bend an oak or the moral failures that corrupt and reform a man. We use some of the simple ideas of God, which fit in with the view that all the realities in the world are individuals; and leave Aristotle's phrase of "The Unmoved Mover" on the high shelf.

So arises the question whether individuals, especially some human individuals, have any stake in the lasting long-run. In that question we are wondering what it is that lasts forever, if not matter and mass. It is the question that was strikingly raised in a play of Thornton Wilder, *Our Town*.

In the higher brackets of evolution there are human beings in whom God, or the aim of some high perfection is implanted or incarnated as a possibility, a purpose, a dream, a Lost Chord. Some of them are full of a sense of need for developing personal and peculiar skills, of working out problems, of chasing mysteries a little further back, of becoming real scientists, of speculating, of arriving at ever new insight and more education. They experience these tugs with a sense of moral and social responsibility. We want to know whether this is just a craving or a part of the blue-print of man. The question itself created that wonderful and bizarre Eastern idea of re-incarnation, in which the pains balanced the pleasures well enough to suggest that more than a mere craving was at work. Just think of being re-born as a pig or a worm!

In comparison with the most inner-purposeful humans we have known, we feel like saying "Pish, Tush" for the second-hand aggregates, for the sometimes beautiful wild conglomerations such as the mountains and the seas, or even for the glorious institutions such as states and governments which the same kind of stout men spend much of their time in building. Even these last grandeurs, so we Americans are in the habit of saying, exist for the people in them and not the other way around. The forefathers did not work to found a system upon which their names would be writ large, a system which would endure only so long as the histories of our times, of our earth, sea, or universe would last. The state exists for the people who are and who shall come. And even so, we may well be led to feel, or to hold open the possibility, that the theme of nature is not to be found in any of her masses or stellar orbs. It is creators, makers of states and of all sorts of mass-effects, servants of use and beauty, that eternally come first in value and position.

Oh, some gardens and landscapes are worthy of much admiration; some businesses, trades, professions, are fine enough to dignify the constructive workers within their ranks; and some works of art are a joy forever. Some governmental systems, working only as well as they do up until now, are still such glorious structures as to suggest that all men, everywhere, were made to grow up and be free. But these are, under God we may say, all of them human instruments, with their beginning and end in the living human. God's end, the end of perfect love, the end of what Whitehead calls "the principle of concretion," is to get himself incarnated over and over, and ever more beautifully in men or supermen. There is an endless vista involved somehow in the very idea.

*　*　*　*

No doubt we have been indulging in speculation based upon a sense of appropriateness and a high estimation of what human beings were adapted or made for. And no doubt this comes under the head of mystery instead of belonging to those clarities of which we first spoke.

It is certainly fortunate that worthy human lives seem to be filled to a considerable extent with fragmentary and clear immortalities: honorable works, well-spent days, good hours, a good fight now and then fought to the finish, the victory of some significant cause. As things stand just now what we call the artistic type of mind is evidently better able to identify itself with these fragmentary glimpses or feelings of immortality than the strictly moralistic type of mind or even the social dreamer's type. St. Augustine said that the heart of man is restless until it finds rest in God, and he did not think that happens fully in this world, where moral corruption is so deep-seated. On the whole, he has led the way for Christian religionists at least. But we have said that in a larger sense all men are meant to be artists; and if we stand by that word, far be it from us to say how much value or eternal life there is to be cultivated by acting on the same principles as those who work with cheaper materials but yet know they are artists. It may be a matter of growth and education.

To go back to the little tale with which we began this chapter, I could still tell the interviewer that I wobble on the topic of the endurance of personality, if by wobbling you mean being struck dumb.

Nobody seems to have just the right amount of imagination or intuition. We all seem to have either too little or too much. If I started to deny the possibility of personal immortality in a sweeping and final way, I feel that I should be struck dumb by a consciousness of the limitations of my intelligence, and (God save the mark) by a kind of authority. After all, William James and others like him knew more about psychology and genes than I do, and he helped open the possibility. In my own case, it would not be the great ones of the religions who would do most to strike me dumb. Among men of religion though, one might mention John Wesley, whose unparalleled labors over long years appear stellar as well as fraught with human limitations. There is J. B. S. Haldane, already quoted, saying that the world "is probably not only queerer than we suppose, but queerer than we can suppose." There is Walt Whitman, saying robustly, "All goes onward and outward; nothing collapses; and to die is different from what any one expected, and luckier." There is Goethe, sometimes called the completest and most rounded human that ever lived, not usually speaking dogmatically on our topic, but saying once to Eckermann[1] that if a

---

1. See conversation of February 4, 1829.

man kept on working hard he was laying the universe under bonds to find him more work to do. It sounds almost as if he were thinking of other literary works to come from the author of Faust. But more often he spoke quietly, as in a letter to Zelter: "Let us work away until, before or after one another, we are called by the World-spirit back into the Aether! May the Everlasting then not deny us new activities like those in which we have already proved ourselves. Should he with fatherly hand add thereto memory and satisfaction in whatever of right and good we have already willed and accomplished, so much the quicker shall we find our places at the loom of life." Call that mysticism and let it go, whoever so feels and wills. We would call it imagination, in one of the many who have too much for most of us to appreciate them rightly.

The most gifted woman I ever knew well, and a highly sensitive and receptive personality, once commented after a funeral ceremony on the lack of hope for personal immortality revealed in it: "Oh, anything is possible in this wonderful world!" Probably we should have some respect for greater minds than our own, for people more highly strung and musically appreciative, if they be still rightly organized and active. There be those who hear harmonies in the air and pull them down for us. Just what kind of respect would you say we ought to have for our betters and our seers? One has already granted that faith in personal endurance is "irrational," in a very common and important sense of that word. But what of that? Do we know all the meaning of the word, or of its opposite? There will be more to say about that in our final chapter.

Nevertheless I confess lack of original faith in this connection or direction. Instead, what never fails is a conviction that, as far as the ultimate fitnesses are concerned, all is well in this matter. The finishes are as well laid on as the foundations, subject to our own measure of freedom and achievement. In this much of the cosmos, in this aspect of it, all is well. And there is something that sustains us in tight places, and in doubts, when we do the very best we can.

* * * *

Practically one of the worst things connected with religious faith in immortality is the dreadful imposition which funeral services and cemeteries inflict upon the human race. Certainly the body which we bury is, or once was, a marvellous symbol

187

and revealment of the spirit. The eye, the glance, the whole face, the gait, the gestures, the attitudes—so long as these remain undecayed—are precious among friends. But the body's value as a symbol and revelation ends with death if not long before. After a man's official death, and sometimes quite a while before it, a portrait, a snap-shot, a framed letter, would be a far better recall of the spirit of the man than a marble slab in a bone-yard or the body that we presently put there with so much ceremony. Socrates once said that if anybody wanted to bury him after he was dead, they "would have to catch him first." Some people have been grinning over that remark since the first time they heard it. Let it echo on!

The calls of life unto life, the overspread of cemeteries and considerations of cleanliness and health of mind, have set many people's thought going towards cremation. And one feels there might be some funeral customs which emphasize the fact that we do not bury the man, because he is beyond our reach. Of course, the preacher often says this in a way, but look at the usual setting of chancel, pall-bearers, coffin and cemetery, as his props and backdrop. Too much of the service also is made to fit the graveyard.

We owe the poet Whittier many thanks for his hymns of the spirit. But he could flop his wings most disastrously sometimes. Yesterday in a church pew one found a calendar containing a Whittier poem called *Forgiveness,* with these lines in it:

> *One summer Sabbath day I strolled along*
> *The green mounds of the village burying place;*
> *Where, pondering how all human love and hate*
> *Find one sad level; and how, soon or late,*
> *Wronged and wrong-doer, each with meekened face,*
> *And cold hands, folded over a cold heart,*
> *Pass the green threshold of our common grave,*
> *Whither all footsteps trend, whence none depart.*

What nonsense for a poet to put forth! Doubtless Whittier had a good sermon about forgiveness in the background of his mind. But his text is all wrong as well as sentimental, and the heavy hand of materialism is all over him. Love and hate do not find "one sad level," or any level at all. There is a difference, and the grave has not one word to say in such matters,

Wronged and wrong-doer may or may not end with "meekened" face: many people would hate the word and doubt the fact. But our footsteps do not tend to a common grave, provided we were going anywhere at all. They end on the road, some road. As for "cold hands over a cold heart," there are hearts which never were cold and could not be. The concluding two lines are sheer materialism, not religion.

What religion says to cemeteries and customs circulating around them is that "the things which are seen are temporal, and the things which are not seen are eternal." We may not have all the meaning of that ready at hand, but it hits a shining mark. It is in tune with mysteries about blueprints for humans and to one particular sort of faith: the faith that, in the whole of nature, life, the positive, has the edge over death, the negative. Life brings itself out of death ever and anon, as in the springtime. Nature is always a story of new life for old. Nature is forever making new beginnings that would overwhelm with surprise if they were not so familiar. It seems as if we should have farewell rites which symbolize the faith, maybe the truism, that Life is ever Lord of Death. It seems as if customs built along this positive line would prove tonic to our feelings when we need a tonic most, gradually penetrating through these musty, clogged, materialistic depths which befog and darken the human sunset.

XXI. In Conclusion

We are certainly not anxious to offend people; and we have spoken bluntly only because silence in the churches . . . is in fact a false loyalty. . . . If there has to be a choice between upsetting some of God's faithful veterans in the congregations or failing to serve some of God's frozen and lovely people on the fringe of our churches, then it seems to us clear which is the choice we must make, according to all that the New Testament teaches.

—T. RALPH MORTON and MARK GIBBS, *in*
God's Frozen People (Fontana Books, 1964)

The true religion of the future will be the fulfilment of all the religions of the past—the true religion of Humanity, that which, in the struggle of history, remains as the indestructible portion of all the sectarian religions of mankind. There never was a false god, nor was there really ever a false religion, unless you call a child a false man. . . . Nothing to my mind can be sadder than reading the sacred books of mankind—and yet nothing more encouraging. They are full of rubbish; but among that rubbish there are old stones which the builders of the true Temple of Humanity will not reject—must not reject, if their temple is to hold all who worship Him who is a Spirit in spirit and in truth.

—MAX MUELLER, Editor of
Sacred Books of the East

WHEN THE PRESENT WRITER was a student in George Santayana's course in Greek philosophy, he was invited to come to the teacher's rooms one day. There he was given a cup of tea and urgently advised to drop either theology or philosophy courses. The present book is a result of not taking that advice. Presently Harvard found him an opportunity to teach philosophy, but, after a good deal of hesitation and a long country walk, the offer was declined. Instead the student "entered the ministry," in which he served for the next eighteen years. Then he made the change from preaching to teaching in college and university, in the field of philosophy, for fifteen years. So his famous teacher's advice had not removed his perplexity about what kind of career to seek. Nor has life itself ever solved that perplexity.

Somehow it has always been my desire to feel, think, and talk about religion in the simplest way, but it has always seemed as if that involved philosophy. For it is philosophy that simplifies a great matter and discovers the principles of it, just as it is science that gets all the learning in the world and gradually clutters up a subject with learning and local peculiarities. Somehow though it has become more conventional for ministers to study science.

Santayana had undoubtedly seen storm and stress on a youth's visage and reacted in a kindly way. He finally gave the student an A in Phil. 8, which perhaps shows that he was not merely trying to push a fellow out of his classroom. Although he himself wrote poetry occasionally, and in his later life novels, there must have been operative in his advice the belief, which we know he held, that there is an inevitable contradiction between religion and philosophy *as careers*. His writings show him thinking that religion belongs in the field of poetry and imagination, and stands over against philosophy and science, both of which disciplines had, in his mind, to deal strictly with prose and facts. As if we did not need both poetry and facts everywhere!

Of course his advice may have been good, and particularly for the case before him. But it never had a chance. The student had both those interests deeply rooted in him and was compelled to go on with both. Religious experience meant something to him; he was not sure how much more there was to that. On the other hand he had come to Harvard on purpose to study philosophy. It is true he had come with some faint dread lest associations at the Divinity School might draw him into the ministry; but that is the story of a kind of divided personality and does not belong here.

One has since discovered more and more people putting up partitions between religion and philosophy, or religion and science, or religion and sociology or ethics. And some of the partitions, probably all of them, might as well be called partitions between religion and life. And it is a common criticism of religion today that it is aloof from life. Those who try to protect religion from philosophy or science may not be exactly the same people who criticize it for being aloof from life, but there is something akin in the two attitudes anywhere at all. Either one of them is enough to divide an individual soul against itself.

Another famous teacher, this one from the Divinity School, nearly upset my career in an entirely different way. I put off taking the course in Church History, required for the School degree but also for the holding of a scholarship, as long as I could; and then Ephraim Emerton gave me a C. That stopped the scholarship. At that period of life I found it simply impossible to take any interest in the course in church history.

And that brings up another very broad topic indeed, the modern impatience, the impatience of the man in the streets today, with what is sometimes given the name of "churchianity." We have dealt with that problem in our chapter on Organization, its Necessity and Dangers. But impatience with the church, with clergy, creed, and dogma, may well be noticed for a moment in its connection with a wide-spread prejudice against all historical studies, particularly in religion, as waste of time.

Mr. Henry Ford made himself famous not only for originating the Model-T Ford car, but also for declaring that history is "bunk." Of course he meant history as written up in books. Napoleon had been equally contemptuous in calling history "a lie that historians have agreed to tell." And Auguste Comte was even more fundamentally dismissive towards the whole historic interest when he divided up the story of mankind into three stages, Theological, Metaphysical, and Positive or Scientific. Comte implied that you did not need to go back into the past at all except to see the three periods of it. Realistic history begins, so he taught, in this scientific age. The inference was that we should study psychology or sociology and leave history alone so far as looking for any light from it to be shed on man's life is concerned—except for seeing how widely misled he had been when "theology" or "metaphysics" dominated his outlook on life. As if theology itself did not have a long and variegated history and evolution, still continuing!

And some of the people of our own times who have defended "history" for certain purposes of their own have not furthered the study of religious history by inspiring us with confidence that history is useful. Financial writers who discover curves in the history of the stock market and who manage day by day either to divide themselves about equally between bulls and bears, or at least to teeter nicely on the question which direction it is due to move in right now, do not inspire wide faith in the appeal to history. Generals who study the last war to learn how to be ready for the next one do not inspire very much confidence. The politicians who recline upon great names of the past, like Lincoln or Jefferson, do not inspire faith in their nostalgic patriotism; for we see that they twist the story and interpret it in the light of their prejudices.

There certainly is "buncombe" in the way men use or misuse history for their purposes and in promotion of their little faiths. And this falls in very comfortably with any prejudice derived from Comte, from Sigmund Freud's kind of psychology, from mental lassitude, or even from mere awe of psychology as a new kind of science, to keep bewildered men and women from having a curiosity about religious history, or in particular the history of Judaism and Christianity. Even more pointedly this prejudice deflates the kind of history that has been appealed to so long in the old and dusty stone building that stands on the typical town square with the graveyard all around it.

As has been apparent from the beginning of this present study, the writer found it impossible to separate religion and philosophy, as impossible as to sever the heart and the mind. What real light there is on theology seemed to him to be found in two places: in the heart or the mystical regions on one hand; and in those clear though sometimes crossed highways of theology which were brought out in Chapter IV, Main Highways in Theology. Incidentally that chapter is full of history in the sense of evolution or growth. The Spirit's manifestation for primitive men began on the level of their mentality and civilization and advanced with man himself.

All our historical chapters emphasized the fact that man's life has grown continually wealthier in a kind of widespread freedom of mind. In fact, what is Science itself, but a new and widening kind of intelligence in which men of our times are practically compelled to "live and move and have their being"? That question is only a way of noticing that we live in a scientific age. Another kind of freedom that has grown, that is to say evolved in history, is freedom for men to govern themselves politically. There has been more and more of that as time has moved on and as Eastern patterns and leadership has yielded to Western. Even the fresh-dyed Communists, like the Chinese, declaim that government is *for* the common people, and that is a step or two away from absolute personal monarchy or dictatorship. It is a new stage of evolution in Africa, where a hundred years ago petty chiefs had the absolute right of life and death over all their subjects, when we come to the time of today in which parading Africans chant not submission to chiefs but a paean to self-government. When a thousand clergymen sign a petition to the pope asking for more representation and democracy in church decisions and the announcements of doctrines, and when we know that a popular and grass roots agitation in favor of birth control is one pouring spring in this democratic freshet, we know it means that man's story is evolving on another broad front. It means that walls which confined human movement are coming down. In almost every aspect of our life the evolution towards more freedom is obvious.

We presented the Church as having developed or come into existence at a stage of religious evolution in Israel, but we did not suggest that it is as yet anything finished or necessarily unreplaceable by other forms of active religious organization. We presented worship as human devotion, you might say as humanity's real devotions, in evolution, paralleling the growth of man's moral sense from honorific rites supposedly owed to gods, and from rudimentary forms of ethics, to widest human sympathies. There is a historical evolution from exorcism and incantation, through the whole gamut of hymnology and dramatics, to prophecy in the pulpit and the championing of human causes. The story of preaching itself is an evolutionary story, running from the reading of a holy book enshrined on its high pedestal with its single revelation from out of the past, to the free mind, speaking the language and the concerns of today and inspired by a Universal Spirit rising up in a consensus that holds pulpit and pew together. Religion is history and revelation still moving on with old and new inspiration.

From the historic Jesus to the universal, timeless, enshrined, Son of God—not limited to any one name and perhaps hailed under a thousand names, is an evolution.

In our own experience, we are always taking a hand in important historic evolution. Some of it moves almost too fast for us. But our range of agency is increased somewhat. Even when we scorn history, meaning perhaps the story of St. Paul's travels, we are using principles exemplified all over history and geography for plotting our own future course. We cannot go forward without looking backward and around. That does not mean we should enter into competition with old timers to see how many times we can read the Bible through from cover to cover. It is not even saying what kind of books we should read most. The idea is simply that we should *use* the Bible, and all the sacred books of the East, as well as all histories that have ideals combined with practicalities and human heroes, to help us to see and feel our way further.

History is companionable when we are not slaves to any historian or book but merely humble conscious debtors to the past. It furnishes us the best possible ground for feeling confident of our opinions, once we have examined them in the light of history and in the presence of the best teachers of life we can find—the best men to inspire devotion that makes integers of men within themselves and unites them with other people in the widest struggles that are in progress. Above all, historical study teaches us that we and the people of this age are not struggling alone, but as part of a great stream of on-going life on this planet and in the total mystery of things.

In one of Disraeli's novels there is a sage or Nestor who is approached by a young man seeking light on religion. He tells this young man that "all thoughtful and sensible people have the same religion." "And what religion is that, Sir?" asks the youth. "That," replies the sage, "no thoughtful and sensible person will tell."

Knowing something about Disraeli himself, one supposes this could be the wily old statesman's own personal answer, as he found himself dealing with political questions which involved all sects. He did not want to stir up unnecessary prejudice and antagonism while he was engaged in manning the bulwarks of the British Constitutional System with the help of the Tory Party, the House of Lords, and the Established Church. Of course his answer could be from a wider aristocratic point of view, thinking of religion mostly as a tool for maintaining public morals and the established order. It could even be that Disraeli was verging into the challenging attitude of that intelligentsia which disbelieves in the common people's intelligence, which opines that ordinary humans think with their emotions or their bellies, and refers to them often as "the mob," or "Tom, Dick and Harry," or the "booboisie." Involved in this last approach is the straight notion that you have to manage people by slogans and tricks and that you cannot change human nature. But the Tory leanings of Disraeli were in many ways somewhat out of tune with his own age.

Disraeli's seer, and all these other people who in their own way distrust the common people, are of course not far in their faith, or in the lack of it, from Marx and Lenin. Marx wrote in favor of making all the people, including the peasantry, beneficiaries of the government; but in no smallest sense was he in favor of making them all agents of it or now giving them the decisive voice in government. Of course his disciples believe in managing the news and making it a sin to disbelieve in the communist line or creed, which is decidedly much like other people coddling their religion. Democracy on the other hand appeals to history and believes that "you cannot fool all the people all the time," that governments derive their just powers from the consent of the governed, and that the common people need to make mistakes in governing themselves as a part of the process of growing up to political maturity. And the analogy between politics and religion seems inescapable.

I may well confess that in holding on to hope for religion I have often been simply astonished to see how resistant to change religious tradition can be. However, the influence of science-teaching in our colleges is unmistakable. Constant assaults upon boards of university trustees, or assaults of the trustees themselves upon faculties where teachers with live minds influence the brighter students or start their original intellectual processes to growing and, naturally, to questioning, are indications of resistance to change but also proof of change being here and still more of it in the offing. Splinters are flying off the rocks of ages in all the systems. To tell the whole truth, I am sometimes also visited by that other fear: lest the people, through the younger generations or all the bright minds upon which we have been depending to bring up the rear guard and the majority, may get so radical or at least so newfangled as to lose all interest in the past history of religion. We all have a tendency in one aspect or another of our mental experience, to fly from one extreme to another, especially where words or vocabulary may momentarily seem all important. I have been frightened by people out for something brand new, by people with a new religious or at any rate a new devotional vocabulary taken from some psychologist or sociologist of the hour. A part of the fear is of people coming to think they need too many long words. But our abiding faith is that the Jewish prophets, the books of the other great religions, (in parts at least), Plato and the Stoic and Epicurean philosophers, Dante's if not Milton's poetry, some of the other poets like Emerson and Whitman, William James, Jefferson, Lincoln, will continue to carry weathered religious literature for to study and cherish.

We have to be somewhat concerned about democracy on two counts: that it may move too slowly and that it may move too fast. We are certainly afraid that it will not shed its prejudices fast enough; and uneasy lest its emancipation come like a thief in the night, or a landslide, and bury us old fogies before either we or history can get a hearing. We need to hope there is some kind of balance-wheel within democracy. While it is true that the ordinary human is much given to new fashions, it is also true that the "new" fashion does not itself last too long with him but passes on.

Democracy's strong and clear point is that no other kind of government attends to the real business of government, which is the self-realization of all the citizens. That is near enough to Plato's phrase for the goal of human living. Good government is no substitute for self-government. God's objective, like the state's, is something within and of the individual citizen. We surely need no special application of that great truth to religion or to any one field.

Santayana's and Disraeli's idea of holding out on the people is no permanent answer. It can be justified only as a stalling action, a slowing action, in the same way as when we have sometimes accepted the notion that certain Latin American nations were not yet ready for democracy because they have behind them no Anglo-Saxon heritage and history, and nothing to take its place. Some of us who have at times in the past sympathized with this way of looking upon neighbors given to having too frequent rebellions have been recently shocked in discovering how ready some of these same peoples felt themselves for Communism. And much shocked of late have been the segregationists, gerrymanderers, and others who do not really believe in trusting the democratic process in this country. They have been forced to see themselves as others, as the wide world sees them. We may have come to a point of choice between much less democracy than we have had or more and more of it both at home and abroad. Fortunately it is not a question of winning a literal majority for new moves towards wider human freedom, especially if all the non-voters have to be counted in. Nothing much was ever led by a numerical majority. We need an active minority of the people who actually take an interest. We need leaders who will make followers for themselves and so control many votes. That was Jefferson's own hope of how democracy might work out under our political constitution, with an aristocracy coming up in part from the bottom but no hereditary aristocracy.

A felt religious need and a kind of religious experience was the only "call to the ministry" the writer ever had. He was a clergyman for seven years before joining any church whatsoever. It may be doubted if he was "called" to the ministry. In the chapters which have led up to this one there is almost certainly too much philosophy (even if you should just mean something along the line of Benjamin Franklin's common sense) to please the typical theologian or clergyman. And it is as safe to say that in these same chapters there is too much respect for, and interest in, religious experience to fit well into the vocabulary of the average college teacher of "philosophy." But for better or worse it has always been the desire of the writer to study philosophy and religion together, and to speak all the time in as short and simple words as possible.

It may have been very early indeed in the life of mankind that people who had the intense experiences of life began to be afraid of the people who had the words, the definitions and the pigeonholes, ready to put the experiences into. At the present time we often note that most poets have little ambition to say things plainly or else think that in high matters the attempt should not be even essayed. Many of them aim, too, at saying things in a way that they were never said before. It is as if they wanted the dew of early morning left on all expression. They undervalue other poets who do try to be as plain as they can be. We are all of us wary as well as weary of the statisticians who come at us with more and more questionnaires. The Freudians are not the only ones who seem to threaten our individual and personal depths with too many ready-made pockets.

The short old words and concepts that we have had with us ever since language was invented were of course a kind of shorthand, even when language was started. They were made for primitive uses and so of course had rather rudimentary meanings. Learning to talk at all must have freed human minds much more than it confined them. But there was something of both effects from the start. The situation of the first words was somewhat like that of our Federal Constitution, which had to grow because time moved on and added new problems. Those old words must have seemed very inaccurate, ambiguous, inexpressive, before our ancestors were willing to tolerate the flood of complex and compound words that came along. Come to think of it though, it is marvelous what mileage we have got out of many of these three and four letter words: "god" or "deus," "good" and "bad," "free," "feel," "see," "grow," "love," "life," "poem!" Taking care of new depths of meaning, new bearings, and modern slants, is however as necessary business as it is tricky. When we think of how inns along the highways of travel have to change their names every few years in search of fresh appeal, it is indeed wonderful how many of these old short words have lasted. But it is not wonderful that poets, scientists, philosophers, and plain people have often felt the need of new or supplementary words? No wonder religious people have been afraid of philosophy, scientists afraid of all the old words (their job is making things exact and calculable), and the poets afraid of old ways of saying anything.

Religion seems to be one of the places where we might always remember that all the time we are talking experiences more than words, or at least that the experiences are more important. That would make us less willing to think that great subjects can be polished off in words, or by a terminology. We might recall St. Augustine saying that not to know God means that you do not "see" him, which is a bit like some modern theologians saying that God is found only within religion.

We do often need to be more accurate and to the point than we are. On the other hand there are some old words which are useful for their romance and associations. That is to say they are useful to many people, if not to all. Longer and more exact words keep coming to us from the firing line where meanings are made more exact as well as more limited. But some of the short words have rendered agelong service and are still useful and at home in the bottom of our minds.

Religious experience neither needs any outside witness nor is it dependent in the first instance upon any of our verbal accounts. It is in the first place as near being sheer matter of fact as anything can be. Of course some of it is for psychological explanation (none of it is exactly immune), and some more of it is for general present-day depreciation. Of course it is never more exalted than its own stage of human and personal growth. Whether you are talking about low-level or high-level religious devotion and experience, about that of the Ku Klux Klansman with his burning cross on the one hand or that of Isaiah, of Dante's furthest heavenly visions, or of "Christ" on the other hand, it is all "real" on its own level. Religion itself has moved from darkest witchcraft, partisan war-cries, narrowest sectarianisms and all kinds of close communions to the universal and human vision of highest Judaism and Christianity or whatever. Its outward advance has gone and goes along with that in fields of evolution.

A practical point for today, so easily covered up by verbiage or dependence upon words, is that we now face no difficulty in finding men and women above us in stature—to admire, emulate, and even reverence. And I think we also feel that these people must know more about what life is for or about than we do—because they have plainly made a better use of it. Because life is in them, on-moving, life-giving to others, challenging!

Differences in religion which make little difference are dying. Denominations and religions are approaching one another in spite of all the ancient fences. Everyone notices that sectarian bonds are slipping and that, as people move from one place of residence to another, they frequently slip or slide into a different church connection. To what church group does not that apply? It seems to be something of a reply to Santayana's skepticism about the common people. The broad drive for church unity may soon move on towards a livelier sympathy with some of the other great religions. In fact we already have Buddhist, Vedantist, Islamic, Bahaiist and Zen groups in this our America, and every year sees them become a little more native to the scenery.

Even the "purple-mystery" sects that are always springing up in our great cities reveal two different things: the genuine appeal of novelty and the fact that importation and proselyting are less frowned upon socially than they were. Mormonism and Christian Science, native sons of New York, Utah and Massachusetts, are readily accepted as Christian, or part-Christian with new revelations added.

Missionaries living alongside people of other great religions have usually developed respect for those other religions. We do not find the word "heathen" very much in use today, and when it is used it is likely to be in connection with primitive tribes. Missionaries are often happy to point out also that the other great religions have recently borrowed much from Christianity. Probably wisdom about what to borrow from others in political ideas, in art, economics, philosophy and religion are a part of the ancient main trick of advancing our own civilization. After all, Christianity borrowed with both hands from Judea, Greece, the Mystery religions. We can note however that other religions do not today borrow the Christian creeds, mysteries, birth stories; or use very much the names of Jewish and Christian founders and saints. They have all those things in kind at home, and prefer their own brands. Present emphasis upon medical missions and the feeding and clothing of the poorest is surely in part the result of advancing education, spread of scientific knowledge, and rising recognition of universal human kinship.

Returned missionaries bring the message that everybody should travel. In particular, seeing human need at first hand and seeing the response to medical missions is found revealing about the peoples of the earth and feels like something good to know. Where doctors are humanitarians they make green oases in what looked from a distance like arid human deserts. Such effects of travel and observation are combining with other things to make people of today crave simplicity and humanity where they formerly allowed our human sensibilities to yield before the "divine" or the sectarian. Meanwhile the desire for a philosophy of life in which we can wholly believe and which we can carry with us to the ends of the earth, is all the time making headway.

It seems as though the democratic upsurgence in our world were more to be attended to for the long pull than Santayana's fears of mixing religious mysteries with philosophy, or Disraeli's Toryism or whatever it was. The whole human race now needs to grow up and to do it fast.

For people who are growing up, religion is no longer just mystery and a contact with unknown forces that sometimes produce surprising results. All the time, religion is present with us *as our own moral experience. It is the deep feeling of safety that goes with being right, or as nearly right as we can see how to be. It is the inner experience of truth, wonder, love, beauty.* In spite of his being a kind of mystic, Gandhi said he plainly saw there is no God except Truth. If he could say that and be a great religious leader, it must be possible for others to follow. Instead of its being right or wise to divorce religion from life, religion turns out in truth to be always on the side of life. It is that inspiration to self-fulfillment which is both a Greek idea and what Jesus is talking about in John's Gospel when he says that he "came to bring life." Some artists prefer the phrase "self-expression" as a name for their objective and goal; but they can grow up too unless they already know everything they will ever have to express. A million years ago and before that, humanity had religion in the urge to grow up, just as every tree has it. Religion is now striking off conscious impediments of human growth, mental among other kinds. It is hearkening for the Lost Chord or trying to recover moments of insight. Religion consists of learning to put first things first. It involves the discovery of our neighbors (no doubt of our enemies as well, as Jesus said and for the purpose he mentioned—of learning to love them too). All that is a genuine part of our own life and possible success. There is a love of man which actually turns out to be love of God, just as has been said of old. Worship is the practical moves we make to feed the progressive and widely human kind of life. It involves leavening the whole lump of humanity. Naught else is "worshipping God in spirit and in truth." Social ethics is the biggest field of religion, although not usually or necessarily the beginning of it.

Laying aside pictorial representations of God, the question of whether Superman is to come upon this planet, and that other wider question whether there may be better and more sensitive spirits, spirits of a higher potential, on some of the other planets of all space, it is obvious that as spiritual beings we are no more alone or lost in the cosmos than the very least of things. We too have our widespreading and deep relationships. Like every atom, we as individuals and also the group of us, live within a matrix. Perhaps modern science has made us dizzy sometimes with its visions of distances in space. But through Mr. Einstein and others it has brought along its own medicine. Such distances are a matter of the point of the observer. Really everything and everybody in the whole wide universe is cozily at home. Distance is never where we live and work. And on the other hand we well know that we ourselves can be unimaginably distant from points of view which at present concern us not at all. Distance is where life or duty are not. Where life is, is home. Wonder of wonders at the same time, after science may have done its best to fix and determine us, our personal will certainly appears to count for something. We know not how much, but we conceive no other energy than that of which we are a valid part. Our portion of the universal creativity may have been here and there derailed or driven into a blind alley; but the universal story stands, that God, or the whole, wills within us to do "his good will." God rebukes and in an inward way provides a hell for narrowness, unkindness, littleness, and for folly in general. He provides for everybody, surely, that remorse, some form of it, which is about the surest and strongest revelation that he brings directly home to practically everybody. God reveals corners or parts of our goal, insofar as that is a common and human goal, in glimpses of men and women ahead of us on the road. We come upon their footprints, especially of a morning. Tagore says that the birth of every new babe proves that God is not yet discouraged about the human race. That is poetry but it probably means that God, or the Universal Life, cannot cease to be creative any more than we can give up our human hopes.

Cosmic energy without our conscious collaboration brought our egos on to the scene of action. Without the help of any who are alive now, the cosmic energy produced all the reformers and the historic critics that have denounced and stung men on to improve. After we come upon the scenes as individuals, we are helped out by visions overhead, by divisions and tensions within us, and by a kind of resilience of the ground underneath our feet. Dr. Edward Everett Hale once said: "Live with all your might, and you will have more might with which to live." This is, at least as far as one of those mechanical concepts will take us, the mutuality of action and reaction of things within a grand matrix.

Here we end, aboard the real paradox of life, which we think is to stand some day in place of that narrow one of which the theologians are so fond—their paradox of Jesus and Jesus only, being both God and man. The real paradox involves some

203

original divine force of our own all mixed up with hindrances and helps from below and from above, which hindrances and helps are to be contended with or explored. It includes man made in the image of God with often no more to show for it than you note in a tough political campaign or a cold war. It includes humanity and divinity all in one package. The inclusion of the divinity is a way of referring to the innate possibilities of men. It crams the natural full of the supernatural in a few very practical or pragmatic meanings of those terms that are often so meaninglessly used. It involves that truth the theologians have become fond of referring to: that God is known only within religion. Truly God is not to be found through telescope or microscope, or anywhere else save in the bloom, the promise, the questionmark, that is on the face of all living nature, in the very lines of the faces of good men and women, and in the general kindlings of the desire to do some kind of creative and lasting work.